Good Time Girls of the Pacific Northwest

GOOD TIME GIRLS

of THE PACIFIC NORTHWEST

A Red-Light History of Washington, Oregon, and Alaska

Jan MacKell Collins

TWODOT®

GUILFORD, CONNECTICUT
HELENA, MONTANA

A · TWODOT® · BOOK

An imprint and registered trademark of The Rowman & Littlefield Publishing Group, Inc.
4501 Forbes Blvd., Ste. 200
Lanham, MD 20706
www.rowman.com

Distributed by NATIONAL BOOK NETWORK

British Library Cataloguing in Publication Information available

Library of Congress Control Number: 2019951402

ISBN 978-1-4930-3809-1 (paperback)
ISBN 978-1-4930-3810-7 (e-book)

∞™ The paper used in this publication meets the minimum requirements of American National Standard for Information Sciences—Permanence of Paper for Printed Library Materials, ANSI/NISO Z39.48-1992.

CONTENTS

Contents

ACKNOWLEDGMENTS

A pleasant plethora of people have assisted me in piecing together this history of prostitution in the Pacific Northwest. My hat is, and always will be, off to Professor Jay Moynahan. Jay's delightful series of books about the subject, as well as his tireless research, advice, and resources, have been of great help to me for many years now. His work has revealed an incredible amount of information across the West, including from his home state of Washington, but also Oregon and Alaska. Also for Alaska, I am indebted to Lori Sewald and Mark Gregory of Victor, Colorado; also to my dad, Wally Smith, and my stepmom, Barbara, for their visits to madam Dolly Arthur's house in Ketchikan, Alaska, and for sharing what they learned with me.

Lucky for me, Oregon's prostitution history remains virtually intact in many ways. But I could not have followed my map of research without the assistance of Joanie Bedwell, her daughter Linda, and Phyllis Pearce of the Hazel M. Lewis Memorial Library in Powers for lending clues for me to follow regarding the shady ladies of Coos County. Lacey Pearce and Wade Hurlock, my ever-cheerful neighbors, have offered much in the way of support and their willingness to listen to my many stories (special thanks goes to Wade, who coined the term "Whoregon"). Powers Tavern owner Jill Moore, community volunteer Tish Moore, and Powers resident Deb Woosley also have been kind enough to share what they know about the area. In Coquille, Cathy Vitale of the Coquille Valley Museum was very helpful. Also, a big thank you goes to Burt Dunn, who provided some great information about Sugar, the once reigning madam in Coquille.

In Washington, I must thank La Jean Greeson, whom I first met back when I was director of the Cripple Creek District Museum in Colorado. La Jean was researching her family there and has since become a dynamo of information and a research goddess besides. La Jean's encouragement, assistance, and introduction of madam Lou Graham to me have been a most pleasant and ongoing journey as we continue discovering historical facts together. Also I must thank Edward Nolon of the Washington Historical Society for providing information about the town of Columbia River. Mr. Nolon was kind enough to assist me in finding the scant information about this little "ferry" town.

In closing, I wish to sincerely thank my editors, Erin Turner and Alex Bordelon, for their patience and for assisting me every step of the way in this and my other books. Thank you also to Courtney Hoffman, Nancy Degnan, and countless others for their business opportunities, encouragement, friendship, and support. There are a lot of wonderful people out there who follow me on social media and support everything I do. Thank you to each of you. Special thanks go to my poor husband, Corey, who watched me disappear into my office each day and largely picked up the chores of running a busy household while I wrote this, the fourth in a new series of books about historical prostitution. He also did his best to hold down the "circus," that is, our two rambunctious cats and one elderly dog, and almost always managed to keep things around our tiny house quiet as I worked. That in itself is an undertaking even when we aren't doing anything but enjoying life in the majestic and beautiful Pacific Northwest.

INTRODUCTION

———◆◆◆———

PROSTITUTION IN THE PACIFIC NORTHWEST

"The Girl with the Striped Stockings"
One rainy day I'll ne'er forget
The prettiest girl I ever met.
And when she raised her skirts to the wet,
I saw she had striped stockings on.
She was always out when the wind blew high;
When the weather was wet, she'd walk or die.
By the raisin' of her skirts as she passed by,
I saw she had striped stockings on.
Oh, the color of her hose was red and yeller.
She says to me, "You're a mighty fine feller."
I escorted her home under my umbrella—
The girl with the striped stockings on.
And when we parted in the rain
She said, "We'll never meet again."
And so she hooked my watch and chain,
The girl with the striped stockings on.[1]

Since their beginnings, certain areas in the states of Washington, Oregon, and Alaska have remained fairly remote. Part of the reason is that the climate of Oregon and Washington is conducive to the growth of flora and fauna. Trees, vines, and bushes are apt to cover old roads and trails, bury structures beneath their branches, and grow with an alarming speed that keeps landscapers and gardeners busy with their mowers and snipping tools. In Alaska, temperatures can range between minus fifty degrees in winter to the humid nineties during summer.[2]

Brave were the pioneers who ventured into these places long before electricity, automobiles, and other modern technology made negotiating these harsh regions easier. Oregon is among the oldest states in the West, achieving statehood in 1859. Ten years later, the United States would purchase Alaska from Russia, although statehood would not be achieved until 1959. Washington became a state in 1889.[3] In all three cases, early explorers made their way to these raw, sometimes unforgiving places in search of trade, gold, and other riches. As the region's economies grew, more women came west in growing numbers to settle and eventually raise families or pursue their own careers.

The earliest Anglo visitors to the Northwest encountered Native American tribes with whom they traded while learning about ancient customs. Among the tribes, prostitution was not the buy-and-sell sex trade to which Americans and Europeans were accustomed. Nearly all Native Americans were accustomed to lending or trading their wives and daughters for sex. To those whose culture allowed for a more open lifestyle, it was common for parents to lend out their daughters for sex, always in trade for goods. The more the girls brought in, the greater the respect for them and their families. Furthermore, the girls in many Native American societies often expressed their anticipation, even desire, for such transactions. Only the rare *Wittico-Weeon* women of the Assiniboine, which translates to "fool woman," plied their trade on their own, for pay. Such women "were considered lost beyond redemption."[4]

During the late 1700s, Spanish explorers began arriving in the Pacific Northwest. While few of their records refer to the sex trade as they knew it, they do include instances of rape and kidnapping of Native American girls. It is generally agreed among historians that French immigrants from Canada, as well as white pioneers from the eastern United States, forever labeled prostitution as a commercial—and shameful—endeavor. So it remains today. Attitudes towards the Native American way of trading women were forever changed during this era. While doing so provided a way to procure food and goods from the Anglos, the settlers also introduced a new illness to the Indians: venereal disease.[5]

Prostitution was certainly no stranger to explorers Meriwether Lewis and William Clark, who during their 1805–1806 journey west were treated to six Chinook maidens along the Columbia River near the Pacific coast. A Chinook leader's wife oversaw the "regular prices proportioned to the beauty of each female." The endeavor was initially unsuccessful, since the men of the party had been warned of disease and illness resulting from intercourse with native women.[6] The men also had witnessed venereal disease among the Mandan in North Dakota.[7] Later, when they encountered a tribe of Sioux, the men were amazed at how many wives were offered up for their entertainment, adding that "we observed among them some women who appeared to be held in more respect than those of any nation we had seen."[8]

In spite of the warnings, at least two of the men on Lewis and Clark's team contracted syphilis. Lewis treated both men with mercury, with limited success. Both patients died young, leading to the assumption they succumbed to the disease. Eventually, even Lewis himself contracted what was most likely syphilis, following an encounter with a Shoshone woman on his birthday in 1805. The illness might have explained Lewis's psychotic behavior a few years after the expedition and his subsequent suicide in 1809.[9]

Some decades after Lewis and Clark completed their famed expedition, more Anglo explorers made their way to the Pacific Northwest. During the 1830s, explorers and other male pioneers continued satiating their needs via the Native American women available to them. A number of French Canadians married, or lived with, natives. As in other instances, the young women's families saw no shame in this and considered it an honor and anticipated better lives for the girls and themselves. To the Catholic priests who set about establishing missions around such fledgling cities as Astoria, Champoeg, and other places, however, such people were considered "infidel women."[10]

In the coming years, Anglo prostitutes would pack their petticoats over the Rocky Mountains to the Pacific Northwest outback to ply their profession in remote camps, towns, and cities. Why would women risk such a treacherous journey? One answer of many is revealed in an 1859 survey of two thousand prostitutes asking why they took up the profession. The majority of them revealed that they were simply destitute. The next largest group said they were seduced or abandoned. Some claimed they were treated badly by parents, relatives, or their husbands, and a smaller percentage admitted they were persuaded to enter the profession by other prostitutes. Others said they simply gave in to the various vices at hand.[11] To them, drinking, dancing, drugging, and cavorting with men seemed like a much more entertaining alternative to living the dull life of a common housewife.

The 1859 survey did not include Chinese women, who were certainly a part of the prostitution population throughout the West. Back in China, their culture largely frowned on women migrating to North America, and besides, many were unable to afford passage. Hence a good number of pioneer Chinese males arrived on the continent alone, leaving their wives behind in their homeland. Young Chinese girls, however, were regarded as a viable way to provide financial assistance to their families—by selling them to traders who promised the girls would live their lives freely in America. Many were under the impression that the girls were serving as mail order or "picture brides" who would marry upon their arrival, to an American or Chinese man. Poorer families were especially willingly to sell their daughters in exchange for money, sometimes only a few pennies or dollars. Some of these girls were mere children, as young as ten or eleven years old.

In reality, once the girls reached America, they were immediately sold or auctioned off and forced into sexual slavery. Some of the men who imported or bought them belonged to tongs, Chinese criminal organizations that owned the prostitutes they imported from China.[12] With no way to return home, the majority of "Chinagirls" were forced into prostitution in order to work off the cost of their passage. Arriving in America without the benefit of knowing the English language, they were forced to sign contracts, written in English, promising to prostitute their bodies until their debt to their "benefactor" was paid. Per the contract, a sick day, menstrual cycle, or pregnancy meant additional time would be tacked on to their servitude. To these unfortunate, illiterate girls, there was no end in sight, and no law that could save them. Even if they did marry, their husbands usually ended up pimping them to the tongs anyway.[13]

However they got to the Pacific Northwest, prostitutes were there in great numbers throughout the 1800s and early 1900s. Surprisingly, they were initially accepted to a great extent. Whether plying their trade in the rich boomtowns of Alaska, the blooming metropolises of Washington, or the seaboard cities of Oregon, the ladies, sometimes quite openly, ran or worked in a vast variety of red-light districts. Not until the late 1800s did cities begin trying to crack down on vice with any real enthusiasm—after the wives and respectable women had finally braved the overland trails and discovered what their husbands, brothers, and sons had been up to. The hypocrisy in politics, wherein officials purposely overlooked the law or found loopholes around it, was a preferable, and viable, way to make money. It was easier to reap profits in the way of fines, license fees, taxes, hush money, liquor, and sex from ladies of the lamplight than it was to actually treat them as equals and help them become first-class citizens.

What the men didn't realize, however, is that a good many women in the prostitution industry were able to use their feminine wiles to gain their own sort of special power, which they exercised with a vengeance over the hapless males who fell for them. Not all their stories have happy endings. Many of their names and backgrounds were buried with them when they died. All of them risked everything for their profession: their health, their well-being, their families, their social status, and their reputations. For those women who managed to reign over their own select queendoms, however, life could be quite pleasant—and profitable. Good or bad, right or wrong, the majority of good time girls of the Pacific Northwest lived their own lives, on their own terms.

CHAPTER 1

---•◦•---

Camp Women of Washington

From the Anglo point of view, Washington State has a long and varied history, beginning with the arrival of Juan Perez in 1774. Subsequent explorers found a range of climates, from coastal lands to rain forests, from flat terrain to towering mountains. Like the rest of the Pacific Northwest, Washington is subject to four seasons, with snowy winters, cool and moist springs, warm summers, and autumns fairly bursting with color. Long before the arrival of Europeans, however, Native Americans had resided in the future state. When Meriwether Lewis and William Clark arrived in the area in 1805, they found the indigenous people to be quite different from most other tribes they had seen in their travels. Notably, women in these groups appeared more equal in status to their male counterparts. Lewis theorized that the women gained their equality due to "more evenly distributed economic roles."[1]

Lewis and Clark also could not help noticing that the Native Americans held a very different outlook on their societal roles when compared with that of Europeans. Anglos regarded prostitution as being promiscuous, while Natives regarded the cultural tradition of selling, lending, and trading women to others for sex quite natural. To them, there was nothing wrong with using women for the entertainment of guests or as trade for goods. There was no shame in doing so, since it generated good faith in business and personal relationships with Anglo explorers and traders. Most unfortunately, by the time Lewis and Clark made their debut in the region, a good number of young girls had contracted syphilis from the French and British traders who had preceded the expedition of 1805.[2] In the following years, the European view of prostitution as a dirty profession became common among all peoples in the United States—primarily because of the sexually transmitted diseases brought by the Europeans themselves.

During the 1830s, scant handfuls of Anglo women began arriving in Washington. In the meantime, traders and other pioneers made do by taking Native American wives. When the logging industry became big business in Washington Territory beginning in the 1850s, loggers were imported from as far away as Maine to work in the resulting camps and mills. Few of them, however, brought women with them. By 1858, Charles Prosch of the *Puget Sound Herald* at Steilacoom was writing about the lack of available white women for marriage. A year later, Prosch reported that the fifty bachelors of the village were "eager to put their necks in the matrimonial noose," but the ratio of men to women along Puget Sound was guessed to be nine to one. Those women who were present were already married, largely due to the 1850 Land Donation Act, which promised 320 acres of land to each man but also an additional 320 acres to married women. Socially speaking, however, at least some of the married "women" were as young as thirteen years old.[3]

In 1860 Prosch furthered his cause with an editorial titled "The Scarcity of White Women." He claimed that "at least two thirds of the three thousand voters in the territory wanted to get married, right then," but lacked suitable women to marry—there being largely only "half breeds" who would be "carrying in their veins the blood of men now historic." The subject was well received, to the effect that in February, Steilacoom bachelors gathered to further discuss the matter. There being no immediate sign of Anglo women back East crossing the raw

Washington's good time girls could range from stately and rich to risqué and naughty.
Courtesy Jan MacKell Collins

plains and unforgiving Rocky Mountains to their locale, the men began to "devise ways and means to secure this much-needed and desirable immigration to our shore."[4] Some of the plans were a limited success, while others failed. One thing was sure: East of Washington were a bevy of soiled doves who seemed to magically sniff out the opportunities in the Pacific Northwest, packed their trunks, and slowly but surely headed toward what would become the Evergreen State.

By the 1860s, good time girls had gained a strong foothold in the region. During the latter part of the decade, Captain Benjamin Sprague, owner of the *Gin Palace Polly*, sailed into Seattle. Sprague rightfully reckoned that he could save area loggers the trouble of going to Seattle on Saturday nights by simply taking ladies of pleasure to those logging camps along rivers. The captain and his feminine crew began a circuit, stopping for a day at each logging camp to sell sex and whiskey to the men. The plan worked beautifully until Sprague sold some of his libations to some natives—a big no-no. The captain was sentenced to a year in jail, and his shady ladies drifted off to other destinations.[5] It mattered little that the loggers lost their hero and heroines of harlotry. The prostitutes now had a firm anchor in the land. They were circulating among the camps, towns, and budding metropolises, leaving a trail of colorful stories in their wake.

Some of the earliest camps to have prostitution in their midst included Loomis, named for a local rancher who opened a trading post in the late 1870s. Although ranching was a primary industry, a bad 1879–80 winter killed off three thousand cattle. The ranchers turned to mining. Soon Loomis was known for harvesting a variety of minerals. Naturally, a bevy of prospectors, merchants, saloon men, and working girls descended on the town, situating themselves right along the main street. Children were cautioned by their parents to walk in the center of the street due to the number of wobbly drunks and "terrible painted ladies" lingering on the wooden sidewalks.

Walter Allen, who grew up in Loomis, remembered that the red-light district was situated at the foot of a hill and that "Big Edith" was the best-known of the painted ladies. "I had a friend who dared me to ride my cayuse [a low-quality horse] right into [Big Edith's] parlor," Allen recalled, "and in those days I never backed down to a dare." Indeed, the boy took the bet, riding his horse right up the front steps and through the front door. "Then I rode through the hall and came to a sort of screen of strings of beads hanging in front of the parlor and started through," Allen said. "When my cayuse felt those beads swishing across her shoulders, she bolted." What followed was quite a wild ride. "We went on through the parlor and through the back door that wasn't even open. There was a porch in back, quite high from the ground. My horse turned a somersault and I landed partly under her. Didn't break any bones, but was pretty shaken up." Allen declined to say what Big Edith thought about his big dare.[6]

Another time, Gilbert Alder decided to raise sugarcane, from which he made black molasses. One night Alder brought a jug of his product to show at a local saloon. Loomis's mining boom was just getting under way, and the owners of the Palmer Mountain Tunnel mine had sent one of their employees to Portland, Oregon, to sell stock in hopes of acquiring some worthy investors. James Haggerty, one of the impatient hopefuls waiting for some investor cash, was at the bar when Alder produced his jug. "Well, it's a good thing Loomis can produce molasses," Haggerty sneered. "It'll never turn out any gold from that damn mine!" Several men immediately objected to the man's comment and threw him to the floor while Alder poured his prize molasses over the prone man. Once Haggerty was good and gooey, another man skipped upstairs to a prostitute's room, where he acquired a feather pillow. The pillow was slit open and the feathers allowed to thoroughly coat the sticky Haggerty as he lay on the floor.[7]

Remote mining camps were one thing, but a good number of both mining and logging camps were company-owned and prohibited prostitution within their boundaries. When a logging camp set up on Vancouver Island during the 1880s, a brothel opened a safe distance away. Because the ladies were not allowed in camp to sell sex, they dubbed themselves "magazine subscription agents" instead and invited the men to their place of business to purchase their magazines. When the loggers made it to the brothel, they indeed received a copy of a magazine—the price of which included sexual entertainment. Another company town was Burnett, owned by the South Prairie Coal Company. Although it was founded in 1881, not until 1921 did Burnett finally allow a dance-hall to be built, as well as a garage housing a billiard hall in back. After the town folded beginning in 1927, the buildings were torn down.[8]

A more successful town was the mining camp of Ruby, established in 1886 and very soon known as a "hell roarin'" town. The place also became known as the "Babylon of the West" after a number of prostitutes set up shop in small cabins at one end of the main drag and up the hillside above it. Only a few are identified, if one includes saloon owners Della Marshall and Nettie Covington. Madam Jennie Bright, however, is recorded as having run an unusually upscale parlor house.[9] Guy Waring, later a county commissioner in Ruby, remembered that in March 1888 one of the town's "more lecherous citizens had attempted shortly before dawn to gain admittance to the town's chief bawdy house in a state of complete intoxication." When the madam, identified as Jennie, refused the man entry, Waring said, "the gentleman, according to the report I gathered, took a swing at her."

Jennie immediately went to her room and came back with a revolver, shooting the man neatly through the heart. The body was "found crumpled upon the steps outside the house, and by the time the sheriff could be persuaded to inquire at the establishment for details of the 'accident' the mistress had found time to board the stage for Spokane Falls." Jennie knew, and rightfully so, that news of some other murder or exciting event would soon mask her own misdeed and allow her to return to town and resume business without further inquiry. Waring himself found that "no one cared much about the actual facts of the murder. The chief point of dispute was whether or not the madame had taken a previous dislike to her unwelcomed client because of the damage he had done to her staff of girls, for it was generally known in Ruby, I learned, that the gentleman's much-discussed limp had been caused by neither infantile paralysis, rheumatism, nor any other common form of affliction or accident."[10]

Waring was obviously referring to a sexually transmitted disease the man may have carried. The idea that he may have transferred it to one of Jennie's employees no doubt infuriated the madam, who had all the more reason to shoot him. As for Waring, he had "heard all I wanted to about the deceased and his scandalous limp" by the time he arrived at the county auditor's office. There, however, the man was accosted by "a further version of the murder by an official who, as he casually explained, had been inside the brothel at the time of the shooting and stumbled over the dead body on his way out in the morning."[11] Jennie, it appears, escaped prosecution not only because Ruby's murders were notoriously numerous but also because the general consensus was that the disease-ridden drunk had it coming.

Jennie also was correct that some other event would soon overshadow the shooting. The new county of Okanogan was being formed, and Ruby was vying for the county seat despite the absence of any office buildings or even a safe. Only one other town was in contention: Salmon City, soon to be known as Conconully.[12] A meeting to make the decision was held on March 6 at the ranch of John Perkins. "It was an occasion I shall never forget," said Waring. "The people of Ruby, hearing of the meeting, all turned out to hold a noisy celebration in our honor. Whores, thieves, and drunkards, and other notorious citizens of the mining town were on hand some time before the oath of office was administered.

They were of course agreeably drunk, and serenaded us so loudly that it was difficult for anybody inside the ranch house to hear himself speak."[13]

The rowdy group carried out their antics while dancing "around the house in a bacchanalia fueled by excitement and bootleg whiskey." The crowd obviously wanted Ruby City to win, which it did. The drunken revelers partied for days and made a halfhearted attempt to construct city offices and a flimsy jail in Ruby City. Waring remembered that "since the county had no safe deposit vault, when the treasurer had on hand about eighteen hundred dollars in cash, he put it into an empty baking powder can and buried it on his ranch." Come the following November, however, it was clear that Ruby was the wrong choice for county seat, and Conconully was successfully appointed the position as of February 1889. Although Ruby incorporated in 1890, the silver crash of 1893 combined with low-grade ore in the local mines to do the town in. Ruby was deserted by 1899 and burned in 1900.[14]

Like Jennie Bright, Vena Blanchard also is remembered as running a stately parlor house in the early railroad town of Yakima. Vena was quite wealthy. She favored wearing high-neck satin gowns in summer and "stylish fur hats" with a "long brown marten coat" during winter. Around her neck was an emerald on a gold chain, which she said Jefferson Randolph "Soapy" Smith had given her back when she worked for him in Creede, Colorado. Vena was in her thirties by the time she arrived in Yakima in 1886, but she still took customers alongside her girls. She was quite popular with the prominent men in town. One of them remembered, "When you sat down in the parlor and started talking to Vena, you often forgot what it was you came for."[15]

By far, Washington's most unusual town was Home, originally formed in about 1895 as an anarchists' colony.[16] The town adopted a carefree attitude about lifestyles in general, declaring the purpose of Home was "to obtain land and to promote better social and moral conditions." The town founders submitted that self-regulation would produce "a society so imbued with decency and honesty that no laws were required to regulate its members." To the outside world, however, Home was anything but the ideal picture of social and moral conditions. Home's first newspaper, *New Era*, emphasized that residents of Home were free to live as they chose. Such post-Victorian no-no's as cohabitation between men and women and other abnormal social behavior were acceptable at Home. A second paper, *Discontent, Mother of Progress* published articles with such headlines as "The Rights of Woman in Sexual Relations" and "Is 'Sin' Forgivable?" One article went so far as to call marriage "the lowest form of prostitution," while columnist Emma Goldman blamed the "organized church" for prostitution as a whole.[17]

For a time, Home flourished. When disgruntled government officials sent a US marshal to Home to arrest the staff of the *Discontent* for publishing their naughty articles, the man reported back that it was a most friendly citizenry who greeted him at the ship. He was fed a wonderful supper and treated to a big dance at which he was the guest of honor. The marshal's report may have been the reason the staff of the *Discontent* were acquitted upon being duly delivered to Tacoma. Home did, however, lose its post office, as well as the right to mail the *Discontent* through federal post offices. But the promoters of Home were not done. Newspapers next reported on a Professor Thompson, who showed up in town dressed from head to toe in lady's attire. The outfit was more comfortable, Thompson lectured, as well as "more aesthetic." Thompson's outlandish statement was followed up by author Lois Waisbrooker, who in her book *My Century Plant* boldly explained how to "free the world from the 'disease of sex.'" Waisbrooker next shacked up with her lover, Mattie D. Penhallow, who generated yet another small newspaper titled *Clothed with the Sun*. Once again, post office officials found the paper too brazen, for stating the facts of life. Mattie and Lois were arrested, the latter woman being fined for "indecent acts." Upon her release from jail, Lois immediately returned to Home and generated yet another paper, *Foundation Principles*, which pretty much repeated Mattie's newspaper.[18]

In spite of the opinions and laws of the outside world, Home remained quite a successful endeavor. The community continued to offer "schools of thought," yoga classes, spiritualists, food experts, and other specialized entertainments. Folks continued cohabitating without the sanctity of marriage. Laura Wood chose to live in a wigwam, and nobody blinked an eye. Joe Kapella lived in a tree, and that was alright too. Outside of town, however, surrounding communities whispered horrified rumors of sex orgies and "free love."

A new attack against Home was devised in 1910 during the "Great Nude Bathing Case." Disapproving local farmers were now purchasing land from Home's homeowner's association. Inevitably, someone reported to the county that men and women were bathing, together, in the nude, in public. Four women and a man were arrested for indecent exposure. Veteran journalist and Home homeowner Jay Fox, in yet another newspaper called the *Agitator*, fired off an editorial titled "The Nudes and the Prudes" and suggested that those who had complained to the authorities ought to be ostracized. He was arrested for encouraging interference with the law and sentenced to two months in the Pierce County jail.

Naturally there was an uproar, with rallies and donations to Fox's cause coming from as far away as Boston, but the US Supreme Court upheld the verdict. Fox served six weeks in jail before Washington's Governor Lister pardoned him. The battles against Home continued well into World War I, but children of the town founders eventually grew up and moved away. As late as 1946, however, dozens of self-educated, creative, intelligent, and friendly Homeites remained. Today, the still-unincorporated community serves as a resort with plenty of natural attractions, but the social faux pas of the past have faded in the wake of modern living that permits everything the town once stood for.[19]

Other places along Washington's coast included Port Townsend, where the good time girls operated along Water Street at the water's edge; the local joke was that "sin flourishes at sea level." A leading madam was Lottie Sinnott, who ran a large parlor house on a bluff above town. Lottie was quite popular among the local merchants, who extended credit to her girls on her behalf. The madam was quite wealthy, as were her clients. One night, however, Lottie made an exception for three young men, all cousins, who had no money. Lottie knew that one of them was the son of a local meat and fowl merchant with whom she wanted to establish good trade. The young man explained that although he could not pay for the evening's services, his father would. Lottie believed him, and the threesome spent a night enjoying expensive libations and Lottie's girls.

Lottie waited for the father to pay; when he didn't, she wrote an eloquent and professional letter asking for the money. The next day a reply came, "a rambling stream of abuse" accusing Lottie of blackmail for an event the man was not even aware had taken place. Lottie replied with a more detailed explanation but was once again rebutted with a rude return letter. In frustration, the madam let it be known among the local merchants that the man was not to be trusted, nor was his family. The merchant never did pay, in cash anyway. Soon afterward, Lottie and her girls returned from shopping to find that a dozen "bowel-loosened" chickens had been set to running amok in her parlor house.[20]

Unlike the mining and logging camps of eastern Washington, Port Townsend authorities exhibited some disdain for their wayward women. In March 1904 soldier Pat Cady was arrested for fighting at a local brothel. But the arrest was not because Cady gave three prostitutes black eyes after instigating the fight, but for fighting with another man after leaving the house. In August the "monthly roundup" of soiled doves by Chief Furlong netted seventy-one dollars in fines. The frequency of the roundups had increased, as officers had previously only raided the brothels every three months. But the ladies caught on and got in the habit of leaving town just before each raid. Of those arrested in 1904, Port Townsend's *Morning Leader* described them as "genteel appearing white women, the French women, the negro and the half-breed as well as the thoroughbred. They all looked alike to the chief, and each was assessed seven dollars."[21]

The fines also had increased, as an earlier report that August stated that "inmates" were typically fined six dollars. Madams were fined ten dollars, and dance houses paid fifteen dollars. Another roundup in September netted 108 dollars. In October, prostitute Lulu Severs was fined ten dollars for "making goo-goo eyes" at a stranger on the street after a policeman witnessed the gesture. And in December, a man named DeWill was arrested for "living off the earnings of a fallen woman." A few days later, Chief Furlong "fired out of the city" a prostitute named Ole Scott and her paramour, a man named Daly. The busts continued through at least 1906, when two soiled doves, Jessie Moore and Daisy Leonard, were arrested and put up bail of ten dollars.[22]

Prostitution continued to flourish in Washington during the early 1900s. When Colorado madam Laura Bell McDaniel purchased four lots in the tiny ferry town of Columbia River Station sometime around 1918, she perhaps intended to open a brothel there if the place ever grew sizable enough. It didn't.[23] Prostitution was able to flourish, however, at McCleary, near Olympia. In 1925 it was discovered that "Big Betty, the toast of the moonshine set," was operating a brothel from the second-floor office of a local newspaper. To keep her business private, Big Betty and her girls willingly subscribed to the paper (which, incidentally, was run by three sixteen-year-olds), and Betty placed a weekly ad for the "Liberty rooms, soft drinks, candy and cigarettes." Later, permitting the ad to run was discouraged by city officials.[24]

There were others. Holden, a company town built on government land, had no shady ladies—an edict directed by the USDA Forest

Service. The men of the town, however, could simply row or hike from the nearby community of Lucerne to access the Edgemont Hotel, where plenty of working girls awaited. By accident or design, the area around Edgemont also was known as Pecker Point.[25] A better-known town was Coulee City, established during the 1930s as the Coulee Dam was being built. Hu "Scoop" Blonk, a former reporter for the *Spokane Chronicle*, later remembered "the frequent raids on the madams and gamblers on B Street in Coulee City."

Blonk knew quite a bit about the city sirens. "The whorehouses were always second-story places up above the beer parlors," he remembered. "One summer the girls were complaining about how hot their second-story place was, so Harvey sent up a plumbing crew and put a sprinkling system on the whorehouse's roof!" Blonk also recalled that when the eventual city of Grand Coulee was short on funds, two city councilmen would take a "pillowslip" to the local brothels and "collect enough money to keep the city going. Some streets were graveled with the whores' money, if my memory serves me correctly. There was never anything criminal about it. Those fifty-five women just paid their taxes, I guess." Blonk knew the exact number of women on the row because he once interviewed the doctor from the dam site. "When I asked him how many prostitutes there had been, he said, 'Fifty-five.' Then he added proudly, 'And not one of them infected.'"[26]

Grand Coulee is in the northern part of Washington; even farther north, closer to the Canadian border, was Curlew. Bill Hottell, a teen in Curlew during 1934, remembered a local blacksmith named Harry Lavin. Harry had a wife, who would "get the gun out and chase Harry around the house" when he drank too much. "Just as Harry would get around the corner of the house, she would shoot." Once, on his birthday, Harry also took his wife and a young Native American woman to Grand Forks, where he "rented rooms and farmed them out for prostitution. He had Agnes Seymour as a Spanish gal, and I don't know what he had his wife named as," Hottell said. One of Harry's other "women" was Ann Bush, a feisty young lady who once went over the border to Greenland, British Columbia, with two other men and robbed a liquor store. "The Mounties showed up and shot one of the robbers. Ann Bush drug him into the car and beat the Mounties across the line," Hottell said. "They never did catch her."[27]

Ann was quite the little roustabout. On one occasion, Hottell remembered, she became quite angry with Harry Lavin. The two were living together and had been on a monthlong drinking binge. While Harry napped, Ann "goes out and finds herself a two by four and she comes in and puts it right across the bridge of Harry Lavin's nose," Hottell said. "She throwed the two by four down, runs into the kitchen and grabs this butcher knife and comes at him with this butcher knife. He says, 'I just opened my eyes enough that I could see that butcher knife coming at me and I grabbed it as she pulled it through my hand. She came at me again with that knife and I grabbed it again, and she pulled the knife right through my hand again and cut me clear to the bone. By that time I was starting to sober up, so I knocked her flat on her ass.'"[28]

On yet another drunk, Lavin suspected someone of stealing meat from him, "so he went out trying to protect his stuff," Hottell explained. "Ann Bush and Big Agnes Seymour knocked him down out in the yard and took clubs and just beat him till he was almost coal black. Then they ran in the house and got the kerosene lamp and poured the kerosene on him and set him afire. So he had scars that were over an inch thick on his neck. It took him a long time to get healed up from that." Harry once retaliated against Ann by pressing charges, but bailed her out before the night was over.[29] Scruffy women like Ann Bush and Big Agnes surely had no place in Washington's larger cities, where the shady ladies remained refined and genteel right into the twentieth century. For the most part, anyway.

CHAPTER 2

Scarlet Women of Seattle

One of the best-known of Seattle's good time girls was among the very first—and few—Anglo women in town during 1852. She was Mary Ann Boyer, a lass standing "less than five feet tall." In 1851 she married whaling ship captain David W. "Bull" Conklin while at sea out of her native Pennsylvania. By the time the newlyweds sailed into Port Townsend, the marriage was less than seaworthy. Conklin left his wife standing on the dock and sailed off in search of a more companionable shipmate. Mary Ann, meanwhile, found a friend in one David S. "Doc" Maynard, who unwittingly helped her open a brothel as Seattle's first madam. They called her both "Mother Damnable" and "Madam Damnable."[1]

Originally, Mary Ann was assigned to run the Felker House. The place was named for the owner, Captain Leonard Felker, and was meant to serve as an inn that occasionally doubled as a courthouse. The seaman actually transported the prefabricated building aboard his ship, the *Franklin Adams*, and deposited it on land he purchased on the Sound at First Avenue South and Jackson Street. The property was known as Maynard's Point and was owned by Doc Maynard. Felker House was "the first hard-finished construction on Elliott Bay with milled clapboard sides, an imported southern pine floor, and lath-and-plaster walls and ceilings."[2] The place resembled a big Southern mansion, with two stories, columns in front, and a large veranda. Small rooms were in the back of the house near the kitchen. Had the house been in the South, these might have served as slave quarters. In Seattle they eventually served as cribs for Mary Ann's girls.[3]

Whether Felker or Maynard knew of Mary Ann's plans to turn Seattle's first inn into a brothel is unknown. But the woman's lavish profanity—in six languages—made her something beyond a quaint little innkeeper. Indeed, to the public, Mary was a "demon in petticoats," but she also was an astute businesswoman. Shortly after Washington was established as a territory in 1853, the first legislative session was held at Felker House. Mary Ann charged outrageous prices for food and lodging: Use of the makeshift courtroom cost twenty-five dollars, and sequestered jurors' bedrooms cost ten dollars per night.[4]

Those who objected to the high fares were met with epithets and sometimes the throwing of pots and pans by Mary Ann herself. When one man dared to ask for a receipt, Mary Ann replied, "Here's your receipt!" and flung some sticks of stove wood at him. Still, even more prominent men tended to patronize Felker House after Mary Ann added brothel services, as well as fine food, beautiful furnishings, and a first-class stay. These guests generally stayed during the week. Many of them were unaware that sex was for sale on the premises, but certainly some of them answered that they were looking for companionship when Mary Ann asked pleasantly, "What is your pleasure?" On the weekends, when the loggers came to town, they too came to Madam Damnable's and specifically asked for girls.[5]

Largely due to her exclusive clientele, Mary Ann commanded privacy around her hotel. Navy Rear Adm. Thomas S. Phelps later remembered that during an "Indian" scare, sailors were directed to build extra roads around Seattle and burn any bushes in which an Indian might be lurking. Phelps told of approaching Mary Ann's house, which was surrounded by foliage to assure privacy. But "the moment our men appeared upon the scene, with three dogs at her heels, and an apron filled with rocks, this termagant would come tearing out of the house," Phelps wrote, "and the way stones, oaths, and curses flew was something fearful to contemplate, and, charging like a fury, with the dogs wild to flesh their teeth in the detested invaders, the division invariably gave way."[6]

When she died in 1873, Mary Ann was respectfully interred in the Seattle Cemetery. Local legend states that when the cemetery was moved in 1884, Mary Ann's coffin proved especially heavy. Curious workers opened the lid to find that "her body had somehow 'turned to stone'" and that her features were intact. Felker House burned in 1889 during the Great Seattle Fire.[7]

Beginning in 1861, Madam Damnable saw at least some competition from San Francisco brothel operator John Pinnell (aka Pennell), who opened a "rough-hewn bawdy house" atop some sawdust fill just below Mill Street (now Yesler Way). The place was called the Illahee, a Chinook word for "home place." The Illahee was alternatively known as "The Mad House" and "The Sawdust Pile." Due to its location, girls of the Illahee were sometimes referred to as "sawdust women." The name caught on and became a popular colloquialism for the entire red-light district.[8]

The Illahee was originally a "simple, unpainted frame structure with the usual bar and a dance floor with a three-piece orchestra." Off the main hall were small rooms where prostitutes charged between two and five dollars. At first Pinnell could find only Native American women to work there. Many of them were simply traded from their families for Hudson's Bay blankets and became indentured to Pinnell. Their families were guaranteed that the women would receive "an education, gainful employment, food, clothing, shelter and even baths." The girls would be able to "send some of their earnings" back to their families. To these poor Native American families and even the girls themselves, Pinnell's offer seemed like a dream come true.[9]

Pinnell assured himself a good clientele. He willingly cashed payroll checks for free and charged a mere fifty cents for drinks. Time with one of the girls cost between two and five dollars. The Illahee was so successful that Pinnell was eventually able to pay twelve hundred dollars annually in license fees, while his employees paid a monthly fee of ten dollars. When the growing city needed street repairs, Pinnell and his girls agreed to slightly higher fees until there was enough money for the project. They say that the money was raised in just three days.[10]

During the 1870s, Seattle battled with Tacoma over which city would be a terminus for the Northern Pacific Railroad. When "town father" Arthur Denny received a telegram stating that the railroad had chosen Tacoma, all seemed lost. But it was John Pinnell who "made the largest single cash pledge" to a fund used to entice the railroad to come to Seattle instead. The ploy didn't work; to make things worse, the Northern Pacific virtually kicked Pinnell out of Tacoma, where he had opened a second Illahee bordello. Pinnell got even—by recruiting a dozen beautiful, professional harlots from San Francisco to open for business in Seattle. The ladies arrived, "all dazzling in form-fitting bombazine frocks, French-heeled shoes, silk stockings, and the war paint of their profession." The ladies were welcomed by almost everyone, and immediately set about establishing fine parlor houses and forming what became known as the Whitechapel District. Seattle boomed as "the Las Vegas of Puget Sound." Satisfied, Pinnell married one of his girls, Annie Murray, in 1875. The couple retired from the prostitution profession and moved to an estate in eastern Washington to breed horses.[11]

By 1880 an area called the "Lava Bed" offered brothels, box theaters, gambling houses, and saloons that stretched for blocks and blocks. Madams included Lil DuPree, Goldie McClure, Laura Molloy, Jenny Sills, and Mattie Singleton. As these ladies set up their common brothels, a healthy handful of upper-class madams opened parlor houses. City officials might have objected to the goings-on a bit more but for the well-behaved ladies of the evening. The majority of them paid their fines in a timely manner, rarely strayed into the respectable parts of town, and kept out of trouble. It is said that the money the ladies paid to the city amounted to 87 percent of the budget's general fund.[12]

In 1883 women of all walks of life in Washington Territory won a major battle: the right to vote. In Seattle the epic decision was immediately followed by a reckoning by city fathers that a closer look at Whitechapel was merited. In what was called an effort "to favor the brothels and 'box houses' of Seattle," a new ordinance outlawed "soliciting prostitution upon any of the public streets," and the mere presence of "dissolute Indian women" after dark.[13] To the city's leading madams, the move was a good one and nearly eliminated the competition of low-end ladies who might undercut the parlor houses. But not every woman worked in an official brothel, as evidenced by the 1887 arrival of Francoise DuMonet.

Francoise seemed to disprove all the characteristics of a typical working girl. Immediately upon disembarking from the *Queen of the Pacific*, the stylishly attired lady made her way to the elite Washington Hotel and took a room. There she remained much of the time, receiving no visitors—at first. Eventually, however, it was noticed that "selected wealthy businessmen and highly-placed city leaders" were known to visit the lady. Francoise quietly made appointments with these men, sans a madam or pimp. Yet every time a prominent man was seen leaving her room, Francoise was soon spotted making her way to the Dexter Horton Bank and depositing large amounts of money. Seattle authorities apparently failed to notice the quiet courtesan for about a year. By the time anyone thought to find out more about her, she had made an unannounced departure. She was never seen again.[14]

More obvious ladies of the evening included Mary Chambers, a veteran of the trade who called herself Kittie Beaumont when she began her career in San Francisco back in 1884. By 1886 Mary was in Portland under the name "Little Kittie May." When she came to Seattle a year later, she gave her name as Mary Chambers. Mary tried passing herself off as a seamstress but was arrested for prostitution. None, however, could beat madam Lou Graham, who arrived in 1888 and boldly built her parlor house across from Father Prefontaine's Church of Our Lady of Good Help at Third and Washington.[15]

The evil deeds of Lou Graham and other women were overshadowed in 1889 when, on June 5, a workman accidentally left a pot of glue warming on a stove and started a fire. The flames quickly grew out of control, and within twenty-four hours Seattle's entire business district and the Lava Bed were gone. Both the city and the red-light ladies quickly rebuilt—a bane to city officials as they saw the Lava Bed rising from the ashes. As they built, the ladies and their male counterparts simply operated out of tents. But gone was the old, passé name of the Lava Beds. It was no secret that the area, including Whitechapel, was now officially known as Seattle's Tenderloin.[16]

Over the next several years, Seattle tried to clamp down on the red-light district. Left alone was John Consadine, manager of the People's Theater at Second and Washington. Consadine purchased the place in 1892. Admission was only ten cents, but customers were also expected to buy plenty of liquor. The theater was unique in that only legitimate, professional entertainers were hired, while prostitutes plied their trade separately in "curtained boxes." At some point Consadine opened a second theater, of the same name, in Spokane. But Spokane was less forgiving, and Consadine returned to Seattle in 1897, where he reopened the People's Theater and invested in several other box houses within the red-light district.[17]

The notorious Klondike Kate was known to entertain at the People's Theater. Another performer was Louise Gething, who hailed from a parlor house in Spokane. Louise's act consisted of appearing on stage in a fearful fit of nervousness and singing the one song she knew. The actual title of the ballad has been lost to history, but part of it went, "The boat lies high, the boat lies low, she lies high and dry on the Ohio." On the last note, Louise would burst into crocodile tears as several sympathetic gentlemen came to her rescue. Louise would slyly pick the wealthiest of them and take him up to her room.[18]

Seattle's sisters in sin weathered the ups and downs of the local economy quite nicely. The ladies managed to emerge unscathed during the silver crash of 1893, as well as an 1894 ban on liquor sales in box houses. Even the miners coming from the Yukon gold rush paid off, although many women did leave Seattle to make their fortunes in Alaska and Canada. Alarmed at the cash-cow exodus, city officials repealed the ordinance prohibiting liquor sales in theaters. Ships coming into Seattle were always loaded with plenty of gold—and men. Mayor Tom Humes, who recognized the benefits of both the ladies and Seattle's legitimate businesses, allowed the town to remain "wide open."[19]

By the early 1900s, several madams reigned supreme in Seattle. Rae McRoberts ran two enormous and grand parlor houses in Seattle. One of them was managed by a demure-looking woman named Tillie Mitchell. Rae and Tillie's girls were treated fine. Their board included breakfast served promptly at two o'clock in the afternoon. The fare included choice of eggs, clam cakes with bacon, kidney sauté, shad roe, breast of chicken, buttered toast, coffee, and milk. Rae always ate in the dining room, but her girls could have breakfast served in their rooms if they chose. At six o'clock, everyone gathered in the dining room, and guests were welcome to join the meal. The ladies could visit at their leisure until they were called to the front parlor rooms. A light supper was generally served around midnight.

One of Rae's more unusual clients was known as Uncle Ned. Once a year, usually following the first substantial snowfall of the season, Ned would rent the entire house for the night, at the hefty price of two thousand dollars. The evening's activities began with Rae's girls assembling themselves, nude, around Ned in the music parlor. As one girl played the piano, the others would sing to the man and run their fingers through his hair. After a time, per Ned's instructions, the party moved into another parlor, which contained a small sleigh. Ned would take the reins as two buckets of ice were spread on the floor of the sleigh. As the girl at the piano played a slow rendition of "Jingle Bells," two girls would slowly disrobe Uncle Ned and go to work. Afterward, Ned would thank them all, commenting, "There is nothing equal to a good sleigh ride!"[20]

City officials continued anguishing between cleaning up the vice in their town and regulating it to Seattle's benefit. In 1902 the Tenderloin District was officially moved south of the downtown area to make room for legitimate businesses. The effort may have been fueled by the murder of prostitute Lottie Brace, who met her end at the hands of Zenon "James" Champoux. The two met when Lottie was working in Alaska. Lottie had accepted the man's offer of marriage but changed her mind and headed for Spokane and then Seattle. In Seattle, Lottie went to work as a dance-hall girl alongside her sister, Ella. Champoux tracked her down at the Arcadia variety theater and, when she spurned his advances, stabbed her in the head. During his trial, it was noted that the murderer spoke broken English and insisted on eating his food raw. He also told others that if Lottie "would not love him in this world, he would force her to love him in the next." Champoux was the first man to be legally hanged in 1904.[21]

As Champoux swung from the gallows, Seattle's sirens went about their business. Dave Beck was around the age of eight or nine when he sold newspapers all around downtown Seattle. Rather than fighting other boys for the busiest corners, Beck sold papers along what he called "Skid Road," the location of Seattle's lower-end brothels. The boy was too young to grasp what went on there, but remembered that his mother "would have killed me if she had known I was down there. That was the habitat of all the gamblers and madams and everything else illicit that you can think of. Oh, I saw many madams, but at that time I didn't even know what they were. It was a damn good place to sell newspapers because people were likely to give you twenty-five cents more for a newspaper than you could get north of there. That was the free spending life they were living."[22]

Wealthier prostitutes worked out of expensive hotels, but the luckiest of them ran their own parlor houses. Many of these places resembled grand private homes, with manicured lawns and a demure outside appearance. Madam Lila Young ran one of these places, between about 1904 and 1910, on King Street.[23] One intriguing story about Lila's ladies was a weekly game they called "The Longest Beard." At the beginning of the week, the girls would each contribute one dollar to a pot. At the end of the week, whoever had serviced the gentleman with the longest beard in the last seven days won the money. The girls only had one chance to pick their winning man; should a gentleman with a longer beard appear, he was off-limits to those who had already made their selection.

When a man arrived who seemed like a sure bet, whoever took him upstairs would quip, "He's my favorite jockey!" The girls had great fun with the competition, joking and teasing one another. If one of them was caught with a customer sporting a fake beard, her punishment was to buy champagne for the rest of the house. None of the customers seemed to wonder why the girls at Lila's happened to keep a ruler in their rooms. Lila remained in business through at least 1910. The census that year attests to the grandeur of her business: six men living on the premises worked as waiters, cooks, and a laundryman. Louise Darrah was listed as a hairdresser, but five other young ladies were blatantly identified as prostitutes.[24]

Beginning in 1909, Seattle authorities began cracking down on the red-light districts in earnest. In May, Mayor John F. Miller ordered the "disorderly houses" closed as police raided five brothels, confiscated their liquor, and arrested their occupants. Miller did not appear to want the houses permanently closed; rather, he was seeking "a thoroughly regulated district as the best practicable means at hand of dealing with the social evil." Those arrested included Nettie Clifford on a charge of larceny and Frankie Williams and Freda O'Conners for being disorderly. All three women paid their fines and were released, likely disappearing back into the demimonde.[25]

Miller was succeeded by City Councilman Hiram Gill in 1910. To those in the vice districts, Gill—a known investor in the red-light districts—was a wise choice. The *Seattle Star* warned that Gill would be a "red-light mayor" who will unleash "a carnival of vice and crime." Gill rightfully pointed out, however, that allowing prostitution in the "Restricted District" would keep bawdy women in one area and give the city a means to control them to an extent. "Give 'em the Tenderloin," he reasoned, "and keep 'em out of the rest of town." Gill's opinions were echoed by *Seattle Times* publisher Alden J. Blethen and others. The mayor promised everybody that the all-new restricted district "will be the most quiet place in Seattle" and would "be located in a place where men will have to go out of their way to find it."[26]

Gill's first act was to hire his old friend, Charles W. "Wappy" Wappenstein, as police chief. Wappenstein had previously been fired by John Miller for corrupt activities. The duo next hired Clarence Gerald and Gideon Tupper, veterans in the red-light district, to manage Seattle's two largest brothels, the Paris House and the Midway (the latter being run by madam Annie Redoubt and owned by Gill). The Midway featured one hundred rooms, while the Paris offered seventy rooms. With the Midway and the Paris squared away, Gill next decided to open the largest brothel the world had ever seen, large enough to house five hundred girls. Gill and his cohorts formed the Hillside Improvement Company, executed a fifteen-year lease on Tenth Avenue South, and built their grand, dormitory-like brothel. But the building was never used for its intended purpose. The good citizens of Seattle objected to the plan and managed to recall Gill in 1911 as Wappenstein was arrested for pocketing the monthly ten-dollar fines paid by Seattle's prostitutes. Gill managed to get reelected in 1914, but was forever after suspected of wrongdoing. Meanwhile, Gill's would-be bordello became an apartment house instead and stood until 1951 when an air force bomber crashed into it.[27]

During the tumultuous years of Gill's reign, Dave Beck remembered the working girls being evicted from "the Slot" and relocating "all over the damned area where I drove laundry wagons. I can remember delivering to them down on Lake Union when they lived in houseboats." But everyone was helpless when Washington passed the Dry Law in 1916, outlawing liquor. Even so, a new generation of harlots were hatching plans to work in Seattle. During the late 1920s, Nellie Curtis, another of Seattle's legendary madams, opened her first brothel in the Camp Hotel on First Avenue. In 1942 she took over the LaSalle Hotel after the inn's Japanese proprietors were sent off to internment camps during World War II. The LaSalle was soon Seattle's "leading brothel," and Nellie remained in business until 1951, when she sold out.[28]

One of Nellie Curtis's biggest hurdles was the 1926 election of Mayor Bertha Landes, who immediately set about cleaning up Seattle. Crooked cops were dismissed and gamblers booted from town, but the cleansing tidal wave also hit prostitutes and dance-hall girls. Bertha did not understand that many dance-hall girls were women trying to support their families and that they only occasionally strayed into the prostitution realm. When the ladies themselves appealed to her, the mayor turned to regulating the dance-halls instead. Two years later, Bertha was ousted from office by her campaign opponent, Frank Edwards, who opposed the mayor's "petticoat government." Edwards refused the traditional debate during his campaign, remarking that "any married man knows the danger of getting into an argument with a woman." Bertha was actually favored by the media, but Edwards found support in the corrupt officers the she-mayor had fired. Upon his election, Edwards fired the police chief, rehired his old buddies from the force, and soon got Seattle's government back on its crooked little feet.[29]

The prostitution industry in Seattle remained alive and well for many more years. During the 1930s, newspaper boy Bob Halberg remembered a "mystery house" at the corner of 64th Street. The gate was always locked according to Halberg, so he and the other boys put the paper in a little receptacle poking out from a hedge surrounding the yard. One time Halberg spied some ladies coming from the house. "They looked like movie stars and they had hats and gloves up to their elbows and silk print dresses," he recalled. "They looked just fabulous. Somebody told me they were prostitutes. I thought, 'My God, that's a wonderful profession, look at how nice they are dressed and look how beautiful they are.'" As the boy watched, the ladies got into some vehicles, each with its own chauffeur who opened the door for them. Halberg also remembered a man at the house "who seemed to have a relationship with the madam of the house and seemed to be the caretaker. He cut the lawn, trimmed the hedges, and did the shopping."[30]

During World War II, officials became alarmed at how many soldiers, after being on leave in Seattle, returned to their respective bases at Bremerton, Everett, and Fort Lewis with venereal disease. A commanding officer at Payne Field even wrote to Mayor William Devin, voicing his concerns and threatening to prohibit his men from visiting a seventy-four-block area of the city. The FBI even stepped in, also threatening to take over police operations and close the city brothels. Devin responded by accusing police chief Herbert Kimsey of corruption. Denying any wrongdoing, Kimsey staged a number of violent raids on Seattle's brothels and commanded Capt. Irene Dunham to take over as vice officer. The FBI withdrew its threat to take over. Kimsey's term expired in 1946, and Devin hired more respectable police chiefs and officers. By the 1960s Seattle's prostitution industry was much more discreet, operating on the hill above the downtown area. As before, the madams paid "protection" money to escape raids and arrests.[31] They say that prostitution remains yet in Seattle, though not in any form or shape of the city's pioneer days.

Chapter 3

Madam Lou Graham, Seattle's Leading Strumpet

By far the best-known of Seattle's wayward ladies was Lou Graham, a petite lady who was born Dorothea Georgine Emile Ohben in Germany between 1857 and 1862. Where the woman spent her early life is unknown, but when she arrived in Seattle in February 1888 aboard the steamer *Pacific Pride*, she discarded her given name in favor of her shorter, and more sporting, moniker. The lady had a plan, and she embarked on her new project with vigor. Wearing her best suit, Lou immediately called a meeting with the city's top businessmen. Seattle, she pointed out, was well on its way to achieving status as a world port for shipping and lumber companies. It made sense, Lou said, that the onslaught of important and wealthy men coming to Seattle should be provided with the finest in top accommodations, entertainment, and food. Such a palatial place should rival those in big cities across the nation, not to mention London and Paris. Weary travelers would need a place where cultured, lovely hostesses from all over the world gathered to address the men's needs, discuss cultural and economic issues of the day, and see to their "personal matters."[1]

It was no secret that Seattle already had plenty of fine parlor houses, but the palatial quarters Lou Graham proposed would make them look like hovels. Lou further guaranteed the businessmen that her prices would be fair, her business discreet. Only the most elite of the upper class would be invited to partake in her palace of pleasure, and she was more than willing to share her profits in the way of generous contributions to the city. All she asked was that she be allowed to operate unmolested by city officials or the law. The men, beguiled by Lou's obvious charm, grace, and intelligence, agreed.[2]

Construction immediately began on Lou's beautiful bordello at the southwest corner of Third Avenue South and Washington Street. As promised, the furnishings were stunning, the staff was fine, and the girls were cultured goddesses from faraway places like England, France, and Asia. The brothel was but a block from City Hall, and upon her grand opening, Lou bestowed her own personal gift to city officials: They were, and always would be, invited guests and treated to all the pleasures of the house free of charge. And, as promised, guests at Lou Graham's were treated better than those in the fanciest hotels across the nation. Men who spent the night awoke to find their clothing laundered, starched, and pressed, with breakfast waiting. Richer clients were allowed to rent the entire house for the night if they wished, and Lou had the power to check anyone's credit to make sure he could pay the fee. She wisely invested her money in the hot commodities of the day, namely gold, diamonds, stocks, and real estate.[3]

The success of Lou's first brothel was short-lived, for the whole place burned during Seattle's great fire in June 1889. But Lou had already made enough money to expand her property and build an all-brick structure that was even finer than the first one. The furnishings were even more lavish and included beautiful antique and imported furnishings, imported carpets, tapestries, original artwork, marble and bronze sculptures, crystal lamps, and fine china. Lou would later build her own private home on Madison Avenue, in about 1902. Unfortunately, inventories of Lou's properties after her death fail to differentiate between the two houses. Suffice to say, both Lou's home and her parlor house

The only known image of Seattle's Lou Graham (left) and her ladies
Courtesy Jay Moynahan

contained exquisitely furnished themed rooms. There was, for instance, a Turkish room with matching Turkish decor, a Wine Room, a library nicknamed the "Tapestry Room" due to the seven tapestry panels adorning the walls, a Dancing Room, a dining room with a twelve-foot oak table and service for up to eighteen, a Smoking Room, and a Billiard Room. Bathrooms were located on each floor.

In one house, presumably Lou's parlor house, the bedrooms were identified by their colors—blue, green, and yellow—while two other bedrooms were simply noted as the Front and Back bedrooms. Curiously, the Pink Room was furnished for a child. It is believed to have been occupied by Ulna, the daughter of Lou's longtime housekeeper and companion, Nellie Delmas, who lived with her. Another room, the Gold Room, allegedly featured glittering gold on nearly every furnishing—from fishbowls to the cuspidors to the grand chandelier hanging from the ceiling. Lou had the room polished regularly and refurbished annually.[4]

Lou's became a regular stop on the trolley line, with the conductor calling out, "All out for Lou Graham's place!" (as long as there were no proper women aboard). To advertise her place, and perhaps just to get out for an afternoon, Lou and her ladies would take a weekly carriage ride around town. Unlike other madams and ladies of the evening, who were shunned by the public, Lou's friends were known to openly call out to her, and she would wave or blow kisses in their direction. The carriage rides usually included a stop at a favorite store, where Lou and her girls would pick out jewelry or clothing and charge them to the madam's account.[5]

Shortly after she appeared in Seattle for the first time, in the Washington Territorial Census of 1889, Lou was shocked to suffer a raid by Police Chief Butterfield and Captain Kinley. Prostitutes Amy Conway and Lizzie Murdoch were arrested, along with a client identified as R. J. Johnson. But Lou had a deal with the city, and she intended to make it stick. In court the madam "refused to be responsible for the inmates of her house." It is doubtful that Amy and Lizzie were indicted for any crime pertaining to prostitution. During another raid in August, it was duly noted that Lou Graham's house "was not visited."[6]

Lou kept up her end of the bargain by being a model citizen and contributing to city coffers as needed. In 1890, when Henry Niegmann's wife ran off with a baker, Lou cared for the couple's three children. That same year, when one of her girls fell seriously ill, Lou sent for Father Prefontaine—who happened to occupy the Catholic Church of Our Lady of Good Help just across the street from the parlor house. The priest stayed by the girl's side until she was taken to the hospital. As he was leaving, one of the other ladies of the house asked if he would hear her confession. The two went into the parlor, and other girls soon made the same request. By the time Father Prefontaine left, he had heard the confessions of more than a dozen girls. Lou always claimed that some of her girls began attending the church after that.[7]

Lou's biggest crime was that she flat-out refused to buy a liquor license. She did, however, willingly pay penalties for the deed between 1890 and 1892. Eventually she acquiesced and paid for her licenses. She also began traveling back and forth to San Francisco. One such trip occurred in October 1890. She was obviously known there; in November, post office clerk Charles Ammerman was indicted for opening the letters of others and had "willfully delayed a letter addressed to Miss Lou Graham, also of this city."[8]

Back home in Seattle, Lou's girls came and went over time. One of them, Lettie Stillwell, later moved to Missoula, Montana, and opened her own house. Another of Lou's employees, Carrie Bell, exhibited her own eccentricity by furnishing her entire bedroom in white. On those rare occasions when the police forgot the city's deal with Lou and raided her house, her girls were sometimes arrested. Lou, however, was above appearing in court herself. When prostitute Carrie Goldsmith was arrested during a raid in February 1891, Lou's attorney, J. T. Ronald, appeared in court on her behalf. Carrie was put on trial, only to be acquitted due to lack of evidence. News of her release even traveled as far as Lou's favorite vacation spot, San Francisco.[9]

Lou's wealth and prominence were evident by the men who patronized her parlor house. In October 1892 the Seattle *Post-Intelligencer* tattled that gubernatorial candidate John H. McGraw and others had been meeting at Clancy and Burns Saloon, a building owned by the madam. But the madam was also susceptible to the occasional ne'er-do-well, as well as outright thieves. When Jim Burns and Ed Page were arrested in February 1894 for a robbery, it was revealed that the men had also planned to rob Lou of five thousand dollars in diamond jewelry. Apparently, Lou's valuable frippery was the talk of the red-light circles—particularly a diamond necklace with twenty-one stones, valued at forty-five hundred dollars alone. Burns and Page were arrested, however, before they could carry out their plan to summon Lou to the door under the guise of relaying a message, grab her by the neck, and take the necklace. Lou wisely opened a safe-deposit box.[10]

Lou's elite clientele, meanwhile, was expected to follow house rules. Foul language was not allowed, and the men were expected to maintain a sense of refinement when visiting. There was seldom trouble, aside from normal wear and tear, and a few health problems suffered by clients. Once, a visiting policeman was showing off his new revolver when it accidentally discharged into a settee. Another time, a young man accidentally set a fire on New Year's Eve. The boy's father was a shipping mogul, however, and stepped forward to pay for all of the damages. Aside from the robbery attempt and the occasional skirmish at her parlor house, only one instance infuriated Lou enough to bring charges. Her complaint against a wealthy capitalist named S. P. Williams stated that the man arrived at her door drunk and "tore off the iron rods that protect the glass on the front door." When Lou asked him "what he meant by destroying her property," the man slapped her in the face.[11]

In January 1896 Lou took yet another two-week trip to San Francisco. She might have been there during the census of 1900, when she is curiously absent from Seattle. If the census records are correct, her house may have been being used as lodgings for actors from John Considine's People's Theater. But the lady was soon back, and in about 1902 she built a new private mansion at 2102 East Madison Street. Soon after, however, some unknown problem presented itself to Lou. To console herself, she fled to San Francisco in search of some relaxation, and perhaps in pursuit of further business endeavors. But while she was still there, on March 11, 1903, Lou died suddenly.[12]

In reporting her death, the *Seattle Post-Intelligencer* illuminated that Lou had come to San Francisco and "took possession of a house at 322 Mason Street," but fell seriously ill. She was taken to the German hospital, where she died. "To those who knew of her recent troubles and of the despondency which had possessed her, the idea of suicide immediately occurred," the paper explained. Dr. M. O. Jellins performed an autopsy, however, and determined the cause of death to be a severe stomach ulcer. Others have said the true cause of death was syphilis.[13] Lou was only in her forties.

Lou's faithful housekeeper and companion Nellie Delmas was with her when she died and accompanied her body to Seattle, while the Pinkerton National Detective Agency was hired to safeguard her Seattle property. Only her close employees—Nellie Delmas and her daughter, Ulna, as well as Millie Diez—were allowed to collect their personal belongings. Also, Nellie was given permission to remove a trunk from the basement belonging to one Della Morton, who "resided" with Lou at one time. A week after Lou's death, the *Seattle Star* alluded to an adopted daughter.[14] Was Della really Lou's adopted daughter? The identity of Della remains a mystery.

In Seattle, Lou received a respectable burial at Lakeview Cemetery as bank teller R. V. Ankey was appointed administrator of her estate. In Lou's probate file, Ankey stated that Lou never married, nor did she have children. He also believed Lou had authored a will some five years before her death, but it could not be located. Until her surviving relatives were located in Germany, Ankey and others puzzled over what to do with Lou's sizable estate. A full twenty-nine pages in her probate record were devoted just to the inventory of her property. Real estate consisted of lots in Barkerville, Des Moines, Gloucester, Salmon Bay, Seattle, Snohomish, and Tacoma.[15]

A week after Lou's death, the *Seattle Star* verified the presence of the mysterious adopted daughter (but did not give her name), as well as some sisters and a brother who actually came from a prominent family in Hamburg, Germany. As the heirs were contacted, Ankey was besieged with numerous creditors making claims on the estate. One of them, John Levy, stated that he was Lou's close friend. In the summer of 1897, Levy explained, he went to Dawson City in the Yukon "in search of gold." Before departing, he left several items with Lou, including a fancy watch, a gold medal awarded him by the Seattle fire department in 1884, a gold matchbox, two one-and-a-half-carat diamonds in "solid gold studded settings," and two suits of clothing. Lou had apparently pawned the watch shortly before she died. Levy claimed the two had exchanged letters over time as proof of their relationship, and he wanted his belongings back. He got them. Several other creditors appeared as well, including former employees who had not been paid.[16]

The final value of estate amounted to $1,806.19 in cash, 7,200 dollars in real estate, and 35,000 dollars in personal property—a cool 1.2 million dollars in today's currency. Lou's surviving heirs—Johann Bernhard Ohben, Joanna Henrietta Bertha Ohben-Klaus, and Pauline Ohben Eberhardt—were finally located. All seemed well until the *Evening Statesman* in Walla Walla reported in July 1904 that the state of Washington had intervened, disregarding Lou's family and stating that since she was not a US citizen and therefore could not own property in this country, Lou's entire estate should go to the state. Furthermore, Lou's total estate was now valued at 86,620 dollars. The value was increased to 115,000 dollars, by the Seattle *Republic* in August, when it was stated that distribution of Lou's money to her heirs had stopped, and that the amount was now earmarked to go toward public schools.[17]

Newspaper reports are scant as to whether a public auction was held to sell off Lou's belongings, but her gold bed was said to have been acquired by Hiram C. Gill, a red-light lawyer during Lou's time, an investor in the red-light district, and later the mayor of Seattle. Lou's home on Madison Street was razed in 1966, but her grand parlor house survives. In 1990 the structure was home to the Washington State Trial Lawyers Association. Although she had nothing directly to do with it, Lou probably would agree that giving her wealth to the school system, which amounted to more than the contributions of the rest of Seattle's early citizens combined, was her greatest bestowal to the city.[18]

CHAPTER 4

●◦●

Josephine Wolfe of Walla Walla

In a day when the average prostitute could expect her career to last between ten and twenty years, Josephine Wolfe beat them all. Between 1860 and 1909, Josephine reigned supreme as an outstanding example of a prominent madam who could do very well for herself. The key was to establish oneself within the city, be generous and kind, stay put, work with authorities, and donate money to every cause possible. Running a clean, comfortable house of prostitution was essential as well. Josephine did all these things during the time she lived in Walla Walla, making the lady one of the greatest philanthropists the city has ever seen, perhaps even to this day.

Josephine was from Alsace, Germany, where she was born in 1836. By 1853 she was circulating around the goldfields of California. Eventually, she traveled to San Francisco, where she was described as a "slim, dark-eyed beauty." After finding work in one of many bordellos along the Barbary Coast, Josephine married the professional gambler who owned the place. Because of her new status, Josephine no longer had to service customers but remained madam of the brothel. She is believed to have borne a daughter and determined to raise her "as a lady and a Catholic."[1] Most unfortunately, record of said daughter has yet to be found.

The 1860 census identifies a Josephine "Wolfs" living in Yreka, California, and employed as a seamstress. Her housemate was identified as Anna Brewen, who was employed in the same occupation. In a town consisting mostly of men, the presence of two women working as mere seamstresses seems unusual; also, Josephine and Anna lived in close proximity to barkeeper Victor Blum and his wife.[2] But author Bill Gulick, in his book *Outlaws of the Pacific Northwest*, dispels the notion that Josephine was eking out a living in such a manner. Gulick claims that Josephine's husband was killed during a card game, and that she was able to sell the brothel at a substantial profit. With her seven-year-old daughter, twelve good time girls, several of the house musicians, and even her bodyguard, Josephine headed to the Pacific Northwest in style.

The trip entailed boarding a steamship from San Francisco to the Columbia River, where the group traveled inland to Portland. From there, Josephine and her entourage traveled through the Lower Cascades, the Upper Cascades, and The Dalles. There the party rested at the prestigious Umatilla House before moving on the next day. This time, Josephine and her bunch took a train to Deschutes Landing and boarded the *Colonel Wright* for Lewiston in present-day Idaho. This would have been sometime after April 1859, when the *Colonel Wright* took its maiden voyage.[3]

While on the *Colonel Wright*, Josephine encountered Marta and Hans Stohlhofen, whose party included not just their children but also "six red-cheeked, flaxen-haired, healthy young female dancers." The Stohlhofens were headed to Orofino, Idaho, some forty miles from Lewiston. Gulick suggests that onboard the ship, some competition was evident between Josephine Wolfe and the Stohlhofens, perhaps because their female employees entertained certain passengers and crewmen on the way to Idaho. At Walla Walla, the *Colonel Wright* was supposed to stop for a two-hour layover to unload freight and passengers. But the trip was delayed due to large ice chunks in the Snake River just eleven miles ahead.

Accordingly, the remaining passengers were told they would have to stay the night. It was then that one of the hundred or so single men aboard came up with the brilliant idea to have a party. Soon, Walla Walla's authorities and proper citizens got wind that the *Colonel Wright*'s passengers included a bevy of buxom women. The captain in command, a man named White, gave his blessing anyway, and the rest of the afternoon was spent readying for the party. The lead musician from Josephine's group put together an impromptu orchestra, drinks began flowing, and the soiree was on.

For Josephine's part, the woman entertained the group by performing her "passion-filled gypsy number" from her days on the Barbary Coast. Captain White seemed fine with the proceedings, although he did forbid the wicked women aboard from charging for their favors should they engage in dancing, swooning, and spooning with the young single men aboard. Still, the party was quite successful—especially for two of Josephine's employees, who declared the next day that they had met the men of their dreams and planned to marry them. Josephine kindly acquiesced, but with a caveat: Neither girl, upon marrying, would ever be able to work for her again.

When it was announced that the *Colonel Wright* would be forced to stay over another night, a cry immediately came up for another party. Josephine and Stohlhofens were reluctant to say the least, fearing the loss of more girls. Josephine appealed to Captain White to at least take the ship upstream a bit, in an effort to dodge the growing number of men who wanted a repeat of the night before. White obligingly maneuvered the *Colonel Wright* up the Snake River to Ice Harbor. The party was repeated as the ship remained in Ice Harbor for two more days, during which Josephine lost two more of her girls and even Stohlhofens lost one. The *Colonel Wright* did make it to Lewiston, and Stohlhofens set up business in Orofino. But Josephine found Lewiston too gritty for her taste and returned to Walla Walla.[4]

Originally a fort, Walla Walla achieved township in 1859 and would be incorporated in 1862. Farmers and ranchers frequented the town, and travelers along the Oregon Trail often stopped at Walla Walla for supplies. These lonely men would make great customers, but Josephine also noticed that prospectors from area mining camps made Walla Walla their winter quarters. Buildings were flying up all over town, which was neatly organized and laid out. Josephine chose the second floor of a building, possibly on Alder Street, in which to open for business. Next she enrolled her daughter in school. She also joined and remained devoted to St. Patrick's Catholic Church, although there is a reference to her being excommunicated from the house of worship.[5]

With her priorities settled, Josephine opened a fine "entertainment parlor" for the gentlemen of Walla Walla. In time, the enterprising madam became known around town as "Dutch Joe." Josephine was a most stalwart businesswoman, running a straight and clean house with strict rules for her girls. She refused to take in anyone new to the trade; rather, she hired only experienced women who knew what they were getting into. Anyone wishing to leave Josephine's employ was free to do so, as long as they married and went "respectable"; otherwise, they had to agree to leave town. It is said that Josephine's patrons included everyone from hardworking firemen to the mayor and his cronies.[6]

Not everybody obeyed Josephine's rules. Once, two sixteen-year-olds showed up in town looking for employment. Josephine listened as they fibbed about being of age and having previously worked in a Portland brothel. She knew the girls were lying, but showed each to a bedroom, where she said they should rest until it was time to go to work. But the first men the young ladies saw that evening were their own fathers, whom Josephine had summoned to take them home. Another incident did not go so smoothly; when the madam gave a delivery boy a five-dollar gold piece at Christmas, the child took the coin home to his mother, explaining where he got it. He even pointed out that Josephine had scratched her initials, "J. B.," on the coin. The boy's mother corrected him that Josephine's initials were "J. W." Even as she made the statement, the woman realized that "J. B." were the initials of her husband, and that the lettering echoed his own "distinctive style of lettering."[7] These indiscretions aside, Josephine became known over time "for her many benevolent acts and kindnesses, always taking the greatest care that no one should hear of these things." She also was "recognized as one of the most liberal of the money-givers in matters pertaining to public concern, and her private charities were many."[8]

The 1870 census shows Josephine living alone and "keeping house" on Alder Street. She most likely was engaging in the practice of having her employees work in shifts at her brothel but living elsewhere. Notably, Josephine's two female neighbors on either side of her also were "keeping house." Alone or not, Josephine was reaping profits from those patronizing her business. Her only competitors were madam Clara Harris over on West Main Street and some small "houses of ill repute" on Rose Street. In 1871, when the county commissioners upped the quarterly license fees for "Hurdy Gurdy Houses" from one hundred to five hundred dollars, Josephine could easily afford the difference.[9]

The 1880 census again documents Josephine as living alone but still running her "house of ill fame." She was not the only one. There were other documented prostitutes during 1880, and their living conditions are interesting. Annie Cartwright lived with her seven-year-old son, Willie. Bell Emmerson resided with a man identified as Sherman Ives. Lena Frank and Hattie Gage shared a house, as did Isabel Mumcey and Minnie Wells. Emma Keiser lived with John Cooper. Linda Ladd's housemates were a couple, Gardner and Annie Washburn. Each of these women came from diverse backgrounds and geographic regions before moving to Walla Walla.[10]

Wherever they came from, Josephine's girls and customers were treated well by the madam. One popular story, which has ballooned over time into an unlikely legend, is that one of Josephine's employees was found to have a rash on her face when examined by the city health officer. The doctor pronounced his patient ill with scarlet fever and imposed a two-week quarantine on the house. Nobody, he commanded, was to enter or leave. It so happened that Josephine's customers that day included the mayor, the fire chief, and the police chief, as well as a Catholic priest, an Episcopalian minister, a newspaper publisher, and six local merchants. All were bound by the doctor to remain at the house during the quarantine. Luckily, someone thought to use a basket via a second-story window to procure food and other items as necessary. This colorful event might have taken place in January 1881, when there was indeed an outbreak of scarlet fever in both Washington and Oregon.[11]

More believable is that during the 1880s, the local police made a habit of visiting Walla Walla's brothels on their rounds to assure that everything was peaceful. Each officer was given a drink on the house, a cigar, and two silver dollars. The bribe may have been slightly illegal, but madams like Josephine didn't mind paying for the extra protection. It was commonly known that anyone presenting a bill for payment or asking for donations, including city officials, should visit each Friday between four and six p.m. The payments would be made, in cash, as the men enjoyed a drink, hors d'oeuvres, and even a little entertainment. Josephine's forthright business tactics allowed her to stay in place at her Alder Street brothel. Sanborn maps for 1888 show seven other brothels surrounding her place, as well as some Chinese businesses, but the madam had little to fear from them.[12] She was now an institution in Walla Walla, and she intended to stay that way.

By 1900 two of Josephine's employees were living at her place—or at least were found there when the census was taken. Notably, Josephine was now a naturalized citizen and owned her brothel free and clear.

Josephine and her girls—twenty-two-year-old Lottie Daily from California and twenty-seven-year-old Lena Russle from Oregon—all discreetly
gave their occupations as "dressmakers." Most interesting is that, up
to this point, Josephine Wolfe does not appear to have ever made the
newspapers. In a time when local papers enjoyed capitalizing on the ups
and downs of their fallen women, Josephine remained unscathed. Her
absence from the papers denotes the firm hand with which she ruled her
little kingdom. In fact, only the 1902 city directory verifies that she was
still in Walla Walla at all. None but her clients, friends, and employees
came to visit her, and her only known relative, an unidentified cousin,
died in Germany in 1907.[13]

Josephine eventually did make the papers, when she died on April
14, 1909. The Walla Walla *Evening Statesman* simply reported—on the
front page—that "Josephine Wolfe, better known as 'Dutch Joe,' one of
the pioneers of this city, died at her home 11 West Alder Street at 3
o'clock this afternoon of pneumonia, after an illness of several weeks.
The deceased is one of the largest property owners in Walla Walla and
owns a great deal of valuable land elsewhere. No heirs to the valuable
estate are known." A second article the next day said that Josephine had
actually passed away at St. Mary's Hospital.[14]

At her death, Josephine owned the lot on Alder Street, as well as
"some valuable wheatland in this city," guessed to be worth around fifty
thousand dollars. Father Van de Ven of St. Patrick's Catholic Church
was made administrator of her estate. The rumor at the time was that the
bulk of Josephine's money would be given to the church, while "other
reports are to the effect that the money will be used for the founding
of a home for dogs and cats, this having been a favorite hobby of the
deceased." As whispered rumors of her true wealth floated about town,
Josephine's funeral was held on April 17 from St. Patrick's and attended
by "a number of friends." Josephine's wish that "her burial be observed
with solemnity" was met.[15]

In the end, the total value of Josephine's property was appraised at more than thirty-one thousand dollars.[16] Those placing bets on where the money would go were surprised to learn that her will included upward of twenty local beneficiaries and was "as unique as anything ever placed on file." Josephine left the bulk of her belongings—consisting mostly of diamond rings, clothing, and cash—to "many prominent business and professional men about town, to well-known young women, hack drivers and others." Two thousand dollars went to the city firemen for the erection of a monument. Five hundred dollars and Josephine's "household goods" were to be given to Stubblefield Orphan's Home. She also left one hundred dollars for the care of her two dogs and gave her parrot, "Hot Lake," to the owner of a prominent jewelry store.

Josephine's will was obviously very thorough. Another four thousand dollars was dedicated for "monuments to herself." The "sister superior" at St. Mary's Hospital received her cross and chain. The rest was left to Father Van de Ven, whom Josephine called an "irremovable rector" of his church. Per Josephine's instructions, the priest was to "sell at public auction" the rest of Josephine's estate, and an additional five thousand dollars was to go toward refurnishing the church. Her daughter, if she really had one, was not mentioned, but ten dollars was offered for "anyone who can prove they are related to me." To the bane of historians, Josephine also decreed that any and all images or portraits of herself be destroyed. Her gifts were accepted by all—except for a few people who, worried that they might be associated with the notorious madam, openly refused to have their names connected to Walla Walla's wealthiest woman. [17]

booths. Who these women were remains undocumented, but one of them was said to be known only as "Tacoma May."[6] When complaints about the bawdy entertainment drifted through the theater doors, Harry Morgan merely upped the quality of his performers. His celebrity guests included comedian Billy O'Day, singer Jesse LeSeur, and even tight-wire walker Nettie Holland. As Tacoma grew, Morgan—whose businesses stood right in the booming downtown area—prospered. The man seemed successful enough, with only one known exception. On June 28, 1887, his "show for the benefit of the fourth of July fund was to have taken place at the Opera House here this afternoon, but only about a dozen people attended and they were given back their money and the show did not take place."[7] But even this instance seems to have endeared Morgan to his customers. He did, after all, refund their money when the show fell through.

During 1888, Mayor Weisbach tried to blame the Chinese element as the reason for Tacoma's economic troubles. Local citizens, however, pointed out the goings-on on Pacific Avenue, and Harry Morgan's name was frequently mentioned. After running most of the Chinese out of town anyway, city officials eventually began focusing on Tacoma's red-light district. Arrested were madams Mollie Rosenkranz of the Star Lodging House and Mrs. Lizzie Howe, also known as "Mother Brewer," on C Street. Both women had been in town since around 1887. Later, Mollie would make the papers when it was reported that a "notorious woman of Tacoma, named Mollie Rosencranz [sic], had got herself tangled up with Judge Allyn, and the result is that she will get the worst of the wrangle. He ordered her to close up her shebang, which she declined to do. He issued a warrant for her arrest for contempt, threw her in jail, and placed a Deputy Sheriff in charge of her place." But while Mollie and Lizzie were dragged into court, newspapers also noted that the men participating in illegal gambling activities were "neither arrested nor taxed."[8]

By 1888 there were forty-two saloons in Tacoma. Harry Morgan, said the Tacoma *Ledger*, "runs a vulgar and obscene variety theatre and gambling hell.... This gambling hell is a disgrace to the City of Destiny." Morgan and five of his gambling clients were at last arrested during one of several raids in June. But the unflappable man simply posted the fifty dollars in bail money and carried on. Now, however, it was no secret that Morgan's Board of Trade and Theatre Comique were known as a "gambling dive and variety theatre."[9]

The *Ledger* in particular favored publishing exposés on the corrupt activities that took place at Morgan's—including those swindled by con artists. When one perpetrator was convicted in court, however, Morgan's lawyer appealed on the grounds that some of the jury members were women who objected to places like Morgan's no matter what the issues were. The attorney won his appeal. Around the same time a Mr. Barton, the *Ledger*'s city editor, along with reporter Albert Joab, were dining in a Pacific Avenue restaurant. Three of Morgan's men, including a former faro dealer named Billy Quinn, came in. The men approached Barton and Joab. Quinn had taken umbrage at an article Joab had written claiming the dealer had attempted suicide. Quinn wanted a retraction, which Joab refused to grant. An angry Quinn began telling the writer off quite loudly before Joab stood up and knocked the man to the floor. A fight ensued with "a general rolling over the floor and swinging of chairs, smashing of crockery and the breaking of a chandelier." Quinn ended up out on the sidewalk, where he chose the better part of valor and walked off while Barton and Joab "resumed their supper."[10]

Quinn clearly lost his fight, as did Harry Morgan in time. As of mid-November, Sheriff Wilt had "a man on guard" at Morgan's "gambling dive" to make sure no betting games were in progress. Next, in January 1889, the Women's Christian Temperance Union descended upon Morgan in court. Better known as the WCTU, this nationwide ladies' organization made it their business to try to close down saloons, gambling dens, and bawdy houses. At issue this time was the sale of the Board of Trade and the Theatre Comique by Morgan to one H. H. Cline. The new owner wanted the liquor license transferred to his name. The WCTU wanted the license of the "hell-hole" revoked, no matter who owned it. Morgan's place was labeled "a source of demoralization to young men, a sink of depravity, and can be regarded in no other sense than appalling disgust."[11]

The sale apparently fell through, for it was Morgan who was named two weeks later, when his license was indeed revoked. Three days after that, Morgan was thought to be shut down for good—until an incorrect date on some court documents caused the case to be dismissed and gave him a brief reprieve. Once everything was straightened out, Morgan's license was revoked once again. Throughout the rest of the year, however, Morgan and city officials continued their tug-of-war with the issue as Morgan's license was restored and revoked several more times.

In answer to the bad press he received, Harry Morgan purchased the *Morning Globe*, a local paper with which he intended to jab back at his adversaries. Next he hired the Portland *Oregonian*'s William Lightfoot Visscher as editor. Some called the endeavor "Harry Morgan's whiskey organ," a true statement, since Morgan duly instructed Visscher to write "something nice about vice." The *Ledger* responded to the news with an editorial entitled "Sodom and Gomorrah." Unfortunately for Morgan, too much newspaper ink ran through Visscher's veins. He tried to appease the boss but found so many other interesting subjects to write about, including Washington becoming a state, that Morgan's instructions often fell to the wayside. The newspaper was sold a short time later.[12]

Morgan fell back on his variety theater. "The only variety theatre in Tacoma," his ads read. "Good Talent of All Kinds Solicited." Then, in October 1889, he proposed building a fairgrounds and a one-mile racetrack. Business at the Board of Trade and the Theatre Comique, meanwhile, went on as usual. Carl Dupuis, who arrived in Tacoma in 1890, remembered that Morgan's gambling house, the Theatre Comique, and his saloon were "all connected at South 9th Street and Pacific Avenue." Dupuis recalled that in "the back rear of his place he had screened booths on a balcony where loggers and sailors were served by jezebels, and they were frequently drugged and robbed of their rolls. It was a tough joint, and gamblers, bartenders and bouncers working for Morgan were a vicious lot." Still, the entertainment was good. Boxer John L. Sullivan "once gave a sparring exhibition on his stage," Dupuis recalled. "Sullivan hung around the place for some time associating with the sporting element and made quite a hit while he was here."[13]

It would have been mighty interesting to see what happened when Harry Morgan added the racetrack and fairgrounds to his list of businesses. Neither, however, came to fruition before the man died after a brief illness on April 26, 1890, at his place of business at 724 D Street. At least the Yakima *Herald* had something nice to say about him. "While not an educated man he had shrewd business sense," the paper commented, "and not withstanding his kindness of heart, which induced him to be continually helping the needy, he had accumulated at his death a fortune of two-hundred-thousand dollars." According to one of Morgan's employees, Frank Cantwell, the gambling house alone took in between twenty thousand and thirty thousand dollars a month. Much of the money, however, was spent on payroll, bribing officials, court fees, and paying off the press. A more conservative amount of twenty-eight thousand dollars was placed on the value of the estate.[14]

Harry Morgan's funeral took place at his D Street address. Reverend W. E. Copeland of the Episcopal Church officiated. Perhaps to the surprise of Morgan's adversaries, throngs of people turned out for the services, and an amazing seventy-five carriages joined the funeral procession. It was, they said, the largest funeral Tacoma had ever seen—yet Harry Morgan's burial place remains unknown. Perhaps the greatest honor bestowed on the man occurred after his death. In his memory, all saloons closed for one hour, between two and three p.m., before the mourners raised a toast to Tacoma's best-known businessman.[15] That was surely a first for Tacoma.

CHAPTER 6

---◦●◦---

Sin in Spokane

S oon after the city was established in 1871, the small settlement
began to grow very quickly. The growth was encouraged, especially
after the Legislative Assembly of Washington Territory authorized the
incorporation of towns and cities in 1877. Officials of Spokane Falls
wanted their town to become a first-class city. But their goals were
marred slightly as good time girls from other regions began their migration to the Lilac City. The red-light district would eventually be located
along Main and Front Streets, between Mill and Market Streets.[1]

One of Spokane Fall's first madams during its infant years was Eve
Johnson. She had formerly worked in New York at an area alternately
known as the "Seven Sisters" and "Sisters Row." The area was so named
for the seven sibling ladies who ran a set of side-by-side brothels in an
upper-class residential neighborhood on West 25th Street. The class of
these women equaled their surroundings: Male guests were invited via
engraved invitations, and formal evening wear was a must. The sisters
happily raked in the profits and shared them with others in need. On
Christmas Eve, the house proceeds were traditionally given to charity.[2]

Whether Eve was able to achieve the quality status of Sisters Row,
and how long she even remained in town, is unknown. But she was certainly onto something. Spokane Falls was about to blossom, bringing

in plenty of business for the red-light ladies. By about 1880 Spokane Falls was bustling with lumber mills, the National Iron Works, and other male-dominated businesses. The population included more than one hundred Chinese immigrants, plus nearly five hundred people of other ethnic backgrounds. Spokane Falls needed a waterworks to meet demand, and incorporated in November 1881 to gain funding for the project. Later, the city's name would be shortened to just Spokane.[3]

By the late 1880s Spokane was known as "the fun center of the Inland Empire." In between numerous restaurants, taverns, hotels, and gambling halls nestled numerous common brothels in an area sometimes referred to as "Skid Row." Chinatown was in place as well, with more brothels and opium dens. Parlor houses also had debuted for the wealthy men living in or visiting the city.[4] One of these was owned and managed by Florence Crayman in about 1888. Florence's luxurious bordello on Front Street even had her name painted over the front door. Florence invested much of her money in sterling silver, and her house was highly insured. She was actually making plans to relocate to a new silver boom in British Columbia when her parlor house burned in a mysterious fire. The madam duly filed an insurance claim, but a few days later a character known as Crookedly Ike admitted that the woman had actually paid him two hundred dollars to set the fire. An investigation revealed that Ike had shipped much of Florence's silver collection to Canada the day before the fire, and that he had lost the telltale two hundred dollars in a poker game the day after the brothel burned.

A flustered Florence quickly hired attorney Frank Graves, and the twosome went before District Attorney Sam Hyde. Graves tried to make a mockery of Crookedly Ike's testimony, but it was Florence who saved the day. When she was called to the stand, Hyde instructed a bailiff to lay out the madam's remaining sterling silver, which had suffered no more heat than a little hot water. "Madam," asked Hyde, "is this your silver?" In a shocked, innocent voice, Florence answered, "Why, yes, sir, it is. And how glad I am to see it again. I haven't seen it since that day when Crookedly Ike stole it and then set fire to my place to conceal his crime!" The judge ruled in the madam's favor. Florence collected both her silver and her insurance money and moved on to Canada to go into business as planned.[5]

Other reigning madams included Julia Spencer, who eventually took up with her favorite customer, a buggy salesman identified as Raymond T. Kressler. The man had previously fought a duel on behalf of the lady. He won the match, and also Julia's heart. Kressler moved into Julia's brothel and acted as her "live-in protector" before the couple retired to a farm in Pennsylvania.[6] Plenty of other naughty women remained behind. One of them was Irish Kate, who is believed to have accidentally started the fire that burned Spokane in August 1889. Plenty of other theories remain in history books as to how the fire started: from the spark of a passing train, at Bill Wolfe's lunch counter on Railroad Avenue during a grease fire, or at a lodging house and restaurant.[7] But Kate's story is far more colorful and bears illumination.

On August 4, 1889, twenty-four-year-old Irish Kate was in her room above a saloon on Railroad Avenue, identified by one source as Sam (not Bill) Wolfe's Lunch Counter. The young lass was fussing with her hair when a drunk man wandered in. Kate, who also had been drinking, spurned his advances. In the ensuing scuffle, the kerosene lamp where Kate was heating her curling iron was knocked over. Kate was able to escape, but the inferno in her room spread quickly; the resulting fire burned most of the downtown area.[8] The circumstance is not unusual; other shady ladies throughout the West were known to be the cause of fires that wreaked havoc on their towns.[9] In Kate's case, however, documentation about the real cause of the fire remains scant, and her story does not appear to have made it into the local newspapers.

Irish Kate remained in Spokane as the city rebuilt. In 1892 she was living at a lodging house in what was identified as the Panhandle Block, under the name Kate Thompson. On May 28 she committed suicide by taking carbolic acid. The Seattle *Post-Intelligencer* reported that Kate chose to end her life after a "quarrel with her lover, who is the proprietor of a well-known harness and saddle store." Kate was alternately identified as Kate Barrett in Washington's death records, the daughter of one John Barrett Smith. She was buried in Greenwood Memorial Terrace.[10]

Spokane was not so forgiving of women like Irish Kate. Following the fire, as Spokane rebuilt, city officials began making it hard to obtain permits to build and outlawed construction of wooden buildings. Unwelcome in the city proper, the gamblers, harlots, and saloon men relocated to a "shantytown" near the railroad tracks upriver. The move hardly fazed women like madam Josey Tripp, whose entertainments featured two "redheaded Creole girls" from New Orleans. Josey favored taking the girls for a ride around town in her fine coach. The rig would travel down Riverside, from her house on Post Street, on the way to the local markets.[11]

By the early 1900s downtown Spokane had grown into a first-class city. There were two reputable stage theaters in town, but also three vaudeville theaters: the Orpheum, the Pantages, and the Washington. The Davenport Hotel offered a five-star stay, although in later years the hotel basement was outfitted with a speakeasy and gentleman's club, accessible from the hotel's Early Bird Lounge. The city's good time girls had slowly managed to infiltrate the downtown area as well. One of them, Abbie Widner, worked out of the upstairs portion of the Colonial Hotel. Like so many other prostitutes, Abbie was trying to save money until she could marry and live a better life. In 1905 one of her clients, identified as "Johnie," had gone on to Seattle. But he also wrote letters to Abbie for at least a short time. Abbie's responses talked of missing him, while expounding on her life at the brothel. The money was good, but Abbie did admit that "every time a man touched her," she wanted "to stab him in the heart."[12]

In one letter to Johnie, dated February 24, 1905, Abbie begins by saying "I was surprised for I didn't get your letter so soon," and

An interesting puzzle: This image has been identified as a "box theater" in Spokane, but also as the Topic Theater in Cripple Creek, Colorado.
Courtesy Cripple Creek District Museum

admonishes him "to be a good boy and don't get in to any trouble." A second letter, penned on March 2, complained that "I have had an [awful] time since you left, first I was taken sick while to breakfast and was brought home in a hack I was so sick I [didn't] know anything, and that night my purse was stolen and all I had left was a dollar. I had twenty dollars in my purse. I tell you I felt pretty blue but I am alright now." Johnie might have regarded the letters as simply personal correspondence, but a third letter, dated March 11, probably gave the man pause. "There was a [couple of fellows] up here that night and had a scrap over me," Abbie explained, "both was [jealous] and they [quarreled] in the room and I made them go out and then they acted something [awful]." Unfortunately, this juicy piece of news is the last known letter between Abbie and Johnie. What happened to the relationship remains unknown.[13]

Spokane authorities may have required prostitutes to move to more discreet quarters as the city grew, but they also acquiesced to the knowledge that businessmen, farmers, loggers, and miners visited the city frequently. Their money was spent not just in the brothels and saloons (which paid their fees and fines and purchased licenses), but also the hotels, shops, and restaurants Spokane offered. Not until 1910 did the city's "fine system" cease as the modern West began seriously frowning on the prostitution industry and prosecuting wayward women.[14] By 1911 city authorities were downright unfriendly not just to prostitutes but even the organizations that tried to help them. Some years before, the Salvation Army had opened Liberty Home, a place for unwed mothers and other women who had "fallen" from social graces. Before long, however, the Liberty Park Improvement Club claimed that the "class of inmates" at Liberty Home was "objectionable to the residents." A suit filed against the home proved successful. The presiding judge assessed that, indeed, "the cries of women in agony and the wails of infants in distress have been wafted over the neighborhood." Furthermore, "women awaiting maternity move around on the porches of the house and in the yard, in plain sight of all who pause." Liberty Home was ordered to relocate.[15]

Three years later, as Washington State contemplated outlawing alcohol, Spokane officials got the jump by limiting the distribution and consumption of alcoholic beverages. In November 1914 the city voted to "go dry" as authorities next fixated on restricting gambling. Bootleg liquor could still be found in speakeasies and parlor houses, the latter "disguised as cheap rooming houses and regular functioning businesses on the outside" with liquor and girls on the inside. But nobody in Spokane could overlook Washington's statewide prohibition act of 1914. A number of speakeasies quite literally went underground, and some of these illicit places managed to stay open until national prohibition was repealed in 1933.[16] As for the city's prostitutes, the bad girls of the pioneer era eventually died, married, or moved away, leaving behind only traces of their past.

CHAPTER 7

---•◦•---

Nellie Curtis, the Belle of Seattle and Aberdeen

Like their counterparts across the West, Washington's wayward women had the luxury of moving from place to place as they pleased. Some flitted from camp to camp and town to town, sometimes to suit themselves, at other times to elude trouble or the law. Others settled in their chosen hometowns for years before inexplicably moving along in search of greener pastures or a better life. Nellie Curtis, the madam who reigned supreme in both Seattle and Aberdeen, fell into this latter category.

Virtually nothing is known about Nellie's early life, except that when she was born in May 1899, it was likely under another name. Nellie's documentation in the Social Security Death Index implies that she came from Wisconsin, but she told the 1940 census taker that she was born in New York; also, that she was a widow. Information on her husband, however, appears nonexistent. Complicating matters further is that throughout her career, Nellie used at least three aliases: Nellie Gray, Yetta Solomon, and, most whimsical of all, Zella Nightingale. But even these elusive names fail to show up on official records about her.[1]

Wherever she had been before her arrival in Seattle in 1932, Nellie had apparently gained the necessary acumen for running a business—a brothel business, to be exact. Her first bordello was the Camp Hotel, at the corner of First Avenue and Virginia Street. Admittedly, the Camp Hotel was not much to look at. Constructed in 1904, the simple wood-frame building consisted of a store with a hotel upstairs. Nellie's first years at the Camp Hotel appear to have been quiet ones, for she does not appear in newspaper articles.[2]

Only the 1940 census tells a bit more about Nellie, who stated she was forty-four years old. Her education had consisted of one year of high school. She also said her business was that of a rented hotel, but her employees—thirty-year-old Patricia Stefeney, twenty-eight-year-old Opal Milligan, and forty-four-year-old Anna Laverne—were each listed as prostitutes. Sixty-five-year-old Bake Ramsey was employed as a porter, while one M. Pinch assisted Nellie with operating her "hotel."[3]

Between 1941 and 1942, Nellie found a most unique opportunity. With World War II ramping up, Japanese citizens everywhere were being incarcerated at internment camps, including the Kodama family of Seattle. The Kodamas later leased the Outlook Hotel at First and Pike Streets. One source states that Nellie's Camp Hotel had been closed, but she was able to buy out the lease on the Outlook. The building was old, having been constructed in 1909 and hosted thousands of guests in its fifty-five or so rooms over time. New plumbing and wiring was needed. Nellie contracted for these updates, plus a new coat of paint and all new, classy furnishings. She renamed it the LaSalle Hotel and instructed her girls to go down to the docks to distribute new calling cards reading, "LaSalle Hotel, Friends Made Easily." The LaSalle was proving quite profitable in no time.[4]

Nellie was so busy that at one time, she enlisted the help of her nephew, Max Elias, in running the LaSalle. Notably, the brothel featured an average of seventeen "permanent guests," presumed to be Nellie's employees. "If they stayed a week," the madam once said, "I called them permanent." Sometimes, however, the "rooms changed hands three times a night." Nellie disregarded the frequent turnover, saying only, "I never asked any personal questions." It apparently didn't matter to her, for she was raking in money—either from her permanent employees who lived on the premises or from street prostitutes, and even the men themselves who wished to rent a room long enough to conduct business. A frequent and likely exaggerated story about Nellie is that she kept two rooms for herself, one for her collection of hats and one in which to keep all her money.[5]

Nellie is remembered as dressing well and rubbing elbows with local politicians and prominent businessmen. Her interest in politics in particular was important in order for her to remain open and unmolested by the authorities, at least in the early days. As time went on, however, Nellie knew she had enough power to hold her own against any authority. In a letter written to her nephew in 1948, Nellie illuminated that "I have been at the same deal, with tougher ones and mean ones and I am still in the same place doing the same, and I took my ups and downs, worse than at present and come out on top so it doesn't matter to me who gets in. I will always find my own outs, and go as I am."[6]

Eventually, Nellie tired of life in Seattle, possibly because the military had banned their soldiers from visiting the LaSalle. The hotel was put up for sale, and in 1951 George and Sodeko Ikeda purchased what they believed to be a legitimate business. The Ikedas were experienced hotel operators who found the sale of the LaSalle a bit fishy right out of the gate. When it was brought to their attention that the hotel and all its furnishings were offered at 25,000 dollars, they made a counteroffer of 17,500 dollars in September 1951. Then they waited. And waited. Nellie seemed indifferent to the offer and did not bother to respond. Ikeda and his colleagues visited the LaSalle a few times, but were always told that Mrs. Curtis "was too ill to see anyone," and besides, she worked from eight p.m. to eight a.m. every day. Ikeda did talk to Nellie's day clerk, a "colored" woman named Gladys Westbrooke, who verified that there were "thirty-four or thirty-five permanent guests" and the hotel filled up on the weekends.[7]

In early October, the Ikedas were finally able to meet with Nellie, who told them the monthly income from the LaSalle was between nineteen hundred and twenty-two hundred dollars. After a bit more negotiating, the Ikedas finally took over the hotel on October 18. The brothel had been operating all night for such a long time that the key to the front door was apparently lost. Sodeko remembered watching Nellie look for it. "She couldn't find the key," Sodeko remembered. "I saw a lot of money in every drawer she pulled out . . . she had a vanity and a dresser. She pulled out the lampstand drawers too. And in every drawer she pulled out she had a lot of cash."[8] It was soon apparent that the LaSalle was not just a simple lodging house for respectable people. As more and more evidence came to light that the LaSalle had in fact operated as a house of prostitution, the Ikedas filed a lawsuit against Nellie, charging her with "fraud in the sale of a hotel property."[9]

Apparently, on the day the sale was final, Nellie gave Ikeda a sheet showing there really were only twelve permanent residents. Trouble began as Ikeda worked his first day at the hotel desk. No fewer than eighteen young men came in looking for girls. Ikeda tried to explain that "it was under new hand and I don't have any girls." One of the men, according to Ikeda, even advised him that "'you don't have to be scared, I am a seaman. And he pulled out their identification cards and everything, but I say, 'I am sorry, I don't have any girls here, see.' And they said, 'Where is Mrs. Curtis; where is Gladys?' and I told them 'I don't know, they left no forwarding address; I don't know how to locate them.'"

A couple of days later, some other men approached the front desk and rented rooms. One of them later called down, asking for a girl. "I say, 'I am sorry, I don't have any girls,'" Ikeda testified, "and he just took off." The Ikedas' son, Bob, also testified to similar experiences when he worked the Saturday- and Sunday-night shifts, reporting that between thirty and fifty men would appear and ask for girls. Per his attorney's instructions, Ikeda posted a sign at the front door reading, "No Girls." Business at the LaSalle immediately came to a standstill, with the Ikedas making nowhere near the income Nellie had claimed.

In court, a ledger from the LaSalle dating back to 1946 was produced as evidence of income. But the numbers didn't add up, and the Ikedas' attorney blatantly asked Nellie if the money came from "the whore house business." How could Nellie answer without officially incriminating herself as a whorehouse madam? She couldn't, and so responded, "I refuse to answer." The attorney queried further, finally asking whether Nellie refused to answer "on the ground of self-incrimination." Nellie replied, "Yes." The damage was done, and Nellie found herself having to explain that sometimes her income increased because she rented out the same room two or three times in the same day. The court concluded that "the chief source of revenue to defendant from the LaSalle Hotel business during the period of her ownership was from use of the premises for lewdness, assignation and prostitution; that the defendant used the said hotel primarily for her business of trafficking in lewd women; and that said hotel was regularly resorted to by prostitutes with defendant's knowledge, consent and approval." Although Nellie never disclosed "the true nature and character of the business conducted by her at the LaSalle Hotel," the court found that she did mislead the Ikedas by failing to tell them the correct income generated by the LaSalle. The court decided in favor of the Ikedas, awarding them seventy-five hundred dollars in damages.[10]

As Nellie waded through the court proceedings, she worked to relocate to Aberdeen. Founded in 1884, the city was once called "the roughest town west of the Mississippi." By the turn of 1900, the red-light district, dubbed "Paradise Alley," was located in an area bordered by Heron and Hume Streets between F and G Streets.[11] The place was described as a "narrow dirt street" with "a long row of tawdry saloons,

A bevy of bathing beauties as they would have appeared during Nellie Curtis's time in Seattle and Aberdeen
Courtesy Jan MacKell Collins

brothels, sailors' outfitting stores, cheap tailors shops, squalid boarding houses, shipping offices, and the local headquarters of the Sailors Union of the Pacific."[12] One source says that upper-echelon parlor houses were named the Harvard, Columbia, and Yale, all located on "College Row." Lesser-class places included the Palm Dance Hall, which employed forty women and was known for "its wild fights."[13]

For years, corrupt city officials, men in the vice districts, and a bouquet of good time girls battled it out as Aberdeen's two thousand loggers and sailors came ashore regularly to drink, gamble, visit houses of prostitution, and fight. The town was soon known as the "Hellhole of the Pacific."[14] The "Black Friday" fire of October 16, 1903, burned fifteen city blocks, but the city quickly rebuilt. In Paradise Alley, numerous small brothels and bars were eventually located on the east end, with the city jail and fire department on the west end. In the midst of the absolute mayhem that was Aberdeen, the city's murder rate exceeded that of similar Wild West towns. Some of the killings were attributed to the roughnecks who routinely did each other in via fights, guns, and knives. But a good number of other deaths were largely due to a serial killer named William "Billy" Gohl, who is believed to have murdered upward of 130 men in Aberdeen alone.[15]

Gohl's story might have no place here but for his marriage to dancehall girl Bessie Hager. Gohl had been in town around three years, committing murders at random, when he met Bessie. The man was a great fan of Aberdeen's bawdy houses and contracted syphilis from one of the girls. The story goes that one night during a drunk, Gohl "got fresh" with Bessie. The woman "landed one on his chin that knocked him down, then she kicked him in the ribs." For the twisted Gohl, it was love at first punch. The couple married in 1905 at nearby Montesano. It was a good match, since Gohl could now be of assistance at Bessie's boardinghouse.[16]

Did Bessie know her husband was a serial killer? There is nothing to show that she did, but after bragging one too many times to others about the murders he committed, Gohl was finally caught in 1910 and went to trial. During the proceedings, he was allowed to remain at home with Bessie. On May 12, however, Gohl was found guilty of murder. He was sentenced to life imprisonment and sent to Walla Walla State Penitentiary in June 1910. Bessie proved to be a model prisoner's wife. She not only solicited lawyers for her husband but also attended the court proceedings as the case unfolded. She never did take the stand, however. After Gohl was sentenced, Bessie moved to Walla Walla with plans to live with her brother and either train to work as a nurse or open another boardinghouse.[17] Unfortunately for Gohl, the idea of seeing her husband on prison visits eventually failed to appeal to Bessie. She filed for divorce in 1912. Gohl died of his venereal disease in 1927. Bessie never remarried, dying in Walla Walla in 1945, just six years before Nellie Curtis moved to Aberdeen and heard the whole awful story.[18]

In Aberdeen, Nellie bought the Cass Hotel for twenty-five thousand dollars. Like the old Outlook Hotel before it became the LaSalle, the Cass also was run-down. Nellie spent ten thousand dollars renovating the place and renamed it the Curtis Hotel. An article in *Look* magazine in 1952 tattled that Aberdeen was still a broiling hotbed of sin, but from all appearances, the Curtis Hotel ran just as smoothly as the LaSalle. This time, however, Nellie kept six full-time employees, with another five during weekends and around payday.[19]

Times were changing by 1959, when police captain Nick Yantsin decided to crack down on the Curtis Hotel himself. Nellie, it seemed, was wielding too much power in political circles, and Yantsin wanted it stopped. On January 31 Yantsin walked into the Curtis under the guise of a customer with a tape recorder hidden in his clothes. With him was Reverend Lloyd Auchard and carpenter Jack Mecak. The men watched as a "hefty" woman appeared at the top of the stairs and invited them up. "Come in fellas!" she said. "These are nice girls; you can hear them better with their clothes off." One of the girls of the house, Lora Summers, next took Yantsin by the wrist and began leading him down a hallway. "Coming through!" she called out cheerfully.

Lora led Yantsin to a crib, where she explained the price for services was five dollars for the "old-fashioned way." Yantsin pulled out some money, Lora began unzipping his pants, and the officer whipped out his badge. "You're under arrest," he proclaimed. Lora's response was to holler for Nellie, who "burst into the room reportedly wearing dark glasses, diamonds on her fingers, pearls, and what Yantsin later referred to as a "Bella Abzug hat." Nellie demanded to know what the man thought he was doing. "You're pinched," the officer responded, and proceeded to arrest Nellie, several of her girls, and eighteen customers.

When Police Chief Pat Gallagher came to work the next morning, he was met by the angry ladies and their embarrassed customers. But he was most disappointed in Yantsin, who had conducted the raid without official permission and thereby angered Aberdeen's mayor, Ed Lundgren. Yantsin was busted down to beat cop on the graveyard shift as Nellie filed charges against the officer for entering her home without a warrant. Yantsin, she said, illegally entered her hotel and seized evidence. He had, in effect, invaded the "privacy of her home." As in the case with the Ikedas, the defense attorney tried to get Nellie to admit to being a prostitute. When the attorney asked if Nellie had ever been a prostitute, she honestly answered, "I never was." It was true, since Nellie had never sold her own sexual favors but was a madam whose employees were prostitutes. When she was asked whether she was a madam or employed prostitutes, Nellie pleaded the Fifth.

The case was dismissed, but Yantsin continued his campaign by suing Nellie. This time she was found guilty of running a house of prostitution and fined five hundred dollars. Astute businesswoman that she was, Nellie had had enough and decided to retire. In 1964 she deeded her hotel to the city of Aberdeen in exchange for eight thousand dollars and moved back to Seattle. Unfortunately the woman found no peace; in 1971 the Internal Revenue Service claimed that Nellie owed 251,000 dollars in taxes, including penalties. Nellie settled the claim for 120,000 dollars. She died in May 1976 and was mostly forgotten.[20] For the last few years, however, the Pike Brewing Company Pub, located in Nellie's former LaSalle Hotel, has served up several handcrafted beers named for the lady herself. It's a fitting enough tribute, and one that Nellie herself would have probably liked.

CHAPTER 8

Jane Barnes, First Maiden of Oregon

The doves brought comfort
To the roughness of pioneer life
The softness and frills of the bawdy house
Took the edge off of some of the strife.[1]

Oregon's founding fathers would surely turn over in their graves if they knew that the first Anglo woman to arrive in Oregon was not the wife but a mistress of one of the state's first pioneers. Her name was Jane Barnes, and she was the hired traveling companion of Donald McTavish. In 1813 McTavish was appointed governor of Fort George at today's city of Astoria. Alternately known as Fort Astoria, Fort George was given its name by the North West Fur Company. The company was established shortly after John Jacob Astor arrived in Oregon and opened a trading post.[2]

McTavish was in Portsmouth, England, loading his ship, the *Issac Todd*, in preparation for the trip to America when he hired Jane. The British miss was but twenty-three years old and worked as a barmaid in McTavish's hotel. A business deal was struck whereby Jane would accompany McTavish to Oregon. He, in turn, would buy her a whole new wardrobe of her choosing. Upon returning to England, McTavish

GOOD TIME GIRLS OF THE PACIFIC NORTHWEST

also promised to pay Jane a "generous annuity" for life. The proposal held great appeal to Jane, who agreed to the deal. At Portsmouth, McTavish bought several new dresses for Jane and ensured that her cabin aboard the *Isaac Todd* was as comfortable as possible.[3]

It took a year and one month to reach Astoria, during which Jane and the ship's crew weathered storms, crashing waves, coastal winds, and other threats. Jane appears to have survived the trip quite well, dining on "bottled porter, excellent cheese," and tinned English beef. On April 17, 1814, the *Issac Todd* dropped anchor at the mouth of the Columbia River. Alexander Henry Jr. was one of the first to meet Jane, in McTavish's cabin, "after which the morning was pleasantly spent in smoking and chatting."[4]

Still, Jane's presence came as quite a surprise to the men at Fort George. When McTavish invited the fort's officials to dine aboard the ship that night and meet her, they agreed. Jane turned out to be as charming as she was beautiful. Only Henry seems to have been offended when the men of the party launched into a "vile discourse" regarding "the subject of venereal disease and Chinook ladies" in front of Jane.[5] Clearly, the Anglo men of Fort George had already been engaging in sex with the Native women, and probably continued to do so once they realized that Jane was there solely for McTavish's enjoyment.

Still, the men were enamored with Jane Barnes. In 1831 former Fort George clerk Ross Cox would remember her as a "flaxen-haired, blue-eyed daughter of Albion" who "had rather an extravagant wardrobe." Cox described Jane's daily mode of dress. "One day, her head, decorated with feathers and flowers, produced the greatest surprise," he wrote; "the next, her hair, braided and unconcealed by any covering, excited equal wonder and admiration."[6] Shortly after the dinner, all parties decided to change the name of Fort George's sloop from the *Dolly* to the *Jane*. The decision was indeed an honor, for the *Dolly* had presumably been named for John Jacob Astor's wife. A grateful Jane next spent the following week making sporadic excursions from ship to shore.

66

But when McTavish made plans to move ashore with her, Jane politely declined. At the time, the lady felt that Fort George held no comfortable quarters for her. Besides, she was aware that McTavish intended to end their business deal and would eventually send her back to England.[7]

There are two versions of what happened next. In one of them, Alexander Henry was so smitten with Jane that he offered her an adequate place in his quarters, and she accepted. In another, McTavish, ready to end the relationship, dumped her on Henry. Either way, the "longboat came with Jane, bag and baggage," Henry wrote in his journal. "About sunset the jolly-boat took Mr. D. McTavish on board alone," he said. "Jane, of course, remained, having taken up her lodging in my room."[8] The move suited Jane a great deal. Soon she had the run of the fort, flirting with the men and doing as she pleased. By May 17, Henry noted in his journal, McTavish had found himself a Chinook woman who was the ex-wife of Astorian Benjamin Clapp. Later accounts suggest that McTavish regretted his decision.[9]

If there was indeed a tug-of-war over Jane, it was brief. On about May 22, both McTavish and Henry, along with other men, drowned during an attempt to cross the Columbia. Left alone, Jane spurned the advances of at least one man, Dr. Swann, who was Fort George's surgeon.[10] But she also enjoyed parading around the fort in her beautiful wardrobe as the Chinook ladies looked on in "fear, envy, awe and admiration."[11] Jane drew the eye of every man, white or Indian, and she knew it.

Not every man, however, approved of Jane's antics. Cox remembered an edgy debate between the woman and another clerk. Jane had expressed her dislike of the open sexual behavior of the local women. When the clerk commented, with a sideways look at Jane, that the native women's "conduct was no worse than some of the white women he had known," Jane rebutted. "O, Mr. Mac!" she exclaimed, "I suppose you agree with Shakespeare, that 'every woman is at heart a rake'?" The clerk corrected her that the phrase had actually come from the English poet Pope. "Pope! Pope!" retorted Jane. "Bless me, sir, you must be wrong;

'rake' is certainly the word. I never heard of but one female Pope."[12]
Jane made her ignorant statement while shaking out a newspaper from
the ship and pretending to read it. The clerk noticed, however, that the
paper was actually upside down.[13]

Jane caused more of a stir when she initially accepted the advances
of Cassakes, son of Chinook leader Comcomly. Another of Comcomly's
sons, dubbed Duncan McDougal, was soon in hot competition with
his brother. McDougal proposed marriage to Jane, with the promise of
sending "one hundred sea otters to her relations" and making sure Jane
would never have to lift a finger as she lounged around in her fine dresses.
But Jane declined that proposal and several others from McDougal, who
finally went off in a huff and declared "he would never more come near
the fort while she remained there." A plan to kidnap her also failed. In
fact, Jane spurned all other advances up to the day she boarded another
ship, the *Columbia*, bound for Canton, China.[14]

At Canton, Jane did eventually find a man she wanted, an "English
gentleman of great wealth, connected to the East India Company." The
man offered Jane "a splendid establishment" and eventually took her
back to England. In spite of the new relationship, Jane wrote a letter to
the North West Fur Company requesting the annuity that McTavish, "a
representative of the company," had promised her. Whether she got it
remains unknown, but she did eventually marry Anthony Robson, captain of the SS *Columbia*. And she willingly sailed back to visit the Columbia River again in 1818, this time with her husband and their two young
children.[15] It has been easy for some historians to make fun of Jane, the
fancily dressed, free-loving flirt who masked her illiteracy with charm and
chatter. Compared with other women of her caliber in the early 1800s,
however, Jane is to be admired for her adventurous nature, her willingness to risk everything in hopes of success, and even preserving what
remained of her honor until she found a man worthy of having it.

CHAPTER 9

————◦•◦————

Astoria, "The Most Wicked Place on Earth"

Jane Barnes's departure from Fort George was eventually followed by the arrival of other Anglo women as the settlement of Astoria developed. Oregon was not yet a state, but a series of treaties between 1818 and 1846 finally established it as a territory of the United States. Fort George was eventually abandoned as Astoria proper became a major fishing and shipping port. The first US post office west of the Rocky Mountains was established there in 1847. During those years, immigrants came to the area in droves. Their ethnic backgrounds were an interesting mix of European settlers, and Chinese. Most found work in the fishing industry and established their own neighborhoods near the docks. The shores along the Pacific Ocean and the Columbia River were soon dotted with everything from bunkhouses and shanties to cultured neighborhoods with fancy homes.[1]

By 1883, Astoria's neighborhoods included "Swilltown," an area along Bond Street near the waterfront. Here, saloons, bawdy houses, and gambling places were free to operate. City officials imposed liquor license fees and were quite willing to let Swilltown be, for at least a time.[2] When Astoria's first major fire started on July 2, the flames traveled from building to building between the waterfront and 17th Street. Notably, the saloon owners carried their liquor to safety, only to have it stolen by "the rougher class of onlookers." Looting and other damage took place as drunken revelers wandered the burning town. Eventually "the scene of disorder was transferred to" Swilltown, where things got even uglier.[3] Local fisherman, who had been among those partaking in libations, were "soon relieved of their money by the denizens" of Swilltown. Angry at being taken advantage of, the men threatened to burn the rest of the town in retaliation.[4]

Thankfully, the men did not succeed. The mayor, urged by citizens to restore order, quickly decreed that all saloons must close at midnight, every night. But one of the taverns was owned by two former policemen, identified as Riley and Ginder, who "barricaded themselves in and shot at the police." The two were captured and threatened with hanging if they didn't leave town. The men gathered their belongings and skedaddled. With Riley and Ginder run out of town, a committee next decided to try to get rid of all the remaining inhabitants of Swilltown. The wild men and shady ladies were given twenty-four hours to leave Astoria.[5] Amazingly, the edict worked with the exception of one man, an English bloke named Boyle, who refused to go. But a committee of men simply captured him, gave him a good whipping, and booted him from the city limits anyway. Boyle, who recognized three of the men from the committee, filed suit against them for damages. He won an undisclosed amount of money, raised by "general subscription" to his satisfaction.[6]

If Astoria's committee thought they had rid their seaport town of bad men and wicked women, they were wrong. The presence of good time girls was evidenced by prostitute Kitty Burke, who began appearing in newspapers as early as 1885 when she was "brought up on charges" in Astoria. Two years later, in June 1887, Kitty was fined ten dollars for using "abusive language." The last anyone heard of her was in 1888, when the *Daily Morning Astorian* reported that a "fire last night about 10:30 in Miss Kitty Burke's establishment, after considerable racing and chasing around, was found to have scared the denizens and burned a bedstead; fully insured."[7]

Kitty's antics aside, a number of saloons and bawdy houses were back in business by 1890, to the extent that Astoria became known as "The Most Wicked Place on Earth." The city's population was now more than six thousand people as better access roads were built. Property prices rose as more settlers came into town. Popular madams of the time included a jaunty little curly-haired miss named Mollie James. By the age of twenty-five, Mollie had enough money to leave the profession and buy a traveling circus back East. Mollie actually ran the circus herself, until it was eventually acquired by P. T. Barnum.[8]

Other stories of Astoria's red-light women are not so sweet. In October 1891 Esther Roeder, "a woman of the street," went to bed drunk with a lit cigarette in her mouth. Sometime later, smoke was seen billowing from her room. Esther was rescued and hospitalized with burns on her neck, face, breast, and shoulders.[9] In May 1895 the *Daily Astorian* reported on Rose Jackson, who "quarreled" with a Greek fisherman. "The brutal Greek clutched the fair damsel by the lily-white throat," reported the paper, "and gave it such a grip that great red and blue marks were apparent for some time afterwards." But Rose was nobody to fool with. The gasping woman managed to grab a "slung shot" [sic] and hit the man over the head, "leaving an ugly gash from which the blood flowed profusely." The fisherman fled and ran into a Sheriff Hare, who took him to get stitched up at Dr. Strickler's drugstore.[10]

Like other places in the West, many prostitutes in Astoria and the neighboring town of Warrenton used slick, untraceable nicknames like "Big Nell," "Bulldog Annie," and "Dutch Lena."[11] Nellie Lamont was also known as "Black Nell" and "The Spanish Queen."[12] As Nellie Lamont, the woman was identified in Portland's *Sunday Oregonian* when she jumped off a wharf in Astoria in 1904. Nellie was drunk, upset, and only saved by her husband, Jack Battson. It was he who "plunged in after her and, with the assistance of the crowd that soon gathered, succeeded in getting her ashore."[13] Two years later, Nellie was in Weiser, Idaho, when she shot saloonkeeper Albert Wenrich in the head, killing him. Nellie next "shot herself through the throat" and was in critical condition, according to the *La Grande Evening Star* of December 13, 1906. A later article revealed that "Wenech" [sic] was formerly a police officer in both Sumpter, Oregon, and Butte, Montana. Nellie, who was not expected to live, claimed that the man had tried to shoot her first.[14]

Perhaps the saddest story of all was that of Hope Clayton, an actress who had performed on the professional stage and accepted a job in Spokane, Washington, circa 1902. When she arrived for the engagement, however, Hope discovered that the job was actually at a common bawdy variety theater. With no other choice, she was bound to remain in Spokane, where she determinedly listed herself as an actress in the 1902 directory. By 1903 Hope was in Astoria when she donated ten dollars during a benefit for the opera house.[15] But she could only find work in another variety theater, and was unkindly referred to later as "an inmate of a downtown resort."[16]

Hope Clayton suffered from a common problem: Although some of the women who worked in dance-halls and variety theaters across the West were chaste, they tended to be lumped in with other performers and actresses who sold sex on the side. Hope does not appear to have sacrificed her morals in any way, but the only room she could find in Astoria was on Sixth Street, very near the red-light district. The *Morning Astorian* described her as a "very beautiful woman, of more than ordinary intelligence." It also was noted that she was "highly accomplished, of pleasing personality and charitable almost to a fault," and that those "who knew Miss Clayton entertained for her the warmest feelings of friendship."[17]

Stuck in Astoria with little chance of regaining her former fame, Hope became depressed and began talking of suicide on July 24, 1904, after another variety actress snubbed her. The public slight obviously had a sad and profound effect on her. It was already common knowledge that Hope was "disgraced" by her life, but her acquaintances were unprepared for what happened next. Around 1:15 a.m. on July 25, Hope was seen hurrying down Sixth Street toward the wharf. Several witnesses, including two police officers, watched in horror as she jumped into the river. She went under before anyone could save her. She was only twenty-six years old.[18]

Reports of Hope's actions initially included the juicy rumor that she was wearing a set of diamonds worth fifteen hundred dollars when she jumped into the water.[19] But the *Morning Astorian* immediately clarified that her jewelry consisted only of a small ring at the time of her fatal leap. The paper also revealed that "the water seems to have brought her to her senses, for she cried piteously for assistance." Furthermore, the paper declared, Hope "could perhaps have been saved had much effort been made." Unfortunately, she drowned and disappeared under the water before help reached her. A hundred-dollar reward was offered for the recovery of her body.[20]

Very little was known about Hope Clayton. She was believed to have been born in either New York or Indiana.[21] The administratrix of her estate was Maud Morrison, a "particular friend and companion" who was probably Hope's landlord. Mrs. Morrison, herself a twenty-five-year-old widow, had been running a lodging house at 77 Sixth Street for at least four years. Going by Hope's probate record, it was obvious that Maud felt the loss of her friend and grieved for Hope's family when they were at last located. Hope's mother, it was discovered, was Nellie Sadler, who was supporting her three children—Charles, nineteen; Lavina, seventeen; and Andrew, six—in Big Rapids, Michigan. Maud immediately arranged to send Nellie one hundred dollars as Hope's estate was settled.[22]

The estate papers revealed that Hope's real name was Shirley Rowe. An inventory of her room indicated that the lady had once lived rather lavishly. Her jewelry included a gold watch and chain and five diamond rings, which she kept in a jewel case. Two cut-glass vases and two vases with gold finish also were among her personal effects, as well as a set of "toilet articles," five fur rugs, three sofa cushions, and an Indian blanket. Her literacy was attested to by the presence of a pen holder and paperweight, plus "one lot" of books. These items had traveled with Hope in her steamer trunk, two suitcases, a bag, and her purse.

Also of interest was Hope's wardrobe, consisting of six dresses and the accompanying "wearing apparel," an opera cloak, a set of furs, one Panama hat, and a hand-painted parasol. She was obviously a woman of modest means; her bank account contained 285 dollars, which would be worth around 4,600 dollars today. Altogether, Hope's estate was appraised at 1,762 dollars. After minimal expenses in settling the estate, Nellie Sadler and her children each received about 258 dollars. Maud also saw to it that Hope's personal belongings, including her clothing and most of her jewelry, were sent along as well. Not until August did a fisherman, Victor Davidson, finally find Hope's body and received the one-hundred-dollar reward. Hope was buried in Greenwood Cemetery in Astoria under her given name.[23]

More women made the papers in Astoria over the years. In February 1908 Lottie Lewis, a black prostitute, got into a knife fight with her white neighbor, Effie Moore. Lottie later claimed Effie came at her first. Her story was evidenced by a bad cut, which she said she received while taking the knife away. But Effie fared much worse, suffering a slash across her abdomen, down her back, and on her arm. Lottie was found guilty of assault and sentenced to six months in jail.[24]

The authorities in Astoria appear to have been as fair as possible during such proceedings, and their goodwill extended to Oregon's government. When Elizabeth and Albert Vance were convicted of robbing a man at one of Astoria's "resorts" in September 1911, they were sent to the state penitentiary in Salem. But newly elected Oregon governor

Oswald West declared he planned to pardon Elizabeth. One of his reasons was because she had a child in Washington. "If she will go home, take care of the child and be good, I see no reason the state should pay $100 a month for her support," West explained. More importantly, the governor blamed Albert Vance for "forcing his wife" into a disreputable house, which was owned by a man named Kelly. For that reason, Albert Vance was not pardoned. Unfortunately, West's sympathy toward women like Elizabeth fell on deaf ears. The *Daily Capital Journal* in Salem mentioned on May 2, 1912, that Elizabeth was in an asylum at Salem.[25]

On December 8, 1922, another fire broke out in Astoria. The conflagration began in the basement of Thiel's pool hall near Twelfth and Commercial Streets around two a.m. Most of the surrounding buildings sat on pilings, making for excellent tinder as the flames lapped up from underneath them. People were killed and twenty-five hundred were left homeless. Due to the fire, as well as progression of the city, many of the old red-light district buildings and boardinghouses were no longer standing by the 1940s. Sadly, one of the remaining red-light hotels was the formerly grand Hotel Astoria, which was now a seedy apartment building at the southeast corner of 14th and Commercial Streets. The hotel had such a reputation for prostitution that it was off-limits to soldiers during World War II. In 1951 the building was renamed the John Jacob Astor Hotel for the city's founder but was eventually condemned. Fortunately, the elegant building was placed on the National Register of Historic Places in 1979, renovated in 1984, and remains a well-known landmark in Astoria today. Few know of its bawdy past.[26]

CHAPTER 10

---•●•---

Naughty Ladies of North Bend and Marshfield

Astoria was not the only port city where prostitution easily flourished. Farther south was today's Coos Bay, which began settlement after the Coos Bay Commercial Company arrived from the Rogue Valley in 1853. Three small settlements quickly sprang up: Empire (county seat until 1896), North Bend, and Marshfield. By 1867, when the population was around three or four hundred people at Marshfield, there was a trading post and an inn, as well as a small tavern run by a Captain Hamilton.[1]

By 1870 the region's economy was largely fed by coal mines, farms, and logging companies. Their goods were piled onto commercial ships for transport to other places. All three towns were located close to the water; at Marshfield many buildings were constructed on wooden pilings over the marshy land constituting the shore. Marshfield's post office opened in 1871, and the town was the first in Coos County to incorporate in 1874. The area was ripe for hooliganism. Roderic Millidge, who served as Marshfield's town marshal in 1877, occasionally doubled as a logger but also as a saloonkeeper and gambler. And in March 1878, town marshal William M. Lind was reprimanded by the town board after he was caught being "present at a disturbance of the place of the said town by riotous and disorderly conduct, assaults and battery, drunkenness and other misdemeanors committed by sundry persons" but "willfully neglected and refused to quell said disorderly conduct and to make arrests for the misdemeanors aforesaid." Lind not only failed to break up the party but also declined to arrest J. Linch for assault and battery. The board also accused Lind of spending too much time on his mining claim, leaving Marshfield without a law officer. He was forced to resign within a month. William M. Lind's successor was constable William Henry "Bill" Noble, who had taken office by June.[2]

By 1879 Marshfield's Front Street was a veritable party resort, described by one man as having "alternately saloons and houses of prostitution, interposed with some businesses."[3] The mostly male population needed places to blow off steam in their leisure time, and Marshfield willingly supplied all the entertainment they needed. On the night of September 20, 1879, W. A. Luse showed up at the Palace Saloon and was joined by W. E. Moore. The men proceeded to trash the saloon, making "night hideous with their bacchanalian orgies" and throwing glasses through the windows and at pictures hanging around the place. For added effect, the twosome shot up the walls. Oil from shattered lamps spread across the floor, caught fire, and nearly burned the tavern down. Luse and Moore were arrested the next morning for destroying personal property—a felony in Marshfield. The local newspaper facetiously reported that the men were given the "ENORMOUS bond of $50 each." In the end, Luse was fined fifteen dollars for damages, costs, and disturbing the peace by firing his pistol. Moore was fined ten dollars.[4]

Four nights later, the *Coos Bay News* noted, there was another "racket at the Palace Saloon last Thursday night. Nobody hurt; no damages done except to fixtures of the saloon. There were five shots fired, a few tumblers broken, etc. As the matter is pending in court, we defer comment." Ironically, barely a month later W. A. Luse became a US deputy marshal and employed his buddy Moore as his bodyguard. Town marshal Bill Noble, who had been trying to restore order for about a year, resigned a month later.[5]

Gunplay seems to have been a most popular pastime in Marshfield. The *Coos Bay News* reported on November 29 that a big party was in progress at a "well known resort on Front Street" when a man named Gunn decided to playfully fire his gun off close to another man's head. The shot was a little too close, and the victim actually lost his eye. Gunn, a known troublemaker around Marshfield, immediately gave a heartfelt, tearful apology. He had explained that he "never intended injuring any-one" and was headed for the door when a Mr. Shingle informed him cheerfully "that an eye equally as good as the one supposed to have been lost could be purchased for about twenty dollars."[6]

First mention of an actual harlot in Marshfield occurred in the January 3, 1880, issue of the *Coast Mail*. City Marshal Henry "Harry" Rhodes approached the brothel of madam Augusta Scales, looking for stolen goods. Finding the door locked, with the proprietress refusing to open it, Rhodes "forcibly brought one of his boots against the door to remind her again that he was there." The kick was rather hard; Rhodes's boot went through the door, and "a moment later one foot was in the house and the other outside." Augusta finally unlocked the door. Rhodes suc-cessfully entered the house and found the stolen items in a closet. When the census was taken on June 5, twenty-eight-year-old Augusta was iden-tified as a "mistress" but worked as a seamstress. The census taker also noted that she was divorced and "not in good health."[7]

Healthier and wealthier women of the night would eventually make it to Marshfield. During the 1890s, Fannie Cardwell ran a bordello on Front Street. Fannie's brothel was one of the most popular in town, and especially during holidays the madam found herself out of rooms for her customers. There being nowhere in the surrounding vicinity to acquire additional property, Fannie came up with the novel idea of purchasing seven small "float houses." These were moored at the docks directly

Marshfield as it appeared long before the city was renamed Coos Bay
Courtesy Evelyn Fisher

behind her building and used as needed to accommodate the overflow of customers. During slow times, the boats were moved to the south end of the bay until they were needed again. In time, the houseboats became known as "Fannie's Flotilla."[8]

Between 1891 and 1895, according to former Marshfield marshal Harkness W. "Hark" Dunham, there were nineteen saloons and four brothels in town. A town hall was built in 1892, but officials did not seem inclined to worry about the presence of good time girls in their town. The ladies' names and activities are noticeably absent from local newspapers, perhaps because it was acceptable for lawmen to cavort in and work among the brothels. One former marshal, David Hutcheson, owned the Arcade Saloon in 1896 while also serving as district constable.[9] Not until 1897 did one prostitute, Ada "Sallie" Thompson, make the papers.

Sallie worked in a crib at the north end of Front Street. She also was the abused victim of J. "Doc" Tucker, aka "N***** Doc." One day in November, Tucker tried to slash Sallie's throat. When the woman tried to protect herself, the razor struck her arm with such force that a piece of the blade broke off in the bone. A few days later, Tucker kicked in the back door of Sallie's crib. She shot at him but missed. That time, a night watchman was summoned and told Tucker to leave. The next day, however, Tucker returned again. This time he grabbed Sallie by the throat and tried to throw her on the bed, but she managed to shoot him in the abdomen. In the room at the time was C. Hazelwood, who verified what had happened. Sallie immediately surrendered herself, and her revolver, to the authorities and claimed self-defense. Officers went to her crib, where they lay Tucker on the bed. Not yet dead, he began expressing heartfelt goodbyes to those around him. He also "expressed no desire to prosecute Sallie for shooting him." Tucker died a day or two later. Sallie was never charged.[10]

Marshfield's red-light district was rivaled by North Bend's scandalous "fancy ladies." Between 1907 and 1914, the women plied their trade all around the corner of Washington and Stanton Streets. Jay Wilcox's saloon seems to have been the focal point of the area. Called the Gem Restaurant and Bar, Wilcox's palace of pleasure "mirrored San Francisco's famous Barbary Coast." Wilcox had actually been in town since 1905. He also had recruited at least five of his soiled doves during a trip to San Francisco to staff the Gem, which also functioned as a dancehall. The place suffered the first of many raids in December 1907, when Sheriff Gage of Coquille paid a visit. Unfortunately for the officer, several gamblers were advised of the raid ahead of time and made themselves scarce before Gage arrived. In May 1908 the Gem came under siege again when Wilcox was convicted of selling liquor to a minor. The case was unusual at the time, as locals recalled that "underage drinkers" were a common site as they staggered around the downtown area.[11]

Wilcox would eventually cave in to a crusade that began in August 1910 to rid downtown North Bend of its naughty ladies. The bawdy houses along Stanton Street, including Wilcox's, were commanded to close. Wilcox simply moved his businesses. He sold the Gem, and the name was changed to the Coos Hotel sometime between 1910 and 1914 under the new owner, Charles Metlin.[12] Not all saloons were intended to double as houses of prostitution. In 1908 the Thom

Building, constructed by Charlie Thom, was originally home to a brewery. Upstairs were rooms to let, and much to Thom's chagrin, some of his renters used them "for immoral purposes."[13]

A few years later, the *Coos Bay Times* printed a front-page shaming article directed at the Royal Theater, a premier and upstanding playhouse of North Bend. In March 1911 a review of a performance involving showgirls noted that the "show throughout was suggestive, but when one of the so-called chorus girls attired in flesh colored tights and a gauze undershirt attempted the hoochy-koochy, it drove the women in haste from the theatre. Men who have traveled and seen the hula-hula and other vulgar dances pronounce last night's performance at The Royal one of the most coarsely vulgar and immoral exhibitions ever seen on a public stage." Royal owner Robert Marsden Jr. did not retort, and perhaps didn't need to. The theater remained immensely popular—at least until the following month, when an actress was badly hurt onstage. Public sentiment for the performer caused an attack on Marsden for failing to do enough for her.[14]

Marshfield and the Coos Bay region continued growing in population, which was starting to include more and more of the female sex. Proper ladies in particular disapproved of what they saw and heard about the red-light districts. Then, in August 1911, Dr. A. W. Porter— who claimed to be a corn doctor and manicurist—was caught in the Chandler Hotel in Marshfield with a sixteen-year-old girl from Coquille. The sordid news made the front page of the *Coos Bay Times*. The innocent girl, Marcella Smalley, called Dr. Porter a "real nice man" who had promised her a vacation, and the two had accordingly registered for two separate rooms. A Sheriff Gage, however, had already fingered Porter as a "white slave" trafficker. During a midnight raid, Gage and Marshal Carter discovered Porter and Marcella in the doctor's room, where they had "retired for the night." Porter was arrested and made to pay Marcella's way back to Coquille. Porter was taken there too, where he was convicted and sentenced to three months in jail and a two-hundred-dollar fine. As for Marcella, who worked as a waitress and came from a prominent family, it was discovered that her parents were on vacation. She was given a good talking to by Gage and expressed "remorse and regret" at her decision to accompany Porter to Marshfield.[15]

Something about the Porter incident stirred the general populace. "Marshfield is just now harboring scores of *maquereaux* [a French word for pimps], a thing that no other city on the coast will tolerate," bellowed one newspaper. "This city is becoming the paradise of this most undesirable element that exists off of fallen women." Shakedowns in Portland, the paper explained, were causing undesirables to flock to other Oregon cities, namely Marshfield. "If the authorities will do their duty and exercise the powers vested in them there would not be a *macque* in Marshfield at sundown today," the paper concluded.[16] The authorities must have read the paper, for in September some arrests were made. On September 7 prostitute Hazel Cameron was arrested along with a man named Joe Gaynor. It was the second time in a week that Gaynor was fined twenty-five dollars for "frequenting houses of ill fame," and this time he gave officers quite a time as they tried to wrangle him. Hazel herself put up the fifty dollars in bail money. The same day, the paper reported that Ralph Jackson and a Miss Ingram were arrested at the Rogers rooming house and taken to Coquille "for the grand jury to handle."[17]

The authorities were not done, but neither were the illicit ladies. On December 23 the *Morning Oregonian* reported that bartender Charles Murray of the Blanco Bar in Marshfield was enjoying libations at the Owl Saloon when a woman came through the side door, called him out, and shot him through the lung. The lady immediately expressed her remorse, helped tend to Murray, and offered to pay his medical expenses as he was hauled off to Mercy Hospital. "No I won't give you his name," she snapped at a reporter for the *Coos Bay Times* as she got in the ambulance. "I won't tell you who shot him. Someone that had an old grudge against him. Maybe I'll talk after we take him to the hospital. I'll probably be in jail by then." It was noted that the woman talked to Murray extensively on the way to the hospital, but all that could be heard of their conversation was when she muttered that "no one could do her and get away with it."[18]

In the coming days, the woman was arrested and identified as Goldie Bestcott, a prostitute of Front Street. Murray refused to make a statement against her, but the lady spent Christmas in jail.[19] At her preliminary hearing, witnesses against her included a deputy game warden named C. F. Thomas, who said he witnessed Goldie pulling a gun from her hand muff and shooting Murray in the back. Thomas testified that Goldie had said she only intended to scare Murray. Only after shooting him, he said, did Goldie declare "he was not going to die and that she had not meant to hurt him." In court, Goldie listened carefully as the attorneys argued her case. Her emotions varied between "a cold cynical smile," looks of "horror," and visibly jumping when the prosecutor stated she would be charged with murder should Murray die within the year.[20]

By December 27, Goldie had been released from jail but remained at the Coos Hotel in Marshfield. She spent most of her time at Murray's bedside and was with him when he finally died, on December 29. He never did make a statement concerning why, or even whether, Goldie had shot him. But his death was too much for Goldie, who had eaten little food and had been frantic over Murray's health. Her doctor stated that she was in such bad shape that she should not be placed in jail. Instead Goldie was taken back to the Coos Hotel and put under guard. Her bail was now set at five thousand dollars, which a number of men, including Coos Hotel owner Charles Metlin, tried to post on her behalf. The judge refused, probably fearing that Goldie was a flight risk.[21]

Goldie was not tried until April 1912.[22] There were now three witnesses who claimed they had heard Goldie say things to Murray. "I told ye. I told you I would. Now, I am ready to take my medicine," she was alleged to have muttered to Murray after shooting him. "Now, I guess you'll stay awhile." Others testified that Goldie had intended to leave her life as a prostitute and live with Murray on a ranch until "another woman crossed their path."[23] These testimonies apparently had no bearing on the case, and Goldie was inexplicably acquitted in May. She was thought to have gone to San Francisco, where she had relatives. Were the citizens of Marshfield surprised to learn that just a month later, Goldie married former Owl Saloon bartender Jack Millett in California?[24] Perhaps not. For Goldie, love was not blind—nor was it forever.

By 1913 the giddy girls of both Marshfield and North Bend were making the newspapers quite frequently. At the latter town during 1913, Mrs. Fannie O'Donnell was noted as running a bawdy house above the Grand Saloon at the corner of Sherman and Connecticut Avenues. The *Coos Bay Harbor* newspaper reported that Fannie had originally been operating out of the Pacific Grocery and upon being evicted had moved to the Grand. There, she was running girls but also a restaurant. Her stay was short, only about a month, as the building's owner, Chris Peterson, evicted her after a chat with Mayor Simpson. The article also reported that she was moving again, this time to friendlier quarters in Marshfield. Fannie did not fare much better in Marshfield; soon after her arrival she was arrested along with three men. In December 1915 she would be arrested again for refusing to pay a fine for selling liquor illegally.[25]

Fannie might have returned to North Bend, even as the city furthered its limitations on the local saloons: A new ordinance decreed that only six saloons were permitted per the three thousand people in town. For every five hundred newcomers, an additional bar was allowed.[26] One of the saloons was the El Dorado, located in the "the space once [occupied by] the Castle Restaurant." The El Dorado certainly got around, for it had moved to the Castle Restaurant from another place.[27] Marshfield, meanwhile, was outgrowing its original borders, and real estate was becoming scarce. In answer, the city began filling in Mill Slough and most of South Marshfield.[28]

As Marshfield grew, certain citizens began complaining about the number of brothels in town. But the demimonde was happily ingrained in the city, and lots of other people liked it that way. When a madam was arrested in 1914 for selling liquor illegally, she countered the charge in court by giving "sensational evidence that involved nearly the entire police force." She was set free.[29] The same went for North Bend, where by 1915 numerous downtown buildings were considered questionable due to the "quality and morality" that "tarred each." These included the Coos Hotel, the Oregon Hotel, a place known as "Our House," and the Palace Hotel. A councilman named Wood proclaimed in January that "nearly every rooming house in North Bend was used for immoral purposes." Wood encouraged the council to force the hotel owners to clean up their places, but H. C. Wray, who owned the Palace, defended his business against such attacks.[30]

A plan was definitely afoot, as the state was already planning on enacting its own prohibition law along with six other western states. During the heated arguments between the "wet" and "dry" teams in the saloon business, North Bend adopted new ordinances for those bars remaining open. All saloons were to close at midnight. Women were not allowed in these places, and no gambling was allowed. Finally, as of December 31, 1915, taverns throughout Oregon were to be closed as of midnight.[31] Naturally the New Year's Eve celebration of 1915 was like no other. The *Coos Bay Times* noted that even those who never frequented the local saloons could be found on the last legal day of drinking in various taverns throughout the region. Even the lone prisoner in the city jail, a man named Miller, was released with three minutes to spare—just long enough to gulp down two drinks before the clock struck midnight. Nearly every drop of liquor in town was sold out as people stocked up their private stash for their homes. Everyone was in a jovial mood as they enjoyed their last libation. At midnight, the streets rapidly cleared as the saloons closed their doors for the last time.[32]

In the aftermath, some saloons, like the El Dorado, tried to switch to selling soft drinks but failed. Others found a loophole in the new law, whereby out-of-state liquor dealers were allowed to ship small quantities of alcohol to individuals in Oregon for private use. The law permitted two quarts of liquor and a case of beer per family, per month. Former Gem Saloon owner Jay Wilcox moved to Eureka, California, where he could procure tonsil varnish for residents of Oregon. Because of this and other ways around the new law, few were arrested unless they were openly caught with liquor or being drunk in public.[33] As for the shady ladies of Coos County, they likely were able to secure some illegal hooch to sell within the privacy of their rooms, a practice that occurred in other places throughout the West.

Bootlegging liquor aside, the party hounds of Marshfield and North Bend quieted down over the next several years. Then, on July 23, 1922, the city of Marshfield pretty much burned to the ground. The fire began in J. Guildesheim's junk store. Twenty-five businesses and four homes burned, including City Hall. The city fathers, after some consideration, decided to move the town just west of its original location on the water-front. A new city hall was constructed in 1924 at Central Avenue and 24th Street. Included was a jail with five cells, three for male prisoners and two for female prisoners.[34]

When Marshfield burned, it would seem as though the good time girls packed what was left of their belongings and departed, for the most part. Newspapers remained quiet about the prostitution industry, although there were known attempts to close down the naughty houses of North Bend as late as the 1940s. It was guessed, however, that there was only one house of ill repute left in town. In 1944, when the citizens of Marshfield voted to change the name of their town to Coos Bay, much of Marshfield's bawdy history was, for the most part, quietly swept under the rug.[35]

The only clue that the prostitution industry was still alive in Coos County at all was a meeting called by District Attorney James A. Norman on September 3, 1952. Norman pointed out that, at least in some cases, each city in the county had quietly acquiesced to prostitution because the industry boosted the city economies. He also pointed out that, like it or not, selling sex was illegal. In conclusion, Norman said, each mayor should take it upon himself to close the local brothels. He gave them a week to do so. The plan worked, and every working girl in each town was notified to close up shop. At the end of the week, the only brothels remaining in business were those in outlying areas like Bridge, Coquille, Green Acres, Myrtle Point, and Powers.[36] The mayors of those places apparently missed the meeting.

CHAPTER 11

Oregon's Camp Followers and Circuit Riders

Aside from the fishing trade, the pioneer Pacific Northwest held riches in the way of three other industries: logging, mining, and ranching. Occupations in these professions could be not only dangerous but downright dreary. Longtime historian and journalist Stewart Holbrook described the logger lifestyle as one often spent among the swamps of Oregon: "The isolation of logging camps, combined with an occupation so dangerous to life as to remove all but the toughest and most alert, conspired to produce a unique race of men whose dedicated goal was to let daylight into the swamp and thus, as they saw it, permit the advance of civilization."[1]

The same statement could be applied to mining and ranching; the hours could be grueling, and the sight of a woman—any woman—must have brought some comfort to the men in these industries. Fortunately for them, Oregon's good time girls found their way over the craggy mountains, desolate hills, and roaring rivers to give them that comfort, plus a dash extra in the way of sexual encounters. The ladies could travel from larger cities and from camp to camp, settling for a while if the prospects looked good. The Western slang word for these women was "camp followers." In Oregon they were also known as "circuit riders."[2]

By the 1860s and 1870s, hundreds of camps and fledgling cities were springing up all over eastern Oregon. They included Clarksville in Baker County, which had a population of only two hundred by 1862. Even so, Florence and Fannie Bloom, who claimed to be sisters, ran a successful brothel in Clarksville. The structure was actually a large tent with a dirt floor. Inside were rooms divided by partitions with a stove, table and chairs, and two beds. The Bloom sisters wisely set up shop near an area where the miners worked, assuring them that each man returning to town would see their place. One day, one of the girls was sweeping the dirt floor when she found a sizable chuck of gold. The ladies spent the rest of their day panning for gold on their own floor, netting five hundred dollars for the effort. The girls decided to stake a claim on the floor—and sold it. Allegedly, one of them returned to her family back East, telling them that her "boardinghouse" in Oregon had done quite well.[3]

There are many stories of the kindness shown by Oregon's shady ladies. Sometime after a railroad was built through La Grande in 1884, a tale emerged about madam Julie Harbor. One of her clients, a businessman, had recently acquired a whopping fifty thousand dollars in cash. Fearful of some men he thought might rob him, the man asked Julie to keep the money overnight, until he could get it to the bank the next day. She agreed, although she was rightfully nervous at the idea of having that much cash in the house. Her feelings only worsened when the man failed to return within a few days.

At last, after about a week, Julie heard that, true to his prediction, the man had been beaten severely. He was under a doctor's care at a hotel in Baker City. Julie hastened to the hotel by train and located the victim, who told her he believed his assailants had taken his money. When Julie informed him that she had his money and that it was safe, he was "incredulous and grateful." Julie returned to La Grande; when the businessman recovered sufficiently, he came to see the madam and get his money. He also gave Julie two thousand dollars for her trouble.[4]

The good time girls of Oregon always appreciated a good tip, but they also quickly figured out how to make money other ways. At Cornucopia, founded in 1878, one woman known only as Blue Stockings would simply waltz into the saloons, display her ample bosom from a low-cut blouse, and invite miners to "flick" their gold nuggets at her chest. "Toss 'em, boys, toss 'em!" she would call out. The men knew that Blue Stockings got to keep the nuggets she managed to catch in her cleavage. Even so, the participants tended to become so excited while watching the game that the woman was often guaranteed good business afterward.[5]

Prostitution was still rampant in Cornucopia in 1898, when eight-year-old Erma Cole's family moved there. Erma remembered the "sporting ladies" who occupied a couple of houses. One of them was a woman named Fanny, who frequently dined at the hotel where the Coles also stayed. Just off the dining room was a barrel where the hotel cat, Snowball, once had a litter of kittens. One evening Fanny and one of her girls, Nelly, "swept in" for dinner in the company of their own dogs, who stationed themselves under the dining table. The mutts inevitably sniffed out the barrel, and when Snowball unexpectedly jumped out in a frenzy, all hell broke loose. In the fray, Fanny and Nelly leaped onto the table, "and held their voluminous skirts well up out of the way." Erma witnessed the hilarious scene, later commenting, "I was somewhat bold in those days and I couldn't help laughing at them, but they were very upset."[6]

Plenty of action also was available at Canyon City after the town was founded in 1862. The best-remembered madam of the town was Polly Wilson, who showed up circa 1886. Little is known about her early life, except that she was born in England in 1855, married an unknown spouse in 1872, and gave birth to five children, three of whom died.[7] Polly first made the papers in 1886 when the *State Rights Democrat* reported that "a few days ago John Rinehart, a saloon keeper, unmercifully pounded one Polly Wilson. Polly went home, got a revolver, returned and shot Rinehart dead. She is in jail awaiting the action of the next grand jury." Polly was fortunate to find a sympathetic jury, for she was never formally charged for the murder and spent only two nights in jail before being released.[8]

Polly may have been granted a reprieve from justice in the killing of John Rinehart, but by 1888 she appears to have been a downright nuisance. A cryptic note in the *Grant County News* explained that the newspaper "was mistaken in regard as to [who] is making the cost to Grant Co. It is the [notorious] bad man with the big Stare. Instead of the [notorious] Polly Wilson and her admirers. Mrs. Wilson's admirers agreed to leave Grant Co. and all of its respective People in 48 hours time. [sic]" Six months later, Polly was in the news once more when she sued one Thornton Williams, but the matter was not further explained by the papers.[9] Polly seems to have been involved with lawsuits quite frequently. In December 1891 the *Grant County News* announced that one W. S. Southworth had successfully sued the woman for a total of $254.03, an amount Polly could not pay. Accordingly, a sheriff's auction was scheduled for January 23, 1892, wherein Polly's house on Main Street would be sold to settle the debt. By 1900 Polly once again owned a house where she worked as a "lodging house keeper." But the presence of two young ladies in the house—nineteen-year-old Lily Potter and twenty-three-year-old Hazel Evans—infers that Polly was still in business. Today, a life-size mannequin in period clothing at the Grant County Historical Museum in Canyon City represents Polly Wilson.[10]

There is much evidence to support a corrupt connection between the prostitution industry and city authorities. In 1904 the *Roseburg Plaindealer* announced that "the premises lately occupied by a washee-washee establishment on Main Street, near the old Van Houten Hotel, has been fitted up as a boarding school for incorrigible girls and women. A stockade has been built around it and the house moved back on the lot.

The Alfred Block in Baker City and other former saloons with "upstairs girls" are now part of the city's historic downtown area.
Courtesy Jan MacKell Collins

The *Plaindealer* learns that it to be used for honk-i-tonk purposes. Bald headed libertines are prohibited from looking through the cracks to see the glory of the *babi humayun*."[11] The newspaper failed to mention that the new owner of the "honk-i-tonk" was Mabel Cox, who intended to run a brothel there. The Stockade, as it became known, was located on the east side of Main Street between Douglas and Washington Streets.

Because the Stockade was conveniently located right around the corner from the Douglas County Courthouse, Mabel quickly realized that certain customers might shy away from using her front door in view of the fancy Van Houten Hotel and another respectable lodging house across the street. In time, the Stockade was alternately called

"The Highboard" for the type of wood used for the fence. A "sort of baffle" was installed in the fence, wherein Mabel's customers could slip unnoticed onto her property if they were quick. There is no doubt that many of Mabel's customers were employees from the courthouse. They say that some of them included "two city councilmen, a deputy sheriff, and a minister." This may be the reason Mabel never appeared in local newspapers. The city officials kept her secrets as well as she did theirs. She even installed a door in the rear of her house so that certain customers could gain even more discreet access via the livery stable next door.[12]

Mabel Cox made history in her own discreet way, and does not appear to have ever suffered for her actions. The opposite is true of Faye Melbourne, who ran a fancy parlor house known as the Red House in Klamath Falls. Faye, a native of California, had been in town since at least 1910.[13] On a sunny day in August 1911, John Hunsaker spotted a body floating in the Oak Avenue Canal near the Red House. Further inspection revealed the man's head had several marks that were likely made by an ax. Hunsaker summoned the authorities, who soon identified the victim as a logger named Charles Lyons. The man had lately been working at a logging camp on nearby Stukel Mountain. Three days earlier, witnesses remembered, Lyons had received his pay in the amount of eighty dollars and had headed to Klamath Falls with fellow logger Ben Robbs to have some Friday-night fun.

Police learned that when they arrived in Klamath Falls, Lyons and Robbs checked into a hotel before beginning a night of barhopping. Their first stop was a place called the Road House, where Lyons had a few drinks and got a shave. Their next stop was the Red House. To get to the brothel, customers accessed a bridge near the city jail, christened the "Bridge of Sighs" for the famed footpath in Venice, Italy, which lay across the canal. Lyons and Robbs crossed the bridge and arrived at the Red House around seven p.m. Five hours later Robbs, broke and tired, left his friend and went back to the hotel. What happened to Lyons after that remained shrouded in mystery.

Policemen scoured the banks of the canal, looking for a murder weapon as certain citizens took the opportunity to criticize the Red House and brothels like it. Just a month before, the town had laughed up an incident concerning a well-known drunk of the city known as Old Man Haley at another bordello known as the Comet Lodging House. In that instance, the authorities were summoned to the Comet, where they found Haley lying in a bed naked, drunk, and waving around a ten-dollar bill for service while refusing to leave. The policemen had duly escorted Haley across the Bridge of Sighs to the jail so he could sleep it off. Afterward the city had ordered the brothels to close, but the orders were ignored. And now there had been a murder.[14]

Fingers almost immediately pointed at Faye, since her palatial bordello was the last place Lyons had been seen alive. There was, however, no evidence of foul play. The authorities, certain that the Red House and Faye Melbourne had something to do with Lyons's death, decided that the best way to proceed was to first charge Faye with "conducting a bawdy house." This was accomplished in December, and the case was continued in early January. The plan was to force Faye to admit to running the place in order to prove that Lyons had been a customer on the night he died, which was believed to have been around July 15. Chief of Police Samuel Walker was a star witness at the trial, claiming that on one occasion he was called to the house by a young man who claimed he had paid ten dollars for sexual services, but that the girl with whom he had made the appointment had taken off in an automobile instead and returned drunk. The man had asked for his money back, which was refused.[15]

Walker also said that after Lyons's body was found, "one of the inmates admitted that she had spent the night with the missing man." He also stated that he had watched between a dozen and fifteen men coming and going from the Red House in the course of half an hour to forty-five minutes. Most damning was Walker's claim that Faye had consulted him because she wanted to quit the "sporting business" and "wished to get married at Christmas." Faye allegedly told the officer that she couldn't sell the Red House because it had been closed by the authorities.

As Faye watched the proceedings, it was noted that she "sat in her wraps on, occasionally turning around to smile at someone with which she evidently was acquainted."[16] Faye's casual actions may have angered Sheriff Walker, but the man was not prepared for what came next. Faye's attorney responded by outright accusing Walker of taking bribes from the red-light ladies. Under oath, Walker admitted that he had indeed advised Faye Melbourne about just where to build her bordello in the first place. The trial against Faye deflated after that, resulting in a hung jury. A new trial was scheduled as Faye posted a bond of two hundred dollars. In normal circumstances, Faye Melbourne would have returned to her brothel and taken up where she left off. Instead, the madam simply disappeared.[17]

Nobody seems to have realized that Faye was missing until they noticed that her lights failed to come on at night and her mail at the post office remained unclaimed. Her attorney never received his fees, and the Red House remained empty and silent. There wasn't even the slightest hint that Faye had even packed before departing. In February a bench warrant was filed against her. The general public, meanwhile, concluded that Lyons had indeed met his end at the Red House, and that Faye had left town one step ahead of officially being charged with his murder. To others, however, the suspicion surrounding her disappearance lay with city officials, about whom Faye knew things—deep, dark secrets. One of them had already embarrassed the chief of police by being revealed in court. Where had she gone? Nobody knew. Faye was never seen again in Klamath Falls, and the mystery of what really happened to her remains unsolved.[18]

Plenty of women like Faye Melbourne, and their stories, have been lost to history. In Baker City, however—founded in 1864 and a virtual den of fancy resorts and brothels by the early 1900s—the story of one woman stands out nationwide. Her public name was Sally Stanford. Although she did not pursue a profession in prostitution until well after she left her native city, Sally drew her inspiration to do so while she was just a girl in Baker City. Born Mable Janice Busby in 1903, Sally grew up in a poor, hardworking family. One day in about 1912, Sally's mother took her shopping for shoes at the Golden Rule Department Store. But Sally wasn't interested in shoes, choosing instead to languish in front of a case of colorful ribbons. Suddenly she became aware of someone watching her. Looking up, the girl noticed "the most elegant lady I had ever seen. She had a frilly laced front white silk blouse covered by a small sealskin black jacket. On her head was perched an elaborate black velvet hat with great black ostrich feathers which hung dramatically over one side."[19]

Sally and the beautiful woman were chatting amicably about the pretty ribbons when Sally's mother suddenly appeared, yanked the girl over to the shoe department, and admonished her for talking to strange ladies. The twosome finally selected some shoes, but while her mother paid for them, Sally stole quickly back to the lady at the ribbon counter. It was obvious to the woman that Sally loved the ribbons. "Would you like to have some of those hair ribbons, little girl?" she asked. Sally nodded and watched as her new friend ordered "yards and yards of every type of hair ribbon, in every color." Once they were placed in a bag, the woman placed them on the counter in front of Sally, "winking knowingly and smiling very sweetly as she walked away." Sally stashed the parcel in her jacket and hid it in her bedroom. Later, Sally prodded her mother about the nice lady. Mrs. Busby told Sally the woman "was not a nice lady, she was a *painted* lady and I don't want you to ever talk to her again." When Sally's mother eventually saw the hair ribbons, the girl wisely told her they had been given to her by a woman whose husband patronized the golf club where Sally worked. Long after she left Baker City, and following her infamous career as a San Francisco madam, Sally was elected to the city council and eventually as mayor of Sausalito, California. She died in 1982.[20]

Others like Sally Stanford remain as heroine harlots in history. At Pendleton, established to the northwest of Baker City in 1867, the rowdy cattle town featured upward of thirty-two saloons and eighteen brothels by the mid-1800s. Pendleton's best-remembered madam today is Stella Darby, who ran the Cozy Rooms in Pendleton from 1928 to 1967. Stella was a model madam, teaching her girls to save their money so they could get out of the profession as fast as possible. She even kept her customers' extra money for them when they went out on the town, to make sure they didn't spend it all. To keep her girls honest, Stella employed the token system, wherein her customers first purchased a token from her before giving it to the girl of their choice. Most unique about the Cozy Rooms, and a wonderful benefit to any working girl, was that each employee was given two rooms: one for business and a separate bedroom she could call her own. Because she was not a working madam, Stella had only one bedroom for herself—with a secret escape door at the back of her closet.[21]

In 2014 the Pendleton Arts Council embarked on a project wherein bronze statues of local figures were created and placed throughout the city. By far the most controversial of the statues was that of Stella Darby, which was both revered and criticized by various citizens. The statue remains today as a tribute to the working girls of Pendleton's past and is admired by history buffs who appreciate historical prostitution. Pendleton Underground Tours, which sponsored the statue, today operates out of the Working Girls Hotel, where one can stay the night and take a tour of the underground tunnels where brothels, as well as other businesses, once flourished. The Working Girls Hotel is just one of several original bordellos to remain in Pendleton.[22]

Stella Darby's statue is a stark reminder that the prostitution industry was once an important presence in the economy, and history, of Oregon. Thankfully, many of those pleasure palaces that once flourished in the downtown areas of many cities remain as quiet, unrecognized landmarks to a bawdy time of frontier prostitutes, dance-hall girls, and saloon girls who danced their way through the demimonde. Other places, having digressed into rough or poorer neighborhoods once they were past their prime, have been abandoned or even torn down as a means to sweep their disreputable pasts under the rug. One place that has managed to endure over time is Whorehouse Meadow, located in Harney County east of Fish Lake. At one time the meadow sported wood and canvas houses that were working vacation homes to prostitutes from Vale and Boise. The girls would visit the meadow and do business with local cattle hands and Basque sheepherders.

Area resident Harry Telford once told a tale of the ladies coming to Whorehouse Meadow and transacting with several cowboys. Telford described their makeshift brothel as a "traveling whorehouse." The ladies, he said were "middle-aged women; they weren't very fancy whore ladies." This appears not to have bothered the men, some of whom hadn't even seen a woman in months. Soon after the women left, however, their customers came down with venereal disease. "There's one thing you don't do when you have that," Telford emphasized, "is to ride horseback if you can possibly help it." One of the ranch hands offered a cure in the way of "sage-rabbit brush," which could be brewed like a tea. The sage grew in heavily alkaline soil, and when used "seemed to work probably just as good as some of their high priced drugs they put out nowadays."[23]

During the 1960s, after hearing complaints by certain "moralists" who objected to the name of Whorehouse Meadow, the Bureau of Land Management published a map identifying the place as "Naughty Girl Meadow." The cartographers must have been shocked when others immediately set up a debate, claiming the original name should remain. Their complaints reached "federal arbiters," and the argument went on for quite some years. Naturally, the unusual controversy went far beyond Oregon. In 1972 the *Washington (DC) Star-News* reported that "folks in the Wild West wish those Puritan pencil-pushers in the federal bureaucracy would leave their colorful place names alone."[24] After several more years of debate, the name Whorehouse Meadow was officially restored in 1981 and remains today.[25]

CHAPTER 12

---•◦•---

Copperfield, No Place for a Lady, or a Gentleman

Although there is a debate whether there ever really was copper to be mined in Copperfield, one fact remains: The budding gold mining boomtown of Baker County, established in 1898, was built in a "grim, narrow canyon" along the Snake River. There were indeed lots of mines along the Snake, the largest and oldest being the Gold Hill Mine.[1] None of them, however, seemed to ever amount to much. Like so many mining towns, Copperfield rode the roller coaster of boom-and-bust times. During the biggest building boom, in the spring of 1907, workers were brought in to build the Idaho-Oregon Light & Power Company and lay tracks for the Union Pacific Railroad. Baker City realtor James Harvey Graham bought the 160-acre Jake Vaughn farm and finally platted the town proper. Graham immediately sold out to bankers John Schmitz and William Pollman, the latter being mayor of Baker City. The ranch cost ten thousand dollars, but lots were selling at fifty to one hundred dollars. By March 1907 more than one hundred lots had sold. In addition, an acre of land was leased to house railroad workers.[2]

Almost overnight, Copperfield's main street grew to include eleven saloons and the same number of brothels. Interspersed with these were the post office (established in 1899), a barbershop, two hotels, two boardinghouses, and three stores. When citizens ran out of room along the main drag, a tent city was built on the outskirts of town. Two women, "Mesdames Day and Knapp," were credited with hauling in enough lumber to construct their Hotel Magpie. But the most popular buildings of all were the saloons, which were quickly being built to serve the masses.[3]

Both the railroad workers and the power plant workers were a rough bunch; early on, Copperfield was fraught with violence and murders. Victims were often dumped into the Snake River, washing downstream, where some of them eventually surfaced in Lewiston, Idaho. Because of this, it is said that Lewiston "has one of the largest cemeteries in the world with unmarked gravesites."[4] Meanwhile, Copperfield was really growing roots. Two thousand men now were toiling to build a tunnel on a branch of the Union Pacific Railroad from Huntington, as well as the power plant. Just off Main Street were warehouses and a small depot for the train, which came to town three times a week. By January 1909 Copperfield was "wide open" as a wild and crazy party town. According to the *La Grande Evening Observer*, "all the booze necessary can be had and that is about all they want. The shrewd 'sport' is there also, ready and capable of separating the laborer from his coin and it is done in the most scientific way. The gay siren is on the ground, too, with all her gay fluffles and cosmetic beauty." The article concluded that "Copperfield is the kingpin of all the northwest towns. It is the quintessence of all that is foul and immoral."[5]

Opposite of the *Evening Observer*'s view of Copperfield, Portland's *Morning Oregonian* casually noted that the fourteen hundred men of the town, of which only four hundred were "permanent residents," were served by seven saloons, but that "Copperfield of today is one of the best new towns in the whole northwest." It also was noted, however, that while there was a school and a hospital, there was no church to be found.[6] And everyone knew that men's entertainment even extended to nearby areas. One story concerns nine sheep ranchers who were shearing wool in Eagle Valley. According to the tale, "three Copperfield girls arrived and shut down the operation." The young ladies were the daughters of a moonshiner at a place called "Homestead," the oldest being only seventeen years old. The girls approached the men, proclaiming, "Less' have a party."

When one of the men refused the girls' offers of a good time, the young ladies boarded a boat and crossed the river, returning with twelve gallons of moonshine. A gallon was given to each man. Before long, one of the girls was seen in a wool sack with one of them. "You know how big a wool sack is," said the unidentified man relating the story, "and she's down inside the wool sack." Another man playfully grabbed a knife and cut the sack lengthwise, revealing the couple who "never even quit right out on the floor."[7]

Copperfield remained wildly raw and untamed for about three years. It was an entity unto itself, and word soon spread that the remote town was no place for a real lady or gentleman. The two factions in town—railroad workers versus the power plant workers—clashed often in drunken brawls fought with rocks and beer bottles. Sometimes, both sides were so inebriated they forgot what they were even fighting about. Even a judge could not decide who was right and who was wrong, for Copperfield had neither a jail nor a lawman to use it. The closest sheriff was 150 miles away in Baker City.[8]

Copperfield's red-light ladies also were running amok. One time, an Irish immigrant identified as Jim Mulino came through town on his way New Zealand. Mulino had a "long layover" at the nearby town of Huntington and joined a fellow traveler who wanted to see Copperfield. When the men arrived, they saw a most interesting sight: The painted ladies of the town were walking across the street to get their mail, wearing nothing but their high-heeled shoes. "Oh, God. What kind of place is this? Man I ain't seen nothin' like that in my life," Mulino is said to have muttered. Yet the Irishman remained in town for another month before traveling to Seattle, where he cashed in his ticket to New Zealand and returned to Copperfield. And there he lived for the rest of his life, or so they say.[9]

The wild goings-on at Copperfield remained largely out of the papers until July of 1909, when an alleged horse thief named Page Hawley was captured outside of town. Saloon owner J. J. Burns led the posse, and claimed that Hawley had fallen from his horse when captured. As the group returned, residents saw that Hawley had been bound to his horse, with a noose running from the pommel of the saddle to hold his head up. His skull was badly crushed and he was not expected to live. The people were not buying the story that Hawley fell; rather, the *Morning Oregonian* rightfully suspected that the man had been severely beaten. The story was followed for months as Hawley recovered to tell what really happened. In the end, Burns was sent to prison.[10]

At last the outlaw lifestyle of saloon owners and others at Copperfield became known to the general public around Oregon. When a flood unexpectedly struck, many men left town, leaving a shortage of labor for a new railroad tunnel as the power plant neared completion. During the lull, about 1913, even the saloon owners were fighting among themselves. Two saloons, owned by Martin Knezevich and William Wiegand, were destroyed by arson. Wiegand reacted by successfully pushing to incorporate Copperfield so he and his cronies could take over the town. Not surprisingly, saloonkeeper H. A. Stewart was elected mayor. The councilmen, including Wiegand, Tony Warner, W. Woodbury, and J. J. Burns, who had apparently finished his stint in prison, were all saloon men.[11]

The council's first move was to issue licenses to every saloon owner in town except Knezevich, who immediately took his case to the county prosecutor in Baker City. It was no good; the fights, threats, and mayhem were so bad that the prosecutor left town without making any headway. Knezevich next complained to County Sheriff Ed Rand at Baker City.

Rand also visited Copperfield but came away with the same opinion as the prosecutor: So vile and violent were Copperfield's men that there was no way to discern what the problem was, let alone fix it. The victors made their final point by setting Knezevich's new saloon on fire, although this time the flames were quickly extinguished.[12]

Eventually, news of the bad boys at Copperfield made its way to Oregon governor Oswald West. The few good ranchwomen of the town had written to West, complaining of the dens of sin and the influence on the women's sons. The letters were accompanied by a petition signed by fifty-five Copperfield residents, including the schoolteacher, all alleging "that the place was under the control of saloonkeepers and gamblers." Mayor Stewart, for example, was running "a dancehall where intoxicating liquor is dispensed," and the saloons were open all night long. Two of the respectable men who were now on the city council, R. E. Clark and a man named Griffith, had thrown up their hands and left town. The petition pleaded for peace via the governor, since Baker County officials had refused to help.[13]

West's first step was to command Baker County officials to do their job and clean up Copperfield. The officials responded that they could do nothing since Copperfield had its own government. Undaunted, West proclaimed that Copperfield's government officials were mere thieves and crooks of their own nasty little underworld, and that Baker County had until Christmas to get the town under control. West's order fell on deaf ears, even after he gave instructions to close the saloons. The edict was followed with threats to send in the militia to restore order.[14] These also were ignored.

Finally, in late December 1913, West made perhaps the most unusual decision a man of his power has ever made. His reasoning was sound enough when he realized that a personal appearance was more likely to only encourage more of the same behavior Baker County officials had experienced. What Copperfield needed, he theorized, was the firm hand of a good woman. Accordingly, West instructed his private secretary, Miss Fern Hobbs, to prepare documents for Copperfield's city council to resign their positions. A second document proclaimed martial law. Miss Hobbs's third duty was to send a polite wire to Copperfield's mayor, advising him that she was coming and expected to meet with the city council in its entirety when she arrived. Sending a tiny woman to quell a bunch of drunken louts was utterly crazy. West, however, had the utmost faith in Miss Hobbs. "It will be up to her to close the saloons," he announced, "and judging from her past work, I have not the slightest doubt that she will be successful." When questioned on the danger of sending a frail woman to quell a town full of dangerous men, West quipped, "You just watch Miss Hobbs, and keep your eye on Copperfield after she arrives." For their part, Copperfield's officials promised to treat the lady courteously and even put up some pink and blue balloons, ribbons, and flowers in anticipation of her arrival.[15]

The men had no idea what they were in for. Miss Hobbs did not make her trip alone. Seven men accompanied her on the train to Copperfield on January 3, 1914: Lt. Col. B. K. Lawson; Frank Snodgrass, who was in charge of the state penitentiary guards; and five soldiers from the National Guard. All of the men were veterans of the Philippine War back at the turn of the century, and there was not a weak member among them. With Miss Hobbs and her tiny army on the way, Governor West kept the media in the loop. He did not mention the men, but he did make sure to mention that his secretary was a mere five feet, three inches and weighed 104 pounds. She, said the governor, would be taking over where the six-foot-six-inch, two-hundred-plus-pound Sheriff Rand would not. The *Associated Press* soon got hold of the story, and before long everyone across America was reading about the impending crackdown on Copperfield.[16]

Meanwhile, Miss Hobbs and her faction were slowly making their way to "the poisonous toadstool of the badlands." Within a day the train

The demure and genteel Fern Hobbs, as she appeared during her victorious battle against Copperfield

Courtesy Jan MacKell Collins

pulled into Copperfield's shabby little depot as the entire town turned out to see what they were up against. The *Associated Press* reporter on the scene noted that "Miss Hobbs, demure enough in any garb, was dressed in a modish blue suit, and wore a muff and neckpiece of black lynx. She had on black shoes, and a black hat with two Nile-green feathers set rakishly at one side." Her studious appearance was accented by her gold rim spectacles, which gazed complacently at the rabble constituting Copperfield's population.[17]

Miss Hobbs and her party were escorted to a barn at one of the local dance-halls. A curious crowd, some wearing guns, followed. As everyone entered the barn, Lawson and two national guardsmen took their posts at the door. Miss Hobbs immediately made her business clear. In a calm, unhurried, and unwavering voice, she announced the governor's intention that the mayor and city council resign immediately and gave a resignation notice to each man to sign. The men read the documents, grumbling something about their refusal to sign it. The room grew tense, the crowd eerily silent. Miss Hobbs remained steadfast, and after a minute withdrew her secret weapon: the document proclaiming martial law. Lawson then came forward, read the proclamation, and placed the mayor and councilmen under arrest before the stunned crowd. Before they could act, the lieutenant issued a final decree. "You will now disperse in an orderly manner," he announced loudly so all could hear. "As you leave the hall, you will turn over your revolvers and other weapons to my men at the door."[18]

The decree was daring, and foolish, but when the last person walked through the door, the guardsmen had more than 170 revolvers in a neat pile. Outside, the citizens of Copperfield suffered their second shock of the day. During the meeting, the remaining guardsmen had effectively closed the doors of each saloon and gambling house and affixed a sign to each reading, "Do Not Enter." Newspaper accounts do not mention Copperfield's shady ladies, but they were no doubt among those shut down. As residents reeled in disbelief, Lawson simply escorted Miss Hobbs back to the train, where she boarded and waved a genteel goodbye as the door closed. The men remained behind, preventing telegraphs from being sent or received and patrolling the streets through the night. Only one incident marred the peaceful evening, when Wiegan and Warner attempted an escape at the depot under the guise of going to see their attorney. Lawson turned the building into a jail, and the two councilmen made Copperfield history as the first prisoners the city had ever seen.[19]

In the days that followed, ten more guardsmen were sent to Copperfield to dispose of the city's liquor and gaming devices. Orders were sent to inform liquor distributors not to bother with deliveries to Copperfield. Lawson, meanwhile, appointed carpenter Sam Grim as the new mayor. Back in Salem, Miss Hobbs declined all interviews with the press and studiously went on with her duties. Writers worldwide turned to writing embellished stories about her instead, calling her a hero as poems, letters, and marriage proposals flooded her mailbox. She declined to answer any of them. In Baker, the shamed authorities bowed their heads at their own cowardice as it was noted that not a single saloon reopened at Copperfield. A few months later, a mysterious fire destroyed much of the downtown area. The depot closed and everyone moved away, and that was the end of Copperfield. As for Fern Hobbs, the demure damsel eventually moved to Portland, working in various government jobs until she retired. She never did marry and died in 1964.[20]

CHAPTER 13

————— •• —————

Coquettes of Coquille and Other Places

The Coquille River snakes its way through southern Oregon's coastal range, with various forks winding in blue-green ribbons toward the ocean. Along the rivers' lush banks, Native Americans and Anglos alike found ample fishing, ranching, and farming opportunities. Shortly after Evan Cunningham built a cabin on the site of today's city of Coquille circa 1858, a tiny settlement began. But it would be many years before Coquille grew enough to be called a city. The population was only ninety-four in 1860, and it would be ten years before a post office was established. The first official store opened in 1871, and the town's first newspaper, the *Coquille City Herald*, began printing in 1882. The following year at least two liquor establishments, the City Brewery and the Cottage Saloon, were in business. But growth remained minimal until 1884, when a wagon road was finally established between Coquille and Coos Bay. Coquille was incorporated the following year.[1]

One of Coquille's first saloons is identifiable on the 1891 Sanborn Map for the community. A fire in 1892, thought to have been caused by construction of the Coos Bay, Roseburg and Eastern Railroad down the middle of Front Street, burned numerous structures on both sides of the street. It was decided not to rebuild in the area until the railroad was completed. Many businesses relocated one block north to First Street instead of waiting for construction to finish. Others, including approximately six brothels and a couple of saloons, were built on the site of the fire after the railroad was complete. One brothel was located above the McCloud House; other houses of ill repute flourished above various saloons. Exactly when these structures appeared is unknown, as Sanborn Maps for 1894 and 1898 do not reflect a great number of saloons, two-story or otherwise, in Coquille.[2]

Coquille was designated county seat in 1896. The city was now highly accessible via several routes and grew to accommodate the wants and needs of citizens but also travelers and the logging men who toiled in the surrounding forests. By 1900 the "entertainments" in Coquille included burlesque shows.[3] The prostitution industry was apparently also present, for a 1901 ordinance sought to "prohibit and suppress gambling and gambling houses, houses of ill-fame and bawdy houses; provided that, any house or room kept or occupied by one or more woman for the purpose of prostitution shall be deemed a bawdy house within the meaning of this section."[4]

In 1903 the Grand Opera House was built on Front Street. The place was owned by Hattie Bledsoe and towered two stories high. The Louvre Restaurant shared the bottom floor with the theater, with apartments on the second floor. The Grand attracted citizens of all classes, offering traveling performing troupes and "high class vaudeville." In time, however, the acts evolved into the occasional "risqué vaudeville act," wherein only "the most daring" audiences attended the shows. To put it bluntly, the Grand eventually functioned as a burlesque theater.[5] Shortly after the seedy actresses from the vaudeville shows began appearing in town in 1904, the *Coquille City Herald* published an article advising that it was illegal to run or rent a house used for prostitution. Another article in 1912 mentioned that "keepers of houses of ill-fame were arraigned and contributed $100 each in fines and costs."[6] The

This original painting of a burlesque dancer from Coos County remains unidentified due to the faded pencil scrawl across the reverse side.

Courtesy Jan MacKell Collins

city eventually closed the Grand Opera House down, and the building burned in August 1915.[7]

Notably, the citizens of Coquille were quiet about their shady ladies. Their names do not appear in newspapers, or the census, and oral histories about them did not surface until much later. A few stories are worthy of mention, however, especially concerning Coquille's juvenile and probation officer, Hark Dunham, who was hired by the police force in 1917. Dunham "took great pains to straighten out the wayward young people who came to his attention." Rather than prosecute teens who went astray, Dunham preferred to help them. He also kept the names of guilty parties quiet, even though the man himself occasionally ran into a circumstance of misunderstanding.

Once, as Dunham was seen taking a young girl to a local hotel in Marshfield to be looked after by a kindly landlady, a Detective Wilke mistook the man for a lecher and arrested him. Dunham was able to prove he was a police officer and was released. Just a short time later, the officer encountered a young woman he had known in Coquille who had since married and moved to Marshfield. The two greeted each other on the street, the young woman asking Dunham to "come up and see us sometime." A nearby plainclothes police officer overheard her and assumed the lady was soliciting. Dunham was escorted to police headquarters once more. This time, Marshfield police chief Jack Carter recognized Dunham and secured his release a second time. The embarrassed arresting policeman bought a round of cigars in apology. Dunham later joked that he tried his best to "look old and dignified because it wasn't safe hanging around Marshfield when you look like a lady killer."[8]

On March 17, 1918, Coquille suffered another fire. This time, the conflagration started under the Scenic motion picture house and burned three blocks of the business district. Afterward, C. A. Machon built another motion picture house, the Liberty Theater. A two-story addition was eventually tacked on, which contained the "Tourist Hotel" upstairs, a popular tavern called Bill's Place and the OK Barbershop on the bottom floor. A recreation hall in the basement was alternately known as "Hell's Kitchen," "The Bucket of Blood," "The Dungeon," and "The Dugout." This place was host to numerous activities that included live music, boxing matches, and dancing. During Prohibition, patrons of the place smuggled their own flasks in, politely stepping outdoors to take their swigs. Betty Donsted Rutherford, who attended Coquille High School during the 1930s and 1940s, later remembered that she and her girlfriends "used to sneak in there and watch the drunks and 'hard' women dance."[9]

Bill's Place was just down the street from Tommy Wing's Coquille Café, which was in place by 1930. Wing's place could be rough. During the late 1930s and early 1940s, policeman Frank McCrary customarily broke up fights at the cafe. Once, two women got into an argument there that escalated into a "hair-pulling contest." By the time McCrary got there, the whole restaurant was in an uproar, with broken furniture and condiments strewn about. Another time, a man named Bacon Sanders was shot at Wing's but was only grazed. Next door was the Coquille Bowling Alley, later known as Ten-Pin-Alley.[10] Nola Luey, who was a girl at the time, remembered that she was forbidden from going into either Wing's or the bowling alley, the latter being a place where "those old sports" hung out. "What is an old sport anyway?" she once queried of her cousin, historian Boyd Stone. "Do they mean hookers?"[11]

In his book *You Are the Stars: History of the Coquille Area*, Stone elaborated on the innocence of Nola, whose mother made sure she remained unaware of the brothels operating in town. Nola did, however, once see some "sports"—four fancy women wearing makeup—when they rode by in a Model T as she and her mother walked along a residential street. Nola was, at least, allowed to attend shows at the Liberty Theater, where she feasted on Tom Mix and John Wayne movies. One day the girl saw a show poster advertising an appearance by performer Faye Baker after

Sugar's upstairs brothel appears above the cafe sign on this mural in downtown Coquille.
Courtesy Jan MacKell Collins

the movie. Nola was given permission to go see the show. Upon arriving, she "got my regular candy and popcorn and galloped down to the front of the theater." The girl found the first two rows all taken by men, but got a seat in the third row and enjoyed the film. "After the movie was over the stage lit up and a man played the piano as Faye Baker came out with her fans and did a fan dance," she remembered. "She didn't have much talent, but at the finale she raised her fans and there she stood, TOTALLY NAKED!" Embarrassed, the girl made a hasty exit from the theater.[12]

The best-remembered brothel in Coquille by far was Sugar's Place, west of the Hotel Coquille. Tales are numerous from people who remembered Sugar and her girls, who worked on the second floor above Tommy Wing's and Ten-Pin-Alley.[13] LeRoy Swinney, prior to becoming prominent in Coquille's city government, worked along the Coquille River when he was younger. Swinney recalled seeing local businessmen coming out on Sugar's balcony, which overlooked the river. "They'd be smoking a cigar and adjusting their clothes," he said. "Oh, yeah—it was interesting."[14]

During her time above Wing's, Sugar's brothel was known simply as "Sugar's," or "Shoogs" for short. A sign in front advertised the place as the West Hill Rooms. Many a stranger traveling through town mistook the lit sign advertising the "rooms" for a legitimate hotel. One of them was Bill Kniffen of California, who arrived late one evening and climbed the stairs to knock at the door of Sugar's Place. When the madam answered the door, Kniffen said, "I would like a room please." Sugar responded, "I don't have rooms, but I have girls." Kniffen declined to stay.[15]

Sugar probably enjoyed the shock value, as well as the extra business, generated by men who innocently sought a room at the West Hill Rooms. But the madam herself also was occasionally the victim of a practical joke. One Christmas, Bob Slagle, who worked at the local wood mill, called in a large meat order to butcher Harold Dey. Slagle specified the order was for Sugar's Place. Dey worked overtime to complete the order, but upon delivery the angry madam informed him that nobody from her place had placed the order and that she had no intention of accepting or paying for it. "Dey never did know I did it," Slagle later quipped. "He used to pull tricks on me, but I think this topped anything he did." Dey eventually found out, long after his old friend was in the grave.[16] Boyd Stone explained that Sugar managed to stay in business by paying the occasional fine to keep operating.

So who was this enigmatic woman? Historian Bert Dunn, who researched the elusive Sugar, believed that although the madam ran the brothel, it was owned by one of two men: either Clarence Price or William Butler. Interestingly, both men were of African-American heritage. The 1940 census shows Price rooming with fifty-six-year-old Estella Bartlett on Front Street.[17] More telling is Dunn's discovery, through additional research and interviews with longtime residents of Coquille, is that Sugar's real name was Blanche Webster. Blanche's last name was likely Johnson when she was born in Mississippi in 1894. She eventually married Howard Webster, and the two had a daughter. After divorcing Webster for "cruelty" in 1920, Blanche next married Michael Schwemler. She was still using the name Webster when she operated the West Hill Rooms in Portland in 1934. The Schwemlers remained in Portland for some years, appearing in the census there during 1940. In 1941, a state report on places of prostitution noted the West Hill Rooms was still operating in Portland.[18]

In Coquille, Sugar's was likely one of two houses of prostitution identified in a 1941 report on such places throughout the state. The West Hill Rooms remained open in Portland as well. Old-timers remember that Blanche's West Hill Rooms were open for sure in Coquille by 1950. The long-lasting madam was finally shut down in 1953, when Don Farr served as mayor of Coquille. Farr brought many needed improvements to the town, but also shut down Sugar's Place once and for all. According to Dunn and others, she relocated and started over, perhaps in Brookings. She may also have married one last time, to Kenneth Smith. The new brothel only lasted a couple of years, and Blanche appears to have retired. She is believed to have died in Eugene in 1988.[19]

As late as 1991, someone paid tribute to Sugar's Place in Coquille by posting a simple sign near the former site of her brothel reading "Sugar Avenue." At the time, the buildings on the south side of Front Street were being torn down to make way for the widening and rerouting of State Highway 42 through town. Sugar's Place and several other historic buildings are now gone, their sites buried under the highway.[20] One other possible working girl of Coquille was Beatrice Berquist, who came from Marshfield and appeared in the 1940 census working as a manger hostess at a nightclub called the Riviera on Hill Street in Coquille. Stone remembered a few other brothels: The Star at 447½ W. Front Street (once run by Vlasta Bryant), The Alpha, and Box Car Annie's. Another brothel may have been the Chenago, which burned in 1985. Only Sugar's Place, however, survived as the last of "a half-dozen brothels that operated on Coquille's Front Street at one time or another."[21]

As Coquille grew over the years, several smaller communities were established on roads leading to Coos Bay, Roseburg, and remoter places. At Green Acres on Highway 42 headed to Coos Bay, there was once a brothel with the silly name of Giggle-Snappers. North of Coquille during the 1930s, a brothel in Bridge was called Swamp Angels. At the town of Remote along the same route was a place called Sandy's. The brothel was located along Sandy Creek, which some said was named for the lady of the house.[22]

The circuit towns around Coquille naturally included a number of logging camps and towns in the surrounding forests. Because the majority of these places were owned by logging and lumber companies, prostitution was forbidden within their realms. At Doe Swamp, a logging camp above the town of Powers, the activities of any female employees were monitored by "Big Mary" Allen, an itinerant cook who worked at several camps over time. One day Mary noticed a young logger flirting with one of the cookhouse girls as he came to get his lunch. Mary, who weighed in at 250 pounds, warned the man to leave the girl alone. When he failed to obey, she hurled a large piece of wood at him.[23]

Powers, established in 1914, was the concentrated effort of Albert H. Powers of the Smith-Powers Logging Company. Rather than seeing men and their families living in remote and temporary quarters, Powers decided to create a central town in which his employees could live comfortably. Almost immediately, a man named Mathes opened a pool hall, and one Len Cochran built a combination "pool parlor and barber shop and tavern and some rooms upstairs."[24] Both endeavors were short-lived, for in its September 9, 1915, issue, the *Myrtle Point Enterprise* reported that Albert Powers refused to tolerate liquor within the city limits. "A. H. Powers, head of the Smith-Powers Logging Co., has always held that no liquor should be sold at or near the company's logging operations," explained the paper. The article went on to report on two men who were living in a tent on a city lot at Powers when it was discovered they were selling liquor. The men were given one hour to get out of town. When they had not moved by the end of the hour, a cable was attached to the tent and it was literally dragged outside the city limits.[25]

Albert Powers was nobody to fool with. Following the forced evacuation of the liquor tent, several loggers believed to have "patronized the 'blind pig'" were discharged and told they could not work for the company again until 1916 when the whole state goes dry." In addition, anyone purchasing property in Powers was required to sign a clause in their deed guaranteeing that no liquor would be sold on the premises. "Mr. Powers says he has no objection to any of the men getting drunk if they feel so disposed," the *Myrtle Point Herald* explained, "but they must get further away from the works than the town of Powers to have their spree and should they come to camp before they have sobered up they will immediately get their walking papers."[26]

Following the repeal of Prohibition, taverns and restaurants with liquor on the menu gradually made their way into Powers. There also was a brothel, located over the bridge outside of town, known as "The Chicken House." Local legend also identifies upstairs girls who once worked out of the Powers Hotel, and even at the site of today's Powers Market. The Chicken House, and other houses of prostitution like it, remained open, at least for a short time, after 1952 when Coos County district attorney James A. Norman commanded the mayors of Coos County to close their houses of ill fame.[27] Today, only a scant few structures stand as a testament to wilder times in remote Coos County, if you know where to look.

CHAPTER 14

Prostitution in Portland

Often, the best that a good time girl could hope for was life in a big city, where she could settle down and open or work at her own bordello. Historian and journalist Stewart Holbrook noted that "Along with the loggers, even if most historians have rather prudishly ignored it, came a notable migration of fancy women from the old sawdust towns. They had seen altogether too much daylight in the swamps of the lake states; and now the more enterprising among them went out and bought new bonnets with sweeping feathers and one-way tickets to Spokane or Portland or Seattle."[1] For many of these women, Portland proved to be just what they were looking for.

An early product of the Oregon Trail, Portland was incorporated in 1851 with eight hundred residents. The young city initially was as proper as any early Western town. In February 1852 the *Morning Oregonian* advised that in spite of the rainy weather, ladies should maneuver their long dresses through the mud "revealing nothing beyond the top of a well-laced boot." To reveal anything above the ankle and "lift the robe in public is a dangerous experiment," lectured the paper. By 1864, however, even the far-off *Montana Post* knew that bawdy houses had made their debut in Portland and other places. In some towns, city officials were already requiring licenses of their dance-halls, which could cost upward of one hundred dollars each month.[2]

Portland's first documented madam of note was Nancy Boggs, who opened her bordello in 1870. Born in Pennsylvania, Nancy was still married but raising her daughter alone when she first appeared in Portland during the 1860 census. Over time, Nancy tried a variety of careers, including that of a seamstress and dressmaker, before turning to prostitution. During the twenty years she was in Portland, ten of them were spent on the Willamette River—for Nancy's brothel was actually housed on a bright crimson barge, measuring roughly eighty feet long by forty feet wide. The barge was settled in the middle of the river between Portland and East Portland. There were two floors, with a saloon and dance-hall on the first and rooms for ten to fifteen girls on the second. Smaller boats transported customers from shore. Nancy's female employees knew how to handle the sin-ship; during unusually high water on the river in 1876, Nancy and her girls are said to have "manned the unwieldy ship in a masterful fashion."[3]

Nancy's barge could accommodate men on the shores or fishermen in the water from Linnton to Portland and all the way south to Oregon City. Being on the river, the lady answered to no authority. Three river towns—Portland, East Portland, and Albina—each sported its own government, police department, and laws concerning prostitution and liquor. With no bridges to connect the three, Nancy could operate in relative peace without having to obey the ordinances from any of them. In times of trouble, she could simply head her barge into the middle of the river. Thus, during her time on the water, Nancy paid neither liquor fees nor fines.

Prostitution-friendly Portland was tolerant enough of a bordello boat in their midst, but they were not so happy that the city's most unique madam declined to pay for her privilege. Authorities on both sides of the river made several attempts to access the barge and force Nancy to pay her fees and fines. When this happened, Nancy simply hoisted anchor and floated her boat to the opposite side. The police forces of Portland and East Portland, which were rivals, eventually devised a mutually satisfying plan and came at Nancy's barge from both sides. But the wise madam knew they were coming. By attaching a hose to the boiler, the creative courtesan was able to spray scalding steam toward both police boats. Great billows of steam filled the air as officials on both sides of the river bellowed and scattered about as they retreated.

The public display of defeat did not sit well with the authorities, and a successful backup plan was immediately hatched to sneak up to the barge in the dead of night and cut its anchor line. Soon, Nancy's floating house of pleasure was drifting down the river. Only one customer was aboard at the time, but he was too drunk to be of help. Accordingly, Nancy lowered into her own rowboat and headed for shore. She disembarked at Albina, where she found a friendly stern-wheeler skipper to tow her barge back upstream and secure the anchor once more. When the authorities awoke the next morning, the barge was not drifting precariously downstream, but instead floating leisurely back in the middle of the river.[4]

Shortly after the anchor incident, Nancy sold her barge and moved to some property she already owned on Pine Street, between Second and Third Streets, in North Portland. There she opened a grand parlor house and paid the city her dues to the satisfaction of the authorities. Nancy's new pleasure palace was finer than most, but it was not above the occasional skirmish. On February 19, 1880, the *Daily Oregonian* reported that "about half past nine o'clock last night the ladies and gentlemen who attend the soirees at Nancy Boggs' palace on Pine Street became out of humor over some slight incident and began to smash each other over the head with bottles, chairs, beer mugs, etc. Officer Bramman happened to drop in and escorted two of the gentlemen, Alex Kidd and John Fagan, to the city jail." Nancy overcame this and other incidents, remaining in Portland until 1894.[5]

At least one other madam attempted to run a brothel out of a scow on the river. She was Bridget Gallagher, whose customers had the unfortunate luck of getting drunk and falling overboard too often. Most of them, instead of sticking around and spending more money, went straight home once they were fished out of the river. Bridget appears rather brazen: In November 1872 it was noted that the "disreputable woman who practically carries out the masculine idea of being 'supported by men'" intended to vote in the upcoming elections. Four years later, Bridget was fined three hundred dollars for keeping a house of prostitution. By 1880 she was operating a parlor house at 143 Second Street when the census noted that six girls—Lottie Brooks, Fanny Dawson, Florence Taylor, Amy Eaton, Billie Maro, and Willie Starr—were employed as prostitutes there. There also were two Chinese servants, Jim Kee and Jim Sing. The madam may have been regarded by the public as a bad woman, but six months later officials at the Mechanics' Fair were fined two hundred dollars for refusing to admit Bridget to an exhibition. Good woman or bad woman, somebody finally assessed, Bridget Gallagher maintained her right to attend public events. The lady eventually moved to San Francisco.[6]

Following Portland's "Great Fire of 1873," Portland's Tenderloin District relocated to the "north side of Yamhill Street and the east side of Third, and scattered about a general district converging on Third and Taylor." The brothels were immediately attacked by the First Methodist Church, which was located in that vicinity, and accordingly moved to Portland's North End where "frame shacks" had been "built specifically for that purpose." In time, prostitution would flourish in other places too. When the Merchants Hotel was constructed on Davis Street in 1885, the place functioned as a brothel for more than twenty years. However, it was the North End, alternately known as Whitechapel, that remained the best known of Portland's red-light districts by 1889.[7]

Portland's North End consisted primarily of small row house bordellos, but on Burnside Street were grander brothels with lavishly decorated interiors. Above their doors were the names of the madam or prostitute within. In time, the parlor houses grew in stature and elegance. By the 1890s approximately four hundred brothels, from cribs to posh parlor houses, were in operation. As long as the red-light district denizens paid their monthly fines, they were pretty much left alone by the authorities. Only when the moral majority intervened did police occasionally close down one of the fancier houses of ill repute. Sometimes, however, the girls themselves created a public stir, which also resulted in arrests. In September 1892, for instance, newspapers reported on three working girls who "staged an impromptu nude dance" out in front of their brothel on Davis Street. Quite a crowd gathered to watch, including policemen, who eventually arrested the ladies for "naughty capers."[8]

The women performing "naughty capers" were actually advertising their wares, a difficult thing to do in a time when placing ads with local media was out of the question. Other ways to solicit business included the girls riding bicycles up and down the streets, calling out their addresses to the men they saw.[9] In 1894 the madams of the North End brazenly decided to publish *The Guide, A description of amusement resorts of Portland, Oregon and vicinity*. The preface to the book extended joviality and goodwill:

> *This is a guide without avarice tainted*
> *A "tip," as it were, before you're acquainted.*
> *And now, my good friends, you've had my excuse;*
> *I could have said more, but what is the use?*
> *This thing I've "writ" and its dedicated*
> *To strangers and those who're uninitiated.*

The introduction boldly explained that in Portland "is a notorious locality, known by the name of the 'White Chapel District.' It is the home of the most abandoned members of the demimonde, and on a small scale resembles the famous section of London, after which it is named. Within its boundaries are several hundred women, most of whom live in small one story houses or cribs. The inmates of these cribs represent every nationality, with French predominating. On Lower Second Street can be seen Japanese and African women. The district lies north of Ankeny Street, and owing to the surveillance of Portland's admirable police department, is perfectly safe for the stranger to visit, provided he does not get too familiar with the occupants of the 'cribs.'"[10]

Notably, *The Guide* did not feature every known house of ill repute, for the advertisers were only the wealthiest madams in town, who could afford to pay the printing costs of the booklet. Each one received a listing, most with a charming rhyme following her name and address. Altogether there were nine entries. Following is the name of each woman, the poem attributed to her in *The Guide*, and what is known about her.

Miss Minnie Reynolds, 89 Fifth Street.
In handsome parlors, skilled to please,
Fair Minnie waits in silken ease,
And at each guest's desire supplies
Dear pleasures, hid from prying eyes.
With such a haven ever nigh
Who could pass her parlors by?

Minnie was born in Ireland in 1866, and appeared in Portland's city directories beginning in 1885. Her first address was at 128 Fifth Street, and she was still there in 1887 when she gave birth to her oldest daughter, Agnes. By 1893 she had relocated to 89 Fifth Street. In 1894 Minnie gave birth to another daughter, Mary. She was at 94 Fifth Street by 1900, when she told the census taker she was a widow. Surprisingly, Agnes and Mary lived with Minnie at her brothel, which included seven prostitutes between the ages of nineteen and twenty-eight, as well as a servant named Gum Yee. In 1904 the *Oregon Daily Journal* reported that Minnie was one of two madams served with a notice to move due to complaints from some local businessmen. "They agreed to do so," Police Chief Hunt said, "and have been looking for a location since then. They will not resist the order, I understand." Accordingly, Minnie was living at 387 East Burnside in 1909. After that, she disappears from record.[11]

Miss Fanshaw, 151 Seventh Street.
Let's live while we live;
We'll be dead a long while,
And tho Fortune may frown,
Fair Miss Fanshaw will smile,
If a kiss will not sooth you,
She has pleasures that will;
The chalice of passion overflowingly fill,
And your troubles and cares,
You will lightly ignore
When love's rich libation
This Charmer will pour.

"Miss Fanshaw" was Lida Fanshaw, whose Seventh Street "Mansion of Sin" was directly across from both the Portland Hotel and the Marquam Grande Theater. Born in New York in 1857, Lida was already thirty-four years old when she first appeared in Portland, in 1891. Her first parlor house was at 105 Sixth Street. The following year she took over the parlor house at 151 Seventh Street from madam Emma Wingard (aka Louise E. Hamilton). Only the most prominent business and government men visited Lida's, which may explain why her name was seldom in the newspapers. Her customers also paid top dollar for services. "Madam Fanshaw and her girls were extremely polite, but you didn't sit around there a great while without spending substantial sums of money," wrote columnist Stewart Holbrook. "It was no place for the loggers, the miners and the fishermen."[12]

Lida dressed in the best gowns and jewelry money could buy. They said that the madam, described as a "statuesque brunette," was never seen by anyone—inside or outside her brothel—when she wasn't wearing a gorgeous gown from London or Paris, her best jewelry, and her luxurious furs. She delighted in riding around in one of her two fancy carriages: a white rig with "black trim and red roses" for summer and a more demure black-and-gold carriage with glass-paned windows for winter. The madam herself provided entertainment, playing her piano and singing "in a particularly erotic husky voice." Sometimes, Lida made up risqué little ditties about her customers as she sang. During the 1900 census, Lida employed ten girls, ranging in age from seventeen-year-old Katie Richardson to twenty-seven-year-old Frankie Campbell. Also living at her brothel were two Chinese servants and a musician, Frank Powell. The census was taken on June 12, 1900; after that, Lida disappears from record, likely changing her name and retiring for good.[13]

Miss Mabel Montague, 94 Fifth Street Cor. Stark
Here is a mansion, of which is related
That on all this Coast it is not duplicated.
Its well-furnished parlors the fashionable seek,
For comfort is here, joined to the unique,
And the girls who respond to the visitors call,
Are the pride of Miss Mabel, and the pride of her hall.

Mabel Montague's time in Portland was short. From 1893 to 1895 she worked out of the brothel at 94 Fifth Street before passing it on to madam Minnie Reynolds and leaving town. She was in La Grande in 1909 when she left her purse at the Oregon Hotel "grillroom" and it was stolen. She was still there in 1910, when the census recorded her as running a "lodging house" with three young lady "boarders," right next door to Mary Wilson, who also ran a "lodging house" with two female "boarders."[14]

Miss Della Buris [sic], 150 East Park, between Alder and Morrison
Here is a lady of such ways all admire
She no flattery from the best does require
Modest as a maiden, youthful,
Good-natured as she is truthful,
Della Buris has a name
All might enjoy, none can blame.

Della Burris's reputation was equal to that of Lida Fanshaw. Her place "was no joint," said Holbrook. "It was patronized largely by men who have since made their mark in the city's professional and business life." Della was virtually unknown, however, when her advertisement appeared in *The Guide*. The following year, she became the unwitting victim of a moral crusade during which city officials attempted to close down Portland's bawdy houses. It all started when Pastor Charles Locke, a newcomer, came up with an idea to build a "home for wayward girls and fallen women." Soon a home, called the Open Door, was in place on North Fifth Street, complete with a full kitchen, furniture, and linens. Mrs. Lucy Morgan was hired as the "house matron." Not surprisingly, none of Portland's prostitutes seemed inclined to rush into the Open Door. Perhaps officials sought to make an example by arresting the two most prominent women in town in April: Lida Fanshaw and Della, the latter being the first to be brought to court.[15]

Della Burris's grand and stately parlor house at 150 Park Street in Portland

Courtesy Evelyn Fisher

Della's trial went like this: The lady was charged with running a bawdy house. At her court appearance, she pleaded "not guilty." Not one witness showed up to testify against her, and there was no evidence to prove that she ran a brothel. The prosecution argued that it was well known exactly what Della did for a living. Justice Geisler, who oversaw her trial, concluded that "Common fame and general reputation are not sufficient evidence to convict anyone of keeping a bawdy house. The positive fact of lewdness must be established beyond all reasonable doubt. Case dismissed." Ever genteel, Della gently thanked Geisler with a smile and rode her fancy carriage back to her bordello.[16]

Nearly every other prostitution case went the same as that of Della Burris. Officers had been so anxious to make arrests that they did so without proper evidence to convict the ladies. One by one, the good time girls were arrested, brought to court, and their cases dismissed. It was the *Morning Oregonian* that pinpointed the trouble: "The District Attorney gets $5 for every arrest; $7.50 for trial; and $15 for convictions," an editorial read. "In each case, having taken pains to draw all the indictments separately, if there are no convictions, he will make from $500 to $600. The police justices and constables make about $12 out of each case, or as much more, and the county foots the bill. This is the total visible profit of the moral crusade so far—about $1,200 diverted from the pockets of taxpayers to those of officials." With all that money flowing into the men's pocketbooks, who cared if the women were guilty or even convicted?

Meanwhile, at the Open Door, the refuge house did eventually take in a healthy handful of wayward women. But when the local logging camps shut down their annual "Fourth of July Drunk," the loggers sought other entertainments in Portland for Independence Day. Women at the Open Door who missed out on the profits swept right back out, shutting the Open Door firmly behind them. The house eventually closed. As for Della Burris, she remained in Portland for just one more year before shutting her own door on that chapter of her life and moving on.[17]

Miss Maude Morrison, 95 Sixth Street, Cor. Stark
No man in this City who is known as a sport
But will tell you he's seen and enjoyed this resort
It's a house full of beauties, whose rooms dazzling bright
Shimmer and glimmer with mirth and delight.

Little is known about Maude, except that she partnered at one time with another woman, Dora Clark, who also appeared in *The Guide* but was given neither a poem nor an address. The twosome worked together at the Sixth Street house before departing for places unknown. Only *The Guide* remains as testament that the ladies were ever in Portland to begin with.[18]

Miss Ida Arlington, No. 90 Fifth Street
To reign is beauty's queenly right,
And he is but a shabby knight,
Who is not charmed, aye wholly won
by lovely Ida Arlington,
Whose grace of manner and of form
Takes every manly heart by storm.

Ida remained at her Fifth Street address during 1894 and 1895. In September 1899 the Salem *Daily Journal* reported that "Ida Arlington was brought to the asylum from Portland last night. Mrs. Daherty, matron of the Multnomah County Jail, brought the patient." Why Ida was sent to the Oregon State Insane Asylum remains unknown. In its monthly statement for April 1900, the asylum proudly reported that "most of the patients discharged have been under treatment for six months or less." Ida was one of these, receiving her discharge that same month. Unfortunately, she was back by June when the census was taken. The information on her is scant, but telling: Ida was born in July 1864 in Missouri, was single, and her occupation while at the asylum was blatantly listed as a prostitute.[19] When she was released and where she went afterward remain unknown.

Madam Flora, 130 Fifth Street
The gay rose gardens are [illegible]
But blooming Flora is still here
To make us quite forget the rose
Has sighed her gentle adios.

Miss Flora is believed to be Flora Hoyt, who lived about a block west of the fancy Louvre Restaurant with its private booths.[20] Nothing else is known about the lady.

Dora Lynn
If you're out for a lark, or that is your passion,
Just call on this house, so lately in fashion.
With its fairy like nymphs and Dora Lynn its queen,
Where privacy, rest, and all is serene.
There are a great many Doras, but I write this one down
As the best one that ever has lived in this town.

The Guide did not print Dora's address, but it was known that she operated a "fine resort" at 269 Salmon near Fourth Street.[21]

One madam who did not make it into *The Guide* was Mabel Heath, who likely fashioned her alias from a popular British play of the same name. During the late 1890s, Mabel ran one of the nicest parlor houses in Portland. Her clients were wealthy men and political leaders. Her carriage was fine, attended by a "high-salaried coachmen," and Mabel's collection of "imported" dogs was well-known. In a 1940s interview,

Mabel's maid, Sadie Harner, recalled that one of the madam's suitors was a wealthy young man who held madam's hand whenever he could and showered her with candy, flowers, and jewelry. One of the necklaces, Sadie said, was "worth well over $50,000." Mable demurely received these gifts with only a kiss on the cheek in return.

When his business required a permanent move to Southern California, the gentleman wrote to Mabel and asked her to join him. Mabel replied that she would, sometime. But she never did, even after the would-be suitor sent her a love letter via a mutual friend. Years later, long after Mabel had lost track of the man and retired, the friend asked her why she had not taken him up on his offer. Mabel explained that her lover had insisted she quit her profession should they marry. Mabel, who had gained much wealth and respect, said that even an offer of a wealthy marriage was not enough to make her relinquish the power she had acquired as a madam.[22]

Lesser-known prostitutes of Portland included Sallie Brown, who ran the Bella Vista Lodging House and charged two dollars for services. Mary Clark's place was called Ivy Green. Liverpool Liz ran the Senate Saloon and rooms. At Liz's, whenever a patron offered to buy a round of drinks, the bartender knew to press a secret buzzer so the upstairs girls could come downstairs and take part. They knew the customer would most likely buy them a drink as well, increasing house profits. Little else is known about Liverpool Liz, except that the Senate was raided in August 1903.[23]

Madams could expect referrals from the local taverns around them. The largest of these was Erickson's Saloon, which commanded an entire city block at the corner of Second Street and Burnside. Five bars, each with its own outside entrance, ran through the enormous interior and were united by one long bar measuring 684 feet. There were "ornate fixtures, huge mirrors, and classic statuary," as well as a five-thousand-dollar pipe organ and a huge stage. Beautiful showgirls performed there,

and the customers were so wild about the eight-piece, all-girl orchestra that Erickson had to install "an electrified rail" to keep the men at
bay. Above the bar, an upper mezzanine offered "small closed cribs."
Another source reports, however, that only proper ladies were permitted
in the small booths along the mezzanine.[24]

One of the largest and most notorious bordellos was Paris House
on Davis Street, between Third and Fourth Streets. This behemoth of
a brothel towered three stories high, with a restaurant and saloon on the
ground level. Upstairs were rooms for one hundred women, divided by
race: Anglo women were available on the second floor, while women
of other nationalities occupied the third floor. Paris House first started
making the newspapers in February 1903, when the *Morning Oregonian*
revealed that Deputy Sheriff Tim Hoare was reaping a dollar per week in
hush money from every single prostitute in Whitechapel.[25]

Hoare's profits were brought to the attention of Police Chief Hunt
by William Ricker, a "cripple" who was arrested for "running a wheel
of fortune at Third and Couch Streets." Ricker claimed that he too was
giving Hoare a dollar per week for protection from the law. Upon further
investigation, Hunt found that Hoare also visited Paris House regularly.
The manager, Duke Evans, had recently "given orders to all of the renters not to pay Hoare when he came for the money." Several ladies verified they had been paying Hoare for the last three years for protection
from the law, but also unruly customers. The ladies may not have been as
vulnerable as they seemed, however, for during the month of April three
women—Trixie Pillips, Edna Dunlap, and Fanny Owen—were charged
with stealing from their customers.[26]

Paris House was actually owned by several businessmen, including a banker and a former Portland mayor. By June 1903, however, the
brothel appears to have suffered some financial difficulties and closed
for a time. The business was open again by August, when a raid was
staged throughout Whitechapel. The following month, another officer,

Jack Roberts, also was accused of procuring protection money from the ladies of Paris House. Five Japanese women shuffled into the courtroom to testify in the case. "The room reeked of cheap perfumery," noted the *Morning Oregonian*, "and stirred with the rustle of silk." The ladies testified that they paid Roberts mostly because they feared drunks who might hurt them. They also gave the officer money whenever there was any kind of trouble and to avoid being arrested. But the ladies verified the officer never asked them for money and that they paid it of their own volition. Roberts does not appear to have suffered for his actions, but when the brothel reapplied for a liquor license in December, the application was "turned down hard and cold." In February 1904 it was discovered that the license had been signed off on by some unknown party, and that liquor was again being sold there.[27]

Even with two fires during 1904, Paris House remained resilient—although the second fire did cause panic among some the women, who "rushed about in scanty attire, and one or two shrieked in hysterical fright." In January 1905 the owners made preparations in anticipation of the upcoming Lewis and Clark Exposition scheduled for June. Duke Evans was fired after being accused of pocketing too much of the profits. A new manager, James Phillips, was hired to make sure Paris House ran smoothly during the exposition. Sheriff Tom Word had other ideas, however, and raided the place that February. Phillips and thirty-three women were arrested. The manager had to agree to use Paris House solely as a lodging house for men, but the promise lasted only two weeks.[28]

More than 2.5 million people attended the exposition as Paris House and other brothels reaped healthy profits. Phillips continued running the business and even managed to weather a 1906 campaign by Mayor Harry Lane to close the brothels of Whitechapel. The campaign continued into 1907, when a failed attempt was made in January to burn Paris House and several other brothels. In November, Lane finally managed to close Paris House for good, and the ladies of the house moved elsewhere.[29]

The actions of Harry Lane only worked for a short time. Brothels once again flourished with a vengeance by 1909, the year madam Louise Gautier made the newspapers at the Richelieu Rooms at 33½ Sixth Street North. Born in 1889, the Oregon native also went by Goldie Gray and Louise Trouville during her time in Portland. Louise had once worked on the Barbary Coast. But Portland, she said, "was the best town on the coast for her kind of business." The Richelieu, with seventeen rooms, was right up her alley.[30]

An article in a December 1909 issue of the *Morning Oregonian* verified that Louise was running the Richelieu when a man named John H. Johnson asked for a room. Johnson balked at the high price, but instead of leaving, he was discovered by Louise in her room, attempting to steal a purse with fifteen dollars in it. Louise "caught hold of him and screamed," alerting others in the hotel, who held the man until police came. During the 1910 census, Louise wisely told the census taker that she worked as a "seamstress." By 1911, however, there was no question as to what went on at the Richelieu. In August, William Johnson and James Adams of the Oregon militia were arrested there. The men could not afford to bond out but were released after testifying against prostitutes Fay Gordon and May Jackson.[31]

Louise continued openly defying the law. During an arrest in September, it was noted that she "has been arrested frequently and . . . enjoys the protection of Henry Gallet, successor to Pete Bruno, the former reputed 'King of the Tenderloin.'" Under her various names, Louise was arrested for selling liquor without a license and other crimes. Each time, she promised to reform or leave town, but did neither. Another article about her in June 1912 caused Deputy District Attorney Hennessey to comment that "a promise to reform from this woman would be ridiculous." It was also noted that the woman "has been arrested probably more often than any other in the city." Hennessey was correct in his assumptions, for Louise was arrested once again in August for, among other things, soliciting on city streets. Perhaps she behaved for a short time, for she does not appear to have been arrested again until December 1917. Louise was listed in Portland's city directories until 1918 before she disappeared.[32]

Another famed madam was Miranda Hall, who ran a brothel at 310 Flanders Street and happened to be a second cousin of Police Chief Slover. She did suffer at least one arrest, when she and one R. Geisler were apprehended at the corner of Fourth Street and Burnside "on a charge of immorality." There was also Madge "Big Maddy" Cahill, who with her partner, Charles May, "owned and ran" several brothels and saloons along Flanders Street. The twosome headquartered at their Welcome Saloon. In August 1912 they were arrested. May was accused of "setting up a small vice monopoly for himself," and it was revealed that the Welcome Saloon was "one of the worst dives in the city, running as a combo house with women upstairs." The place was often the scene of violence and robberies, to the extent that the couple's bail money was set at two thousand dollars—each.[33]

During 1912 the authorities sought to close down Whitechapel due to public pressure but were appalled to find that many bordellos were owned by prominent bankers, churches, city officials, doctors, lawyers, and, most horrifying of all, members of the very Vice Commission attempting to close the houses down. In a novel attempt to shame them, the city came up with the "tin plate law," whereby property owners were required to display their name and address on a tin plate and post it on their buildings. Most owners acquiesced to the new law, and Portland's citizens had great fun identifying who owned which brothel—until a wise lawyer noted that the law didn't require the names to be written in English. Thus, some of the plaques were inscribed in Arabic, Chinese, Hebrew, and Sanskrit.[34]

Next, during 1913, a report from the Vice Commission revealed that city leaders were profiting from Whitechapel, the saloons, and the gambling houses. The crusades continued into 1917, when most madams finally gave up and closed their doors. One of them was Winnie Gaylord, who had operated brothels in Seattle, Tacoma, and Portland since the mid-1890s. In Portland, one of Winnie's most unusual customers was a man who visited regularly. The gentleman donned his own set of women's clothing and spent his time dusting and sweeping the brothel from top to bottom. Upon finishing, the stranger would change back into his regular clothes, place a silver dollar on the table, and leave. When Winnie was forced to close in 1917, the spinster madam spent the rest of her days touring the world. She was in London when she died in her hotel room. Her will bequeathed five thousand dollars for the care of her cats, Crystal and Toby. In addition, her three sisters and two brothers in San Francisco, as well as her nine-year-old niece, received a large portion of her five-hundred-thousand-dollar estate.[35]

The closing down of Portland's demimonde was bittersweet. During 1936, historian Stewart Holbrook wrote several columns about the dear departed wild women of Portland for the *Oregonian*. At least one attempt was made to document Whitechapel's history, in March 1939. Sarah B. Wrenn of the Federal Writer's Project for the Oregon Folklore Studies began seeking out those who remembered Portland's more sordid past. One of her subjects was William "Billy" Mayer, owner of a cigar stand in the lobby of the Davis building at 220 Third Street. Wrenn assessed that "his manner and dapper clothes suggested he had been somewhat of a man about town in his day and he seemed enthusiastic to talk." During the interview, however, the cigar stand was patronized by several male customers who made Mayer uneasy. "Nah, I don't think I've anything worth telling. Nah, nah. I don't want to be bothered," he said.

Mayer did finally pull what was perhaps the only surviving copy of *The Guide* from his pocket, but changed his mind again. "Nah, I won't let you see it—I wouldn't let my own mother see it," he told Wrenn. "It's a guide to the old bawdy houses in Portland, back in '94." Mayer went on to explain what he knew about *The Guide* and its businesses before relenting. "Ah here," he finally said to Wrenn, "you might as well take the book and copy the stuff. I haven't got time to read it all." Wrenn was able to make copies of the book and presumably returned it to Mayer before generating her report. Today, the notes from *The Guide* remain one of the only firsthand testaments to the bawdy life in Portland.[36]

CHAPTER 15

———◦•◦———

Sirens of Salem

For Salem, Oregon's capital since 1851, sin in the city's midst was unusually permissible. At least one small house of prostitution was once located within a few blocks of the capitol building, although the brothel catered more to laborers than government men.[1] Early in Salem's history, a channel from the Willamette River existed near the intersection of Ferry and High Streets along Pringle Creek. The channel, large enough for boat access, ran "east to the center of the block on State Street south of the courthouse." In time, Ferry Street became the demimonde district between Liberty and High Streets. Even a flood in February 1890 could not stop Salem's good time girls. The ladies of the evening built their houses and walkways on stilts above the channel, and by 1893 the area was known as "Peppermint Flat."[2]

Plenty of women were already working in Peppermint Flat before it became so named. In November 1892 prostitute Lily King of Ferry Street was tried for stabbing Tom Sullivan. The victim testified that one evening he and N. S. Williams "received a message from Lilly [sic] King saying she was very ill and asking them to come see her at once." The men arrived at Lily's brothel to find the woman and several other prostitutes terribly drunk. It was Lily who proposed they all write letters to their friends and kill themselves, hence her message to Sullivan and Williams. Her drunken counterparts agreed to the idea. Sullivan, who appears to have watched the proceedings with some apathy, told the court he went to see prostitutes May Clifton and Ida Chase to say goodbye. Drunken Lily, meanwhile, had borrowed the man's pocket-knife with which to clean her nails.

When Sullivan returned, Lily "used vile language" and lunged at him, stabbing him in the midsection. The wound was thought quite serious, for blood spurted a good two feet when Sullivan opened his shirt. The man fainted and awoke to see a doctor dressing his wounds. Meanwhile, Lily and her companions had apparently changed their minds about committing suicide. Lily does not seem to have been held responsible for stabbing Sullivan; in court, a number of people were present who were actually hoping to keep her from going to jail. Indeed, the next day Lily was released due to lack of evidence.[3]

Two weeks later, Lily contacted the police after a man named Kreutzer allegedly robbed her of some silk hosiery, jewelry, a watch, and "several bottles of consumption cure."[4] What became of Kreutzer remains unknown. As for Lily, she was sent to the Oregon State Insane Asylum for a time in December 1892 "as of unsound mind."[5] The newspapers reported nothing more on the woman until November 1894, when she suddenly flounced into town just as the authorities were making raids in hopes of shutting down Peppermint Flat. "She was constantly up before police court on some charge or another until about a year ago, when she disappeared from view," tattled the *Capital Journal*. The previous year, it was explained, Lily had filed a complaint against one Ira Green but skipped town before the trial. The case had been dropped, and the authorities were not amused. Upon hearing of her return, Lily was charged with "contempt of court, for instituting a proceeding involving the city in cost, and then failing to appear." Lily was charged twenty-five dollars.[6]

More brothels began appearing on Ferry Street. In 1893 it was reported that a house in the "business block just north of Hotel

Willamette," after being vacant for six months, was now functioning as a brothel. The complaint focused on the dining room of the hotel, from which diners could clearly see the "low dive." Furthermore, "ladies passing on the street are apt to be brushed or jostled by the women on the street." The newspaper had discovered that the house of ill repute was owned by "the Hirsch estate" in Portland, and that someone from that city was renting the building. Most offensive was a red curtain hanging in a window "to catch attention from State Street."[7] The newspapers were not done commenting on prostitution in the midst of Salem. The next day another article appeared, blasting authorities for their failure to do anything about the "house of ill fame" across from the Hotel Willamette and predicting that similar businesses were sure to next encroach on Commercial Street. "It is not necessary to state that a Salem business man in good society pays the rent for these women," said the paper. "The facts are not hard to get at. But the city government should act."[8]

A few months later, the *Capital Journal* launched an attack on Salem's Chinatown as well. "Within easy stone throw are three Chinese or Japanese houses of prostitution besides one conducted by American demimonde," the paper stated.[9] The *Journal* was probably referring to Chinatown, located on "the east side of Liberty Street between Court and State." A prominent bell tower was near or at the entrance of the tiny community, a sign that Chinatown had been in place for some time and intended to stay that way. Nearby, or perhaps in, the settlement, were some Chinese houses of prostitution on Ferry Street and around Commercial and Trade Streets. Notably, the latter were owned by one Ed Hirsch, probably the same man accused of owning other brothels in Portland.[10]

On October 4, 1895, a Japanese prostitute named Maggie Toyo (aka Wantawabe) was stabbed to death in Chinatown. She was buried in Salem's Pioneer Cemetery as details emerged about her. An examination of Maggie's house revealed that she was learning English. Her little "reception room" contained a few chairs, a heating stove, and her "large and expensive Saratoga trunk, locked." There also was "a small parlour table, on which were some ordinary nick-nacks such as a woman of her class might keep about her." The table also held some paper on which Maggie had been writing some cryptic words in English: "Philli Coup H. Hair Oil. Meigle Toyo. Miss Meigle Toyo. Mrs. Willie Heppbin."

Also found were several old telegrams bearing the name of William Heppbin, who had been involved with Maggie in some sort of scandal the previous October.[11] But nobody came forth to claim Maggie's body, and her personal items were auctioned off. Several pieces of jewelry, "a whole kitchen," and clothing were sold. Most telling was "an elegant scarlet, wool, plush accouchement wrapper, that had never been worn, but had been prepared in anticipation of becoming a mother," but the paper declined to speculate whether Maggie was pregnant. In reporting on the auction, the *Capital Journal* noted that proceeds from the sale would be held for two years in case any of the woman's family came along wishing to claim it.[12]

The incident in October was indeed scandalous for the time, because Heppbin and Maggie had actually run off together at one time. The *Capital Journal* reported that there was a skirmish between Heppbin and a Chinaman in a Chinese restaurant on Court Street. During the fray, Heppbin apparently struck the man with a teapot, cutting his head, and was taken to court. Two months after that, the *Statesman* reported that Heppbin's "Japanese 'lover'" had had him arrested for stealing a diamond ring and other jewelry from her. The authorities apparently saw no reason to pursue the said Heppbin. In its October 5, 1895, issue, the *Statesman* covered the murder, with the subheading "Mouye [sic] Toyo Yields Her Life to the Passionate Rage of a Chinese Lover." Maggie's actual killer, however, was never found.[13]

As a boy circa 1900, Daniel J. Fry remembered that "Ferry Street was a no-no street. It was really all built up on stilts. Water stood in that part of town nearly all summer long. The people who lived on Ferry Street were the gay ladies of that day. This was a legal profession at that time, and they often drove around in horse-drawn cabs, showing their fine clothes and seeing the city which was about the only way they had a chance of doing so." Fry also recalled a day he fell into some serious trouble on Ferry Street. "There was a very narrow, high walk along Ferry Street over this sunken part of the city," he said, "and I was riding my bicycle along there one day and gawking into the windows to see what I could see, when I ran off and broke my arm. I was very much chagrined because I shouldn't have been there in the first place because we children were never supposed to go that way."[14]

Not all was gay along Ferry Street, as shown by the sad story of Pauline Phillips. Born in New York City as Emma Reisner in 1877, Pauline was living in Denver by 1896. She had a daughter at that time, but whether her husband, James McDogget, was the father is unknown. By the time she arrived in Salem later that year, Pauline was divorced and her eight-year-old daughter was no longer with her. Pauline's circumstances for moving to Salem remain a mystery. Yet there she was, in a strange new city, where she took the name Phillips—likely with the intention of going to work in a bawdy house. All did not go smoothly in Salem. Pauline was recorded as being in court in August 1898. Two weeks later, the *Daily Capital Journal* reported that "Frank Woods was arrested early this morning for assault and battery on a complaint sworn out by Pauline Phillips."[15]

Two years later, Pauline began to unravel. She was working for madam Hattie McGinnis at 142 Ferry Street by June 1900, when Salem's *Capital Journal* reported that Pauline had unaccountably broken the window of the "Misses Goode" millinery parlor on Commercial Street. Pauline, said the paper, "became crazy drunk over night" and was wandering up Commercial Street. At the millinery, she picked up a rock and threw it at the glass, creating only a small hole. Next, she struck the window with her fist "and completely destroyed it."[16] Witnesses next said Pauline slit her wrists with the glass. When night police officer E. B. Smith arrived, he found the woman bleeding profusely. Smith ushered her to the hospital, where a doctor stitched the wound before Pauline was committed to the Oregon State Insane Asylum.[17]

Pauline was released from the asylum after six weeks of treatment, and this was likely when she told others of her past life. But was Pauline really who she professed to be? Possibly not, as neither McDogget nor the Reisners appear on record in Denver. One Edward *Reiser*, however, was arrested on July 6 for cashing a forged check at the brothel of Hattie McGinnis at 142 Ferry Street—Pauline's place of work.[18] Pauline had returned to the brothel after she was released, but soon began threatening to kill herself. Just over a month later, on July 19, McGinnis and her girls were eating dinner when they discovered Pauline had downed a bottle of carbolic acid. Two doctors, Shaw and Robertson, were summoned but it was too late. Pauline's lifeless body was taken to Rigdon & Clough undertakers as Hattie McGinnis arranged for her burial in Salem's Pioneer Cemetery and paid for her headstone. Remarkably, Hattie's services for Pauline even included a card of thanks to the Women's Christian Temperance Union in the newspaper. "We take this means of extending our heartfelt thanks to the ladies of the WCTU for the kindness and courtesies extended on the occasion of the funeral of the late Pauline Phillips," the notice read. "We also wish to thank Rev. Dr. John Parsons for conducting the funeral services." The thanks was signed, "Mabel Rhodes, Mrs. Hattie McGinnis."

It was true that the WCTU was run by prominent society women who sought to close down saloons, gambling houses, and brothels. But the kinder women in this organization often extended an offer of help to women like Pauline who seemed to have lost their way in life. Apparently, the local chapter had indeed made some sort of effort to assist the woman, and it was very rare to see anyone from the demimonde actually thank them for it. But if the WCTU extended kindnesses toward the fallen woman, Salem's *Daily Journal* did not. An article shortly after Pauline's death snipped, "Dickey Woods and Pauline Phillips have gone by the last couple of months. Is the moral status improving?"[19]

By April 1903 Salem was waging a war on both saloons and the red-light district. "Vice," they said, was spreading as far as North Salem, outside the city limits, making Salem authorities helpless to do anything about it. "When the new city boundaries go into effect the city will have authority, and all houses of ill fame can be concentrated in one quarter of the city, where they shall be publicly known for their true character," warned one newspaper. "This is not said in condemnation of anyone, and even with the sincerest pity for those living in moral darkness, but to sound the public warning that the spreading evil may be dealt with."[20]

Two years later, in February 1905, the papers applauded the efforts of Police Chief Cornelius to "drive out the disreputable characters who prey off the unfortunate women of the town." A bill had recently been passed as well, making it a felony to purchase sex from a woman. The authorities began by focusing on a Madam Dollarhide, but when they arrived to arrest her, she had already left town. But Salem wasn't done; if they could not chase every bad woman out of town, they could at least confine them to a red-light district as planned. Cornelius encouraged the formation of an official red-light district, which was likely the already existent Peppermint Flat. "He says let the red-light district be confined strictly to its own precincts," reported the local paper, "and the rest of the community will not make complaint, but the inmates must not walk the streets, frequent saloons or lodging houses."[21]

The crusade to expose men who frequented brothels continued into March, when Elsworth E. Nichols was arrested for "frequenting a house of ill-fame" along with piano player "Professor" H. H. Diener, who was employed there. This was the second arrest for Nichols, who might not have been apprehended at all had he not heard Diener arguing with officers. Instead of remaining in hiding, Nichols revealed himself by "bursting into the room" and exclaiming, "Never mind, Professor, I can pay your bail!" Nichols and prostitute Fannie Davenport, who also was jailed, were released on their own recognizance. Diener posted a twenty-dollar bond—presumably with Nichols's money—but skipped town.[22]

In the battle against the red-light ladies, the city fathers forgot about Hattie McGinnis's kindness toward the wayward Pauline Phillips. The madam had been around since she first employed Pauline, Ida Burnell, and Dora Mason at her Ferry Street brothel in 1900, and possibly even before that. Notably, the 1900 census documented that Hattie had married in 1879 in New York and was the mother of a child. But her husband, James McGinnis, was nowhere to be found in February 1906, when Hattie was charged with vagrancy. In this case, Hattie was able to disprove the accusation by showing the tax receipts she paid on her property. Her case was dismissed, but the city of Salem certainly seemed to have it out for her.[23]

Officials waged their battle against Hattie for three more years. Finally, in October 1909, charges of conducting a bawdy house on Ferry Street were filed against Hattie, Julia Downie, Rose Leland, Dollie Richie, and Emma Thomas. Attorney William Kaiser was retained to defend all five of the ladies. Over the next two weeks, a juried trial commenced as each woman was hauled into court, berated, evidence presented against her, and a sentence handed down. Hattie and Emma Thomas went first. Apparently one U. G. Kellogg of the Law Enforcement League had visited both brothels "for the purpose of securing evidence." The concept of entrapment had yet to exist, leaving Kellogg free to buy "a malt liquor known as beer in these two houses." Furthermore, he said, "the proprietress had behaved like Potiphar's wife, while he took the part of Joseph."[24] The biblical reference, wherein the wife of Potiphar accused Joseph of rape when he refused her advances, struck a chord with the jury. Hattie and Emma were duly found guilty of running a bawdy house.

A week later, four of the guilty women were sentenced to thirty days in jail, while Hattie McGinnis paid a three-hundred-dollar fine. The madam filed an appeal, set for March 1910, during which the "lawful" gathering of evidence was discussed. Only two detectives had evidence or testimony to present, however. Still, the reputation of known brothels in general was discussed at length, as well as the ruling of condemning a person in court based on "common fame." After a month in court, it was ruled on April 12, 1910, that due to her reputation and that of her house, Hattie McGinnis was indeed guilty of prostitution.[25]

Hattie had had enough of Salem, as well as the last laugh. James McGinnis had apparently resurfaced, and when the couple left town, they left an unpaid tax bill in the amount of seventeen hundred dollars. The couple had retired to a modest house at 1295 Essex Street in San Diego by 1920. Any money Hattie had left was gone. The elderly madam was now seventy-nine years old; James, who was ten years her junior, toiled as a carpenter. Shortly after the census was taken, Hattie died on July 10. Ten years later, James was a resident at the Edgemoor Poor Farm in nearby El Cajon. Fortunately, Edgemoor was most unique. Residents dined on fresh vegetables, fruit, and meat raised at the farm, and a slew of volunteers and able residents pitched in to supply everyone with everything they needed. James died just after the next census was taken, on August 31, 1930.[26]

Hattie McGinnis may have left Salem, but others remained. In December 1911, police raided a house and arrested three women: Edith Jerman, Mary Koning, and Maud Vaughn. Mary was charged with selling liquor without a license and would stand trial. The others were charged with vagrancy and fined twenty dollars each, and it was expected they would later be charged with prostitution. The suspicion was not without merit, as all three women were at one time identified as being from the red-light district when they were seen participating in a Fourth of July race along the Willamette River. About a year later, Governor Oswald

West at long last successfully shut down every brothel at Peppermint Flat. Later reports, perhaps in defense of Salem's failure to close the district for so many years, politely stated that the shutdown had actually occurred back in 1904.[27] Those who remembered the shady ladies of Salem, however, knew the truth.

CHAPTER 16

— • • —

Gold Rush Girls of Alaska

The Madam was stood in her parlor when a knock was heard on the door,
Her fairies then gathered around her to display their stock and store.
She peered through the grill in the panel like a panther stalks a deer
And with quick respond to the cute little blond she whispered in her ear:
'He's fresh in from the jungles, dear, with a great big roll of hay.
So stick right close beside him, and make that sucker pay.
I had my spotter down last night to watch the boats arrive,
And my taxi driver picked him up in an east-end bootleg dive.
He'll be my guest while you get dressed in your finest evening frock;
His tonsils anoint in a cocktail joint, but bank his roll in your sock.
Offer your charms to lure him—make sure of your feminine wit;
But get his jack, and then come back. It's a fifty-fifty split.'[1]

History books credit George Holt as the first white man to climb Alaska's treacherous Chilkoot Pass, in 1878. Holt was in search of gold, and when he reappeared with a couple of nuggets given to him by a Chilkoot Indian, the news created a small gold rush. Still, gold prospectors making their way to Alaska during 1880 initially numbered only in the handfuls. They first concentrated on Juneau, where gold had been discovered, with small camps popping up between there and the Yukon

Valley. New strikes were quickly swarmed by camp followers in the way of gamblers, saloon men, prostitutes, and a bevy of others intent on making their fortunes.[2]

Like Holt, many of the prospecting pioneers to the Far North accessed the Yukon via Chilkoot Pass. A precarious and dangerous passageway climbed nine hundred feet to its base. Here, at a place called the Scales, travelers got one last chance to balance their loads before trekking another six hundred feet straight uphill. The climb was so steep and rocky that it was downright treacherous in winter; even summer travelers were often forced to crawl the entire half mile over the top of the pass. Eventually some hardy entrepreneurs managed to carve fifteen hundred narrow steps over the icy trail. Those who used the "Golden Stairs" were not only forced to pay a fee but also to file in one single line as they ascended. Only about two hundred prospectors were hardy enough to make it over Chilkoot Pass by 1886.[3]

At the time of Holt's climb, Alaska was barren of Anglo women. Some of the only female entertainments were "squaw dances," described by geologist Josiah Edward Spurr, who chanced upon "a row of miners who were lined up in front of the saloon." The men told Spurr that a dance was going to be held, "but when or how they did not seem to know." At ten o'clock that evening, about a dozen native women shuffled up, each with a baby wrapped in a blanket on her back. The women resolutely marched into the saloon, sat on long benches, placed their babies beside them, and "sat awhile looking at the ground on some one spot."

When the ladies at last looked up at the miners crowded into the cabin, a fiddler struck up a tune. Spurr watched as "some of the most reckless of the miners grabbed an Indian woman and began furiously swinging her around in a sort of waltz while the others crowed and looked on." Notably, the men and women spoke different languages and so did not converse with one another. The only sounds in the room were the fiddle and the shuffling of feet. After several hours, the women began

A typical gold rush girl of the era. Many images of good time girls remain unidentified; the ladies often wished to remain anonymous.

Courtesy Jay Moynahan

tiring and, one by one, left the dance floor, picked up their bundled child, and departed. The men set out for the nearest saloon for a drink. All in all, Spurr reported, "the affair was one of the most peculiar balls ever seen."[4]

The first Anglo woman to reach Alaska was none other than "Dutch Kate" Wilson, a woman of easy virtue who made the trek over Chilkoot Pass in 1887. Kate was with a small party of prospectors. Among them was John Rogers, who described Kate as "one of those poor, fallen women who are often found casting their lot with the mining class." Rogers was probably mistaken when he assumed Kate wore men's clothing for the trip because she was a "poor creature." Rather, Kate likely correctly assumed that the crossing of Chilkoot Pass was no place to wear petticoats and long skirts. And she surprised Rogers and others when, just before reaching a Native American village, the woman stepped into the bushes where she "arrayed herself in the finest apparel, powdered her face, and arranged her bangs in the most bewitching style."

The woman quickly caught the eye of the tribal leader, who detained Kate at a boat near some water as the women and children of the village ran for wool blankets. These were majestically spread out before the tainted lady so she could walk to the village without soiling her slippers. In the coming months, the tribal leader did his best to romance Dutch Kate. By the spring of 1888, however, Kate had escaped the man's clutches for the new diggings at Fortymile. When that didn't work out, she moved on to the settlement of Dyea. But Dyea also dissatisfied the lady, who sold nearly all the provisions she had lugged around and continued traveling. The last anyone knew of her, she had wound up in the town of Douglas near Juneau, where she opened a dance-hall.[5]

As Dutch Kate traipsed around frontier Alaska, gold strikes big and small were being discovered with more and more frequency. One early camp was Circle City, founded on Birch Creek in about 1893. Within three years, twelve hundred people were provided with eight dance-halls, a music hall, two theaters, and twenty-eight saloons. The growing city was being hailed as the "Paris of Alaska." But that same year, 1896, there was a mass exodus from Circle City as the miners heard of the next great rush in the Klondike. On August 14, 1896, George Washington Carmack discovered gold at the confluence of the Klondike and Yukon Rivers in Canada, close to the Alaskan border.[6]

The resulting rush to the Yukon was one of the largest known in history. The one drawback, however, was that the gold "district" was only big enough to support about four thousand claims. In the next three years, more than one hundred thousand people would attempt the trek to the Klondike anyway. The journey was long and treacherous, especially over Chilkoot Pass. The wise man got to the area early enough to stake a claim, but also needed to know how to make money other ways if there were no good claims left. Winters in the region were cold and icy, with temperatures frequently dipping below freezing. In contrast, summers were mild to hot, with muggy temperatures creating a breeding ground for disease caused by mosquitoes.[7]

Today the city of Dawson in Canada, close to the Alaskan border, is remembered as the place with the largest concentration of miners, loggers, gamblers, and shady ladies. But there were plenty of other camps and towns in Alaska that also enjoyed prosperity for a time. The Red Light in Juneau was opened by Miss Gertie Joseph on February 15, 1896, on Main Street between Front and Second. There also was Skagway, where the dance-hall girls and prostitutes dressed in the latest fashions as they scrambled and fought among one another to snag male customers in the concert hall "boxes." The boxes were private, curtained rooms skirting the balconies of such places where gentlemen could enjoy a show and be entertained by a soiled dove. The ladies successfully worked their wiles on every man they could find. One customer was said to have spent 750 dollars in one night for cigars and three thousand dollars on another night for wine. The fierce competition among working girls echoed down the streets, where shootings took place nearly every night.[8]

Most of the ladies of the Alaskan gold rush during the 1890s were Anglo, but other ethnicities also were represented. Author Jay Moynahan noted that a number of Japanese prostitutes worked in Alaska during the 1800s. Those who have remained in history's eye appear to have worked independently and done well for themselves. Moynahan also speculated the difference between Chinese and Japanese girls was basically cultural; Japanese women came to North America to marry Japanese men, only to find that they were indentured prostitutes instead. In contrast, Chinese women were sold outright by their families, sometimes with the knowledge that they were to serve as sex slaves.[9]

Many prostitutes were ruled over by men, but not all pimps were successful. Elias Jackson "Lucky" Baldwin perhaps got what he deserved when his effort to open his own brothel failed miserably. Lucky's cousin was Verona "Fannie" Baldwin, an elegant and cultured courtesan with "large, dark hazel eyes." Verona was only twenty years old when she shot Baldwin in 1883. At the time, the man was the millionaire owner of the Baldwin Hotel in San Francisco—the scene of the shooting. Allegedly, he had had four wives over time and numerous affairs with other women. Those "other women" frequently sued him, and it was said that "he was named defendant in more seduction and breach-of-promise suits than any other man."[10]

Verona claimed that Baldwin had sexually assaulted her while she was teaching school at his Santa Anita, California, ranch. Baldwin survived, to which Verona commented, "I ought to have killed him. Yes, I ought to have killed him at the ranch."[11] Verona's trial went on until at least 1887. She claimed that her cousin "had ruined her in body and mind," and that after he assaulted her he accused her of "improper conduct" and fired her. Baldwin's attorney, however, claimed that a servant had caught Verona and a guest on the ranch having sex and reported it to Baldwin, who discharged her.[12]

Three years after she was acquitted due to Baldwin's refusal to testify, Verona claimed he had fathered her child and threatened to sue her cousin for child support. Baldwin had her committed to an insane asylum in Napa, California. It was no secret that Baldwin had Verona locked up to shut her up; even lawyer and publisher Horace Bell acknowledged that "our hellish statutes protected him and enabled him to send his victim to the insane asylum." Verona, along with the general public, fought the insanity charge and she was released. She eventually moved to Denver, where she became a prominent madam.[13]

Indeed, woman trouble would plague the playboy Baldwin for the rest of his days. He was actually shot one other time, in a courtroom, during his trial for seducing one Lillian Ashley. The culprit was Lillian's sister. As far as his finances were concerned, however, Baldwin was indeed lucky. But after several years of making several lucrative investments, sometimes by accident, Baldwin's luck finally began running out beginning about 1898. That year, his San Francisco hotel burned down.[14] Baldwin next decided to head northwest, at the age of seventy-one. He first went to Seattle and soon made a plan to hire several prostitutes and open a place in Nome, Alaska.[15] He set sail with a large cargo containing gambling devices, "two ready-cut frame houses," supplies, and fixtures for a saloon.[16] Sarah Josephine Marcus later claimed that she and lawman Wyatt Earp were married by Baldwin aboard his "yacht." Baldwin and the Earps became fast friends, and in about 1900 Earp opened the Dexter Saloon, a two-story saloon with pretty girls for sale upstairs.[17]

For Baldwin, however, the cards were not in his favor this time. Not only did he fail to find any good real estate in Nome, but there also were no good mining investments to be made. Besides, the elderly man was in ill health. Baldwin soon returned to California, leaving his property behind. Some "crooked officials" managed to confiscate everything "on a phony charge of tax evasion." David Unruh, the son of Baldwin's financial advisor, H. A. Unruh, had remained behind in Alaska. With Earp's assistance, Unruh was able to get all of Baldwin's property back and opened the Second Class Saloon on Baldwin's behalf. Unruh quickly sold the place for a profit.[18]

Baldwin never returned to Alaska, dying in 1909.[19] It was just as well—by 1899 Alaska's great gold rush was at an end. There simply was not enough gold to go around, and the prospectors, gamblers, and floozies lit out for greener pastures. Alaska's former boomtowns faded to ghosts or melded into respectable cities. As late as the 1940s, however, Alaska remained relaxed with regards to such societal rules as marriage. Olive Barber, who had docked with her husband in Funter Bay, asked the storekeeper there, "Do you also perform marriage ceremonies?" The man was quick to reply. "Oh," he said, "up here we ain't *that* strict."[20]

CHAPTER 17

——•●•——

The Demimonde of Dawson City

Within a year of the gold discoveries in Alaska, hundreds of camps began springing up throughout the Yukon. By 1897 the population of Dawson City—located in Canada close to the Alaskan border, but often referred to as part of the Alaskan gold rush—had grown from five hundred to five thousand.[1] The influx was simply incredible; in the next two years, the most successful of Dawson's business folks would revel in riches they never dreamed of. Land, liquor, goods, and giddy girls could be had for exorbitant prices equal to or greater than those of today. Through it all, everyone basked in wealth, drunken dreams come true, and a time in history that would never be seen again.

For prostitutes taking advantage of the gold rush, Dawson was a virtual treasure trove. Women flocked into town by the hundreds, initially setting up their tents and shacks wherever they pleased. A red-light or red curtains in the window let passersby know what kind of business went on inside.[2] "I have seen [them], sitting at their windows," wrote Alfred G. McMichael in a letter home, "highly decorated maidens in low neck and short sleeves who winked and beckoned the weary traveler in to rest."[3] One gal, Big Sal, dared to pitch her tent right in the middle of a street.[4] News of the gold rush circulated throughout the American West as wayward women packed their trunks and bags and made their way to Dawson. They were a welcome sight to the lonely miners who were hungry for female companionship. Geologist Albert Brooks observed, "Since prostitutes always had plenty of money, the best accommodations on the steamers and in hotels were reserved for them. This condition made it very trying for the better class of women to travel."[5]

Ladies of the evening found a variety of ways to make money. Some danced in dance-halls or worked as waitresses in the box theaters. A good dance-hall girl could make up to forty dollars a week, plus commissions on drinks. Others worked outright in the sex trade out of tents, cribs, and brothels. Those adept at the trade could make twice the amount of their dancing-only counterparts. One dance-hall girl, Mable LaRose of the Monte Carlo, put herself up for auction as a temporary wife for the winter. She made five thousand dollars. Others sold themselves by charging a certain amount of gold for each pound they weighed. Many of them hid heavy buckshot in their corsets to increase the amount. Men too caught onto the auction idea, opening "matrimonial agencies" and bringing women to the Klondike with the understanding that they would be sold to miners for up to two thousand dollars each. To these ladies, the men were easy pickings. When Mabel Long fell off a boat into the icy waters, a kind stranger rescued her while her husband stood by. The soggy Mabel immediately expressed her desire to go with her rescuer rather than stay with her lay-about husband. The two boarded the stranger's boat and sailed off as the hapless husband watched them depart.[6]

It was amazingly simple for ladies of easy virtue to pick and choose their paramours. Gussie Lamore was a favorite call girl of mining magnate Swiftwater Bill Gates. Gussie loved eggs, a rare and expensive commodity in Dawson. One day, as Gates sat in a local restaurant, in strolled Bessie, arm in arm with a known gambler. The two were seated nearby and ordered fried eggs. Incensed, Gates tried to buy every egg in town to make his cheating trollop jealous. In alternate versions of the tale,

A group of Dawson's shady ladies pose for Larss & Duclose photographers, circa 1899.
Courtesy Dawson City Museum 1962.7.58

Gates ordered the eggs fried, which he flipped out the window of the restaurant to a pack of dogs. Or, he gave them to all the other dance-hall girls to teach Gussie a lesson. However it really happened, Gussie got no eggs—unless another source rightfully concludes that Gates gave her every single egg to win her love.

When Gates left for San Francisco, Gussie promised to meet him there. Alas, the woman was already married, and had been since 1894, to a man named Emile Leglice or Leglise, and had a child by him. It may have mattered little to Gates, for his mission in San Francisco was to recruit new girls for the all-new Monte Carlo Dance Hall in the Klondike. When Gussie eventually followed Gates to San Francisco in about 1898, she refused to marry him. Gates married her sister, Grace, instead. That union lasted only three weeks before Grace threw Gates out of their fifteen-thousand-dollar house in Oakland. Undaunted, Gates married again, to Nellie Lamore, the youngest of Gussie's sisters.[7]

Gates grew even more eccentric. While recruiting girls for the Monte Carlo in Seattle, he lived lavishly at the Rainier Grand Hotel, bathing in champagne and running up at hotel bill of fifteen hundred dollars. His partner, identified as a Dr. Wolf, began having misgivings about the man, which were confirmed further when the doctor returned to Dawson and learned of Gates's crazy antics there. Even when Gates showed up with two scows full of girls, Wolf demanded his twenty-thousand-dollar investment back. Gates paid it, decided to found the British North American Trading and Exploration Company instead, and left for London. What became of the ladies in the scows is unknown. They may have worked at the Monte Carlo, which did eventually open. The "hastily erected" two-story building was large enough to house a front room with a "long polished bar," a gaming room, and a theater. Upstairs were several bedrooms, which could be rented by travelers or prostitutes, it mattered not which. Girls could also ply their trade in the private theater boxes on the balcony in the theater.[8]

Due to the high cost of shipping goods to such a remote spot as Dawson, prices were much steeper than they were anywhere else. As time went on, the dance-hall ladies of Dawson charged, and got, a dollar a dance versus the two bits they received elsewhere, and a hardworking girl could make between twenty and one hundred dollars per night. Prostitutes also profited, charging four ounces of gold for fifteen minutes of their time. The more unscrupulous ladies weighed the gold themselves with crooked scales, netting more than their customers knew.[9]

At Pete McDonald's M & N Saloon and Dance Hall, 125 dances were the norm on an average night. McDonald charged a dollar per dance, giving his customers ivory chips to present to the dancing lady of his choice. At the end of the night, the ladies turned in their chips and received twenty-three cents for each one. The amount seemed low, but some girls stashed enough chips in their stockings "until their legs were lumpy with ivory vouchers." One man actually bought seven hundred chips in advance. The saloon burned on Thanksgiving night in 1897, after a dance-hall girl identified as Belle Mitchell hurled a flaming lamp at another girl. The loss was estimated at one hundred thousand dollars, but McDonald simply rebuilt a new place, the Phoenix.[10]

During the winter of 1898–99, city official James McCook waltzed into the dance-hall with Gertie Lovejoy, known in Dawson as Diamond-Tooth Gertie. She was a favorite in the dance-halls, perhaps because of the diamond she had lodged between her two front teeth. According to the *Klondyke Nugget*, McCook was "bursting with patriotic flavor" as he offered to buy drinks for any "true American." Gertie's colleagues immediately rushed the man, along with several men. When one of them declared himself to be a Canadian and refused the offer, McCook declared he would "make the man an American."

There was a brief skirmish, after which McCook next gave a bunch of money, some nuggets, and a gold watch to the ladies. Next he turned his pockets out, yelling, "Take the whole works!" There was a mad scuffle as the jovial McCook rolled about on the floor. When he got to his feet, according to the newspaper, he "produced a small Stars and Stripes, pinned it to the seat of his pants, placed his hands on the bar, and, leaning over, requested Pete McDonald to give him a good square kick." McCook lost his joviality when he read the newspaper account of the incident. He sued the paper and its owners for twenty-five thousand dollars. But there were too many witnesses; the suit was dropped, and McCook was fired. Diamond-Tooth Gertie probably knew the story was true, and once commented, "The poor ginks have just gotta spend it, they're scared they'll die before they have it all out of the ground."[11]

Prospectors continued arriving through 1898, when waves of men scrambled to the Klondike in search of gold. Dawson's population grew again, to an amazing twenty-eight thousand souls. The dance-halls now included the Combination and Charlie Kimball's Pavilion, which made twelve thousand dollars on its first night in business—which the owner spent like a madman. Over three months, Kimball spent the three hundred thousand dollars he made, and lost his dance-hall. Inside the Pavilion, the Combination and other such places were women wearing silk evening gowns and sporting such romantic names as Daisy D'Avara, Flossie de Atley, and Blanche Lamont—the last probably adopting her pseudonym from the sensational murder trial of Theodore Durrant, who killed an innocent young girl by that name in San Francisco in 1895.[12] Such was the mixture of dramatic flair and black humor during the gold rush.

No matter where they got their names, the girls of Dawson had a common goal: Make money, and lots of it. Flossie de Atley told others that she had a sick brother in a sanitarium and needed money for his care. Whether the story was true is up for speculation, but it is true that Flossie eventually departed Dawson "with enough for a dozen sick brothers." Another woman, who was missing an eye believed to have been lost during a fight with another girl, was simply referred to as the "Grizzly Bear." The Oregon Mare was said to whistle and squeal as she danced, and would occasionally call out to her customers, "Here boys—there's my poke. Have a drink with me, all of you!" The Oregon Mare also loved to gamble, and once spent a thousand dollars in just one hour at the roulette table. But she also saved up fifty thousand dollars, enough to pay off her mother's ranch near Sacramento, California.[13]

Famed dance-hall queen and performer Cad Wilson was believed to have been the highest paid girl in town. Cad was not so much talented or pretty as she was just plain fun. When she wasn't belting out "Such a Nice Girl Too" onstage or dancing at the Tivoli or the Orpheum, she favored running about, "laughing her famous laugh" and pulling her skirts up so men could see her legs. She also told her admirers outright that she wanted their money. Opening one of her acts at the Tivoli, manager Eddie Dolan would tell the audience that Cad's mother had admonished her to "be sure and be a good girl and pick nice friends." As he beckoned the woman onstage, Dolan would yell out, "I leave it to you, fellers, if she don't pick 'em clean!"[14]

Like other women, Cad kept her gold nuggets on a belt fastened around her waist. The belt was said to have been made and given to her by her admirers, and was worth a cool fifty thousand dollars. They said she had the largest belt in the Klondike, so large that it circled her waist one and a half times. And, she had plenty of admirers. One of them once filled a bathtub with wine for her to bathe in, which she allegedly did without allowing him to even watch. Dawson resident Burt Parker commented that if the bath took place as they said, it "would be salvaged, re-bottled and go into circulation again."[15]

One of the most famous madams to appear in Dawson during 1898 was Mattie Silks, queen of Denver, Colorado's Tenderloin. Mattie and her husband, Cort Thomson, were on vacation in London when they read about the gold strike in the Klondike. The couple returned to Denver briefly before setting out for Dawson in the company of eight of Mattie's girls. Upon their arrival, Mattie immediately rented a building on Second Street for 350 dollars per month and opened for business. Another fifty dollars was paid monthly to the Canadian Northwest Mounted Police for protection. The ladies each made about fifty dollars per night. Mattie took half, charged thirty dollars for a bottle of champagne, and raked in the bucks. In his usual fashion, Thomson left Mattie to her business but used her money to support his gambling habit in the local gaming houses. Come late summer, he caught a terrible cold. Mattie had heard about the harsh winters in Dawson and feared Thomson would only get worse, so she closed up shop and headed back to Denver. In three months' time, after expenses, Mattie netted thirty-eight thousand dollars.[16]

It is fun to speculate how much Mattie would have made had she remained in Dawson. Everyone, from madams to prostitutes to dance-hall girls, was making gobs of cash. Two famous entertainers were Lottie and Pollie Oatley. The sisters were nationally popular stage performers who traveled around the West. Their parents, James and Eliza, were natives of England. After two stillborn boys, Eliza successfully gave birth to three daughters: Mary Jane "Pollie" in 1864, while the family still lived in Wales; Sarah "Sadie" in 1873; and Lottie, in Ohio, in 1876. As the girls grew, Eliza recognized their talent for singing and formed the Three Oatley Sisters, which she initially managed. Success did not come easily. Sarah married Charles Harding in 1892 but suffered from St. Vitus' Dance (Sydenham's chorea) and died in Philadelphia in 1893 from "congestion of the brain." [17]

Pollie and Lottie went on, billed as the Oatley Sisters. In 1896 they performed in Victor, Colorado, with their small dog, Tiny, who "sang" along in a soprano voice.[18] In Dawson in 1898, the girls performed at the Regina Saloon, apparently without Tiny, and probably without their mother. The girls would perform "twenty dances with the customers at a dollar a dance" before taking the stage and singing some sentimental ballads, including "Break the News to Mother," "A Bird in a Gilded Cage," and other numbers. "A lot of those songs are graven on the walls of my memory," recalled admirer Bill Parker. "I stood there with my mouth open, listening to the Oatley Sisters sing those sad ballads. I never knew them personally and didn't have enough money in those days to get near enough to get a really good look at them. But they sure helped me to put many a lonesome night behind me and gave me something to think about when I crawled into my bunk at night and parked my weary head on a pillow made of my two high boots."[19]

After they sang, the girls would commence dancing again, offering three dances for a dollar, either with one of them or another of the dance-hall girls in the place. Eventually the Oatley sisters followed "N*****

Jim" Daugherty to Circle City, where he purchased two dance-halls for the girls and married Lottie. The marriage cost Lottie dearly. In 1900 she gave birth to her only daughter, Charlotte, near Dawson. Daugherty went broke that same year and was forced to go to work on the railroad. Why Lottie left him shortly afterward remains unknown, but by marrying him in Canada she had lost her US citizenship.[20] Pollie died in Seattle, Washington, in 1901. Lottie was in Washington too, in 1910, when she divorced Daugherty to marry Vernon Casley. The couple was living in Hollywood, California, when Casley died in 1942. Two years later, Lottie was living in Los Angeles with Charlotte when she applied to have her US citizenship restored. She died in 1961 in Hollywood and is buried among other celebrities in Forest Lawn Memorial Park.[21]

Other famous characters to visit Dawson in 1898 included "Arizona Charlie" Meadows. This illustrious trick rider and shooter-turned-entertainer had already made a name for himself for holding the first rodeo in Prescott, Arizona, and hosting a less-than-glorious bullfight in Gillette, Colorado.[22] In Dawson, Meadows opened the Palace Grand dance-hall with theater performances featuring private boxes. There were troubles; one of the performers, a dance-hall girl named Babette Pyne, played the lead in *Camille* opposite George Hillier as Duval. But Babette hated the man so much she refused to speak to him offstage and "was in a state of nervous prostration" following their love scenes together. One night, Babette's character called for Prudence, played by another dance-hall girl named Nellie Lewis. The actress failed to appear. It was only after the play came to a complete stop that Nellie, "her hair tousled and her face flushed, poked her head from between the curtains of a wine box in the gallery" and slurred, "Madam Prudence isn't here! Call all you like, but Madam Prudence ain't a-coming tonight." Theater employees forced Nellie to come out of the box, but she still refused to take the stage. At the very least, Meadows could always depend on his own shooting skills to entertain his audiences.[23]

Curiously, Dawson's dance-halls, gambling places, and taverns closed at the stroke of midnight each Saturday night. They remained closed on Sunday, reopening at two a.m. each Monday morning. This was an edict issued by city officials, and it was carried out religiously. Dawson citizens might have been an uncouth, rowdy, deliriously drunk party crowd, but everyone appears to have obeyed the law in this respect. The law eventually relegated prostitutes to a crowded little neighborhood bordered by First and Third Avenues and King and Queen Streets. The tiny, jam-packed cabins were built neatly into two rows, containing roughly seventy cribs, and dubbed Paradise Alley. Each shack featured one window and a door, with the girls' names painted above.[24] Images of the alley show wooden sidewalks in front of the shacks, but the women endured a mighty muddy street between the rows, which froze over during winter.

Paradise Alley could be a harsh, lonely place, especially in the hours before four p.m., when the ladies were not allowed on city streets. Many of the women were literally white slaves to men who had paid their passage to Dawson and expected the ladies to pay them back. By now there was class distinction between the dance-hall girls and the prostitutes of Paradise Alley. Prostitutes now made slightly less money than dance-hall girls, who had the freedom to go where they pleased and had a variety of schemes to make money. But all of the women did have one malady in common, and that was the occasional tragedy—usually over a man. During the winter of 1898–99, newspapers reported on suicides like that of Stella Hill, lately of Oregon, who killed herself by drinking strychnine just before Christmas. Stella was upset to find her bartender boyfriend at the Pioneer in the arms of another woman named Libby White. When Libby's lover found out about the affair, he shot her to death at the Monte Carlo before taking his own life.

Another woman, Helen Holden, attempted suicide over a local saloon owner. A most interesting story was that of Myrtle Briscoe, a dance-hall girl who managed to retain her virginity. After Myrtle shot

herself to death in the room of gambler Harry Woolrich above Sam Bonniefield's gambling establishment, a bevy of men testified that they had
shared her bed—but not her body. Even Woolrich claimed that Myrtle
went to her death a virgin. Myrtle received an honorable burial in an
expensive coffin, her memory preserved as the chivalrous men of town
upheld their statements that she was indeed pure.[25]

The giddy girls of Dawson could sometimes prove a detriment not
only to themselves but the entire town. In October 1898, Belle Mitchell,
the same dance-hall girl who had set the M & N Saloon and Dance Hall
on fire in 1897, threw yet another lamp and started a bigger, much more
devastating fire. Hurling flaming lamps was apparently Belle's habit, and
the *San Francisco Call* told all on the woman. "The conflagration was
started by a drunken and infuriated woman, Belle Mitchell, who occupied a room at the Green Tree," explained the paper. "A man named Tony
Page was with her at the time. She threw a lighted lamp at him, and, the
lamp breaking, the burning oil flew all over the room. Her pseudonym
is 'Coal Oil Belle.' Two weeks before she threw a lamp in her own cabin,
and it was burned to the ground. She is also accused of having caused
the comparatively small fire last winter by throwing a lamp." Because of
Belle's foul temper, Dawson "was almost wholly destroyed."[26]

The city had barely recovered from the fire when, on April 26, 1899,
a "tongue of flame shot from the bedroom" of another dance-hall girl
above the Bodega Saloon. The conflagration was far worse than that of
the previous year. The freshly built cribs of Paradise Alley went up in
flames once more. The ladies of the line "poured, naked and screaming,
from their smoking cribs into the arms of the firefighters, who ripped
off their own coats to bundle up the terrified women." Buildings were
blown up to stop the spread of the flames as more structures burned anyway. Perhaps it was just as well, for by 1899 the limited amount of gold
claims to be had had been reduced to virtually zero. Finding nothing to
mine, newly arrived prospectors took off for greener pastures. Rumors

began circulating that new gold strikes were happening in Nome and other places, and Dawson's raucous citizenry slowly began exiting the town. As the population dwindled, a census taken revealed there were 3,659 men compared to 786 women. Of the female population, it was guessed that about half were prostitutes.[27]

Over the next year, gaggles of people continued leaving. Dawson's real estate could now practically be had for the taking, but a few thousand people remained behind. In 1901 the Paradise Alley girls were relocated to Klondike City, formerly known as "Lousetown" and located across the Klondike River away from Dawson proper. Probably due to the violence that broke out in the district with alarming frequency, the new district was called White Chapel—the same name as the red-light neighborhood in London where Jack the Ripper preyed on unsuspecting women of the night. It was also known as "Hell's Half Acre."[28]

All in all, it took about two decades for Dawson's population to downsize to about two thousand people. Dawson's riches remained as late as the 1940s in the form of gold dust and smaller nuggets, which were found as the town tore down the old dance-halls, repaired old banks, and renovated the old theaters. Misplaced, spilled, and forgotten gold was literally panned from the streets.[29] Today Dawson's population is about fourteen hundred, with a museum and plenty of historic buildings to see. As for Paradise Alley, the old red-light district now features numerous little shops for visitors to enjoy.

CHAPTER 18

—•◦•—

Klondike Kate of the Yukon

By far the most famous, or infamous, woman of the Alaskan gold rush was "Klondike Kate"—a beautiful and talented woman described as having "natural red hair, violet eyes, long black lashes, and a splendid figure."[1] Kate's adventures were many, her heartbreaks few. Noteworthy is that she serenaded her way through the throngs of men throughout the West and beyond. No matter that her reputation was at times questionable; Kate skyrocketed to fame, making her a celebrity in her own right who remains famous even today.

Katherine Eloise Rockwell was born to a family with several children in 1876 in Junction City, Kansas. Her father, John, worked as a railroad telegraph agent; her mother, Martha, toiled as a waitress. In 1882 Kate's parents divorced. Martha married her lawyer, Frank Allison Bettis, a Civil War veteran who was destined for a life in politics. The Bettises were in Spokane by 1890, residing at 25 East Third Avenue, where Bettis continued his law practice and became a city councilman.[2] Called "Kitty" as a child, Kate benefited from her stepfather's wealth with private nannies and private schools. She received her education at a variety of boarding schools, none of which worked out. Even at her young age, Kate was "a lively, impetuous girl whose strong will was difficult to control." Her "dancing and carrying on with men" resulted in her being

Kate Rockwell, right, is pictured with her friend Lilly Edgerton in this 1901 image, taken at Dawson City by photographer Major James Skitt Matthews.
Courtesy City of Vancouver Archives

expelled on numerous occasions. The nuns at one school once discovered that Kate had seven diamond rings in her possession and made her return them to the various suitors who had given them to her. Kate's fretting mother tried installing her at schools in Kansas and Minnesota, but the outcome was always the same.[3]

Eventually the Bettises divorced. Martha tried running a rooming house but eventually sold it. With the money from the sale, the frustrated mother took Kate on a trip to see her half-brother, Ralph Morris, from another of Martha's former marriages. Ralph lived in South America, and Kate enjoyed the trip tremendously—especially being on the ship, where she could easily flirt with the crew. En route, Kate announced she was engaged to a young naval officer. Martha objected and installed her daughter in yet another Catholic school in Valparaíso, Chile, before taking a long vacation. She eventually returned to New

York. According to Kate, despite having squandered all her money, Martha objected to Kate's insistence on being engaged to another man, a young "diplomatic attaché from Spain" while in Chile.[4] Mother ordered daughter to sail to New York immediately. Upon her arrival, Kate learned that her mother was poor and about to take a job in a shirtwaist factory. "I was only sixteen," she later said, "but I knew I must help in some way."[5]

Kate's idea of helping out was to apply for a job as a chorus girl under the name "Kitty Phillips."[6] Ever watchful, Martha clocked the time in which Kate could change from her costume and hop the streetcar home.[7] Still, Kate managed to perform in theaters in Manhattan and Coney Island before returning to Spokane. There she began working at the local box houses. Kate later claimed that she "learned to work customers after each show for a commission on drinks," but that she never sipped anything stronger than lemonade.[8] She also worked in Seattle, where "Big John" Consadine hired her to work at his renowned People's Theater. Kate might have made her reputation as a stage performer, but she soon found that working the floor yielded much more money. She used her famous "pixie stare," a feigned portrayal of innocence, to get what she wanted.[9]

When the gold rush hit the Yukon in 1896, Kate made her way north. With a partner named Gertie Jackson, she first performed in shows at the Savoy, a vaudeville theater in Victoria, British Columbia, Canada. During her time there she became "engaged long-distance" to minstrel star Danny Allmon, whom she had met in New York. Long before Allmon could catch up with her, however, Kate had moved on to Alaska. In Skagway she parted with Gertie and struck out on her own to begin a long, illustrious solo career on the road. She wore a crown of candles for a dance in Juneau. She also tried going over Chilkoot Pass but was turned away by Canadian Mounties with the warning that the trail was too harsh for a woman.

Back in Skagway, Kate went to work at a "honky-tonk" owned by con artist "Soapy" Smith. She also performed in the town of Bennett; afterward, an admirer emblazoned her name with champagne corks on the ceiling of a hotel. It was not until 1900 that Kate was finally able to make her way to Dawson. On the way, she said, she donned men's clothing when mounted guards again prevented her from taking a boat down the dangerous Five Finger Rapids on the Yukon River. Kate was having a fine time; she barely seemed to flinch when Danny Allmon died that same year as he tried to come join her.[10]

In Dawson, Kate was soon wooing audiences with her song and dance, wearing expensive gowns and hats and gaining an immense fan base. When rodeo trick rider and theater entrepreneur "Arizona Charlie" Meadows saw her performance, he immediately booked her, giving her the "Star's plush suite" at his Palace Grand. Soon after that, Kate became known under her famous pseudonym, "Klondike Kate, the Queen of the Yukon." Other fancy nicknames included "Queen of the North," the "Darling of Dawson," and the "Flower of the North." Kate raked in the profits, making two hundred dollars per week, plus another five hundred dollars in commission on champagne sales.[11]

Kate worked her male audience to her best advantage. One of them, Ed Lung, recalled that the lady was "truly captivating," with a "complexion like peaches and cream; her voice ranged from velvety soft to musical bells; and yes, she was sweet as honey!" Lung couldn't help digging his hard-earned poke of gold nuggets from his pocket and offering one to Kate, who professed a genuine interest in the beautiful bits of precious metal. "Her lovely hands grasped, fondled, and almost weighed each nugget," Lung remembered, "and then, she chose my biggest one." Later, Kate admitted that she and her coworkers "were not vestal virgins. Far from it." Kate very likely made money from her performances in the way of tips, and occasionally by selling sex on the side.[12] Soon it was nothing for Kate to buy three-hundred-dollar hats and thousand-dollar gowns.[13]

Probably the most famous man to serenade Kate was Alexander Pantages, a Greek box waiter who dreamed of opening his own theater. Pantages had escaped a hellish youth and worked hard to come to America. Kate reckoned that he was the smartest man she ever met. When the twosome met, Pantages was working as a waiter at Charlie Meadows's Monte Carlo and Kate was working the box rooms in the theater. In time, Pantages worked up to the better-paying job of stage manager. Soon, he and Kate were living as husband and wife—but without a marriage certificate.

Together, Kate and Pantages worked their way up the entertainment ladder. Kate continued headlining at the Monte Carlo, supporting her lover when he was in the red. When Pantages opened the Orpheum Theater in late 1900, Kate invested in the company and became his star entertainer. The Orpheum was soon taking in eight thousand dollars daily, and Kate spent lavishly on expensive gowns and jewelry. In spite of public sentiment about their not being married, the couple thoroughly enjoyed each other as they became more and more successful.[14] Kate fondly remembered how "we'd make plans for the day when we would later marry."[15]

When new gold strikes at Nome began drawing people away from Dawson, Pantages suggested leaving in 1902. Kate was unhappy at the prospect, so much so that on a trip with her man to New York City and Texas, she had a fling with an abusive gambler. After scoping out Nome and even reopening the Orpheum, Pantages next set his sights on Seattle as a place to open a national theater chain. Kate remained in Dawson, and the two exchanged letters for a couple of years. They had reunited by 1904, the year Kate is thought to have given birth to a son in Washington after a visit to San Francisco.[16] Kate later claimed the child belonged to "a young tubercular girl she had befriended, who had died giving birth."[17] When asked about it much later, Kate's answer was firm. "I took the baby," she stated. "I kept him until he was three, then I found

him a home and foster parents in the States. I sent the money for his
college education, and he is one of the most successful engineers in the
country today. I have never disclosed his identity. He perhaps has never
known me, but I like to think of him as my son."[18]

Whoever was the real mother of the child, Kate's relationship with
Pantages became more and more strained. Kate left the Klondike for
Seattle, but was soon off playing stages in and around the Pacific North-
west and even Texas. In Spokane, a friend advised her that Pantages had
married a performer at his Pantages Theatre in Seattle, a woman named
Lois Amel Mendenhall. Kate was hurt, especially after Pantages told a
Seattle Times reporter that he didn't even know Kate Rockwell. The
wounded harlot sued for breach of promise to marry, but settled with
Pantages out of court. The amount, depending on the source, amounted
to between five thousand and sixty thousand dollars.[19]

For the next several years, Kate rounded out her career in Dawson
and Fairbanks. In the latter city she purchased a hotel that burned during a big fire in 1906. Afterward she performed on a tour in the lower
forty-eight, which included an excruciating roller-skating act. None
of it was much fun, and Kate grew increasingly envious as Pantages's
theaters became a success. In 1914 her mother talked her into using
the last of her cash to buy a house with land, sight unseen, near Bend,
Oregon. To Kate's dismay, the homestead was "a one-room shack in
the middle of a 320-acre homestead. I never saw so much country in
my life."[20]

Kate's arrival was remembered by a group of teamsters, who were
dining at the Dunn ranch about eight miles from town when they heard
"a great commotion" outside. Upon investigating, they saw a "cursing
driver trying to hang onto a jittery horse with one hand and calm a raging
redhead in a big plume hat, glittering dance-hall gown, flashing jewelry,
and red dancing slippers in the other." The woman, Kate, was claiming
the horse had thrown her and that she had sprained her ankle. The men

helped the woman into the house, Mrs. Dunn installed her in a bed, and she was fed supper. "Yet soon after being fed," writer Ellis Lucia wrote, "she called out to the boys: 'Would one of you nice fellows come in here and hold my head? I feel so sick.'" Kate also had a bottle of alcohol with her, which she offered up. The teamsters politely declined for fear their "womenfolk" would find out.[21]

With nowhere else to go, Kate remained in Bend. She worked to repair her "ramshackle barn," paid to have water hauled in, and tended to her "desert yard." In appearance, Kate could not have looked more out of place. Her entire wardrobe, it seemed, consisted of her beautiful gowns accented by a considerable amount of jewelry. In this unfit ensemble, Kate wandered around her yard wearing her high-heeled shoes. Of the tiny holes made throughout the yard, Kate explained, "I made 'em with my dancing slippers." Although she was past performing, Kate made housewives wary. She was terribly friendly, especially to men, and her gentlemen callers—married or not—were many. And rather than modestly hiding her past, Kate seemed to enjoy letting everyone know of her adventures.[22]

Kate eventually married Floyd Warner, in 1915, at Crook, Oregon. Warner, fifteen years younger, worked as a farmer near Brothers before he registered for the draft for World War I in 1917. In 1918 Kate filed for a homestead on their land. After Warner returned from serving in the war, the couple tried running a restaurant in Prineville. But the restaurant failed, as did the marriage. After they split, even the local sheriff warned Warner not to stick around in order to avoid Kate's wrath.[23]

During the 1920 census, Kate listed herself as married, although Warner was long gone. Her occupation was reported as managing a restaurant. Living with her was thirty-five-year-old Oren Ward, who was employed as a cook. Kate had trouble making ends meet. At one point she gathered enough money to travel to Los Angeles and ask Pantages for some financial assistance, but he was hardly welcoming and gave her only a paltry six dollars. Kate had no choice but to return to Oregon, this time taking up a home on Franklin Street in Bend.[24]

If revenge is sweet, Kate must have felt like a chocolate truffle in 1929, when Pantages was accused of raping a seventeen-year-old actress in California. Although she never got to testify at the trial, Kate gave a scandalous interview to the press that embarrassed Pantages and his family. But much of Pantages's troubles were of his own making. He was sentenced to fifty years at San Quentin but was acquitted following a second trial two years later; in the meantime, Lois Pantages hit and killed a man while driving drunk. She was later "cleared" but paid more than seventy-eight thousand dollars to the man's family. Pantages died in Los Angeles in 1936.[25]

Kate remained in Bend, where folks began calling her "Aunt Kate." Some unkindly called her "our destitute prostitute."[26] Yet Kate became an institution unto herself around town. She eventually managed to purchase some rental properties and build up a little cash. Her quick tongue and temper often surprised and shocked those around her, and she was not beyond waging a battle with neighbors or anyone else who displeased her. And she never missed an opportunity to attend an event or a public dance. One of her admirers once commented, "She was the best dancer I ever danced with; she certainly knew her business." In fact, Kate refused to shy away from those who shunned her. She had no problem begging for vegetables and meat so she could make a nourishing soup for the homeless and hungry. Some days she could be found in the local record store, playing her favorite songs for hours on end.[27]

Kate also retained many of her relationships with old friends and visited them often. When the census taker came by her place on April 6, 1930, she was recorded as owning and operating a lodging house. At the time her lodgers were Dick Hoffner, Frank Hartwig, Tex Hart, and Glendina McCormick. Kate was obviously not home at the time; her birthplace, as well as that of her parents, was simply listed as "United

States." Had she been there, Kate surely would have given the correct information. Where was she then? The census gives the answer on April 10, where Kate was documented as a guest at the luxurious "Rosslyn Million Dollar Fireproof Hotel" in downtown Los Angeles under the name Kate E. Rockwell.[28]

Upon returning home, Kate resumed her normal activities. She loved collecting rocks and talked some local firemen into using them to build a chimney for her. The collection was so large that there was enough left over to contribute a rock fountain near the fire station, a shrine at St. Charles Hospital, and a petrified stump to grace the city park. Kate favored the firemen, once bringing them hot coffee as they fought a fire on a cold winter's night. Sometimes, she might even offer them a snort from her illegal whiskey stash. She also gave the men gifts, ranging from homemade preserves to more lavish items. In turn, the firemen gave her a card declaring her their one and only auxiliary member and allowed her to ride on the fire truck during parades.[29]

One day in 1933, Kate received a letter from Johnny Matson of Dawson. Matson, an older man, had seen her perform in her younger days and had recently seen her picture in a Los Angeles newspaper. Kate responded, and the two were married in 1933 in Vancouver, Washington. Strangely, they never lived together, and Matson never visited Bend. Instead, the two exchanged letters and met annually in Dawson or Vancouver. To the people of Bend, however, Kate presented her faraway husband as the love of her life. She was still Kate Matson when the 1940 census was taken. One of her lodgers was William Van Duren. Two years after Matson died at Dawson in 1946, Kate married Van Duren.[30] "It's April Fool's Day. It's Leap Year, and at my age, I don't think I'll get another chance," Kate explained in her flamboyant way. "I was the Flower of the North but the petals are falling fast, honey." Like Matson, Kate chose to marry her new mate in Vancouver, Washington.[31]

The Van Durens eventually left Bend and resettled in the Willamette Valley, first at Jefferson and finally at Sweet Home. But Kate never forgot her little piece of desert in Bend, visiting there often. When she died in 1957 at the age of eighty, her ashes were scattered there. Notably, her death certificate recorded her legal first name as "Klondike," her middle name as Kate, and her last name as Van Duren.[32] Kate would have liked that.

CHAPTER 19

——◦•◦——

Soiled Doves of Skaguay

L ike other places during the Klondike gold rush, the city of Skagway's history really began in 1897. The city had first gotten its start
ten years before, when Captain William Moore crossed the newly established White Pass to the valley where Skagway lies. The tiny settlement,
located along the Inside Passage at the northern tip of Lynn Canal, was
called Mooresville for the first ten years. In 1897 the first boatload of
gold prospectors converged on the place. The name of the fast-growing
town was changed to Skaguay, as it was first spelled, a Tlingit term used
to describe a beautiful woman. According to legend, Skaguay was the
nickname for a mythical maiden named Kanagoo, who turned herself
into stone in Skagway Bay and blows the wind across the remote little
city.[1]

Skaguay was the farthest one could take a ship inland in Alaska.
Because of this, the town was highly popular with travelers seeking gold
in the Alaskan wilderness. Newcomers sometimes arrived in town broke
and were obligated to stay there until they could earn enough money to
move on. Others used Skaguay as their first stopping point before figur-
ing out where they wanted to go next. All of these people were taken
in by the town's more permanent residents, who offered food, lodging,
liquor, gambling, and bawdy entertainment. Not everyone intended to

stay, but plenty of naughty girls and outlaws were stopped at the Canadian border at the top of White Pass and had no choice but to remain in Skaguay. Soon, proper businesses mingled indiscriminately with gambling houses and brothels. According to one writer, "if there had been any street lights they would all have been red."[2]

Annie Hall Strong, a proper lady and businesswomen, commented on the brave women who dared to travel through rough terrain, crashing seas, and below-freezing conditions to reach Skaguay in 1897. "There is no use trying to discourage them," Annie wrote. "Our wills are strong and courage unfailing." Strong wrote an advice column for women in the *Skaguay News*, commenting, "It takes strong, healthy, courageous women to stand the terrible hardships that must necessarily be endured." Although Strong addressed all women coming to Alaska, her words surely struck home with the ladies of the evening who ventured to Skaguay and set up shop. Although many prostitutes came to Skaguay of their own volition, others were kidnapped and forced into sexual slavery. Also, not all women came to Alaska with the intent of working in the skin trade. But many of them, tired of making a mere twenty-five cents a day as a hotel maid or frustrated at being unable to find respectable work at all, turned to prostitution as a more lucrative way to earn a living.[3]

Skaguay's first red-light district consisted chiefly of cribs that were hastily erected in the alleyways between Fourth and Seventh Streets.[4] Larger bordellos followed, including the Red Onion Saloon in 1897. Located in the center of town, the Red Onion had a unique procedure for selling sex. Customers at the downstairs bar were treated to a line of dolls, each carved to resemble a girl upstairs, on a shelf behind the bartender. When one of the women was occupied with a client, her doll was laid down until she was available again. The clients were free to choose one of the dolls remaining upright or wait for their favorite girl. The price was five dollars of gold for fifteen minutes. Each lady's room had a hole in the floor, with a tube leading down to the bar. After each transaction, the girl would drop the gold down the tube so that the bartender knew to set her respective doll upright.[5]

Within a year, Skaguay's population was guessed to be between eight thousand and ten thousand people. Construction began on the White Pass & Yukon Route Railroad as more and more traffic trailed into town.[6] Before and after the railroad was built, wealthier travelers could book passage on ships to reach Skaguay. One such vessel was the *Islander*, which was chock-full of wayward women. Pioneer E. C. Trelawney-Ansell described the boat as "a floating brothel where all sorts of wild, weird and bestial doings took place twenty-four hours a day." Although Trelawney-Ansell noted the presence of Northwest Mounted Police aboard, there also were plenty of "crooks" and "riff-raff," not to mention "whores, dance-hall girls," and their male counterparts. "The dining saloon and the so-called social hall stank of rye whisky and the cheap perfumes so favored by the 'ladies' and their awful pimps," Trelawney-Ansell recalled. "From the cabins occupied by these prostitutes could be heard all kinds of cries from them and their men, interspersed with the clinking of glasses and popping of corks."

Worst of all, "half-dressed—and often completely naked—women reeled about the passages, looking for lost cabins or for lavatories; laughing, screaming and talking in a drunken babble," Trelawney-Ansell wrote. In the dining room, the ladies "would dance obscene dances" as their pimps passed a hat around for tips. The money guaranteed easier passage and a means to find lodging when the ladies and their consorts arrived in Skaguay. When another steamer, the *Amur*, set sail for Skaguay, the captain forbade the fifty prostitutes aboard to ply their trade during passage. At least one woman, "Big Annie," made her discontent known. "We'll be in Skagway in little more than a week," a preacher (of all people) told Big Annie, "and once there you'll see that things will be a lot better for you and the other girls."[7]

To the respectable women aboard these ships, things could be downright uncomfortable when they encountered prostitutes on deck or in the hallways. There also was the danger of being lured into the brothels by the innocent-seeming promises by prostitutes and their pimps of a good-paying job once the ship arrived in Skaguay. It was Reverend John Alexander Sinclair, not a law official, who rescued two naive waitresses from Seattle who thought they would be hired as virtuous dancers upon their arrival.[8] Canada's 1892 "Criminal Code" created laws against "procuring women for unlawful carnal connection" with men, including making it unlawful "for parents or guardians to encourage the 'defilement' of their daughters or wards." But that, and similar laws in America, were extremely difficult to enforce in Alaska's Skaguay.[9]

By far, the most notorious character in Skaguay was Jefferson Randolph "Soapy" Smith, who had long reigned in Denver, Leadville, and other places of Colorado as a well-known "bunco artist." In 1895 Smith was invited by Joe Wolfe to set up his shill games at the entrance to the only known legal bullfight in America, at Gillette, Colorado. Smith took so much money off his victims that some of them could not afford the five-dollar admission fee to the bullfight.[10] When he arrived in Skaguay in 1897, Smith had brought with him "an unholy lot of footpads, thugs, ruffians, harlots and card sharps." He also opened his own saloon, promising a free first drink to lure customers inside.[11]

Smith initially invested in Clancy's Place, a music hall with club rooms. He may also have invested in another saloon and gambling hall known as The Klondike. But his pièce de résistance was his own place, Jeff Smith's Parlor, a nongaming saloon offering "choice wines and liquors."[12] Outside the saloon, however, Soapy and his associates bilked their way through the pocketbooks of as many suckers as they could. "I beg to state that I am no gambler," he declared in an 1894 article in Denver's *Rocky Mountain News*. "A gambler takes chances with his money, I don't." Indeed, it seemed as though Smith's ruses and rip-offs seldom required investing his own money. Once he charged people five dollars to send their telegraphs off to "anywhere in the world." The catch? There were no telegraph lines in Skaguay at the time.[13]

The telegraph stunt was among many scams Smith and his buddies used to dupe numerous men and women out of their money. The man was quite cheerful about his activities, carrying them out in a manner that, afterward, had his victims feeling they had only themselves to blame for falling for his schemes. Smith and his gang began exhibiting a power in Skaguay that mostly angered only rival gangs. But the murder of Smith's alleged mistress, prostitute Ella D. Wilson, put a sizable dent in his already tarnished reputation. Ella, an attractive mulatto, met her unfortunate end on May 28, 1898, at her house on Holly Street. She was found on her bed. "Around her neck a pillow-case had been drawn tightly, with the ends thrust in her mouth for a gag," reported the *Morning Oregonian*. "Her wrists and ankles were tied together with sheets. Over her head and face a pillow was pressed down, and death had evidently resulted from smothering." The writer of the article also believed that Ella had two thousand dollars, which was missing.[14] A coroner's jury was formed by US Marshal Taylor, but he neglected to complete the investigation.[15]

Enter Mattie Silks, famed madam of Denver, Colorado, who had opened her own bordello in Dawson City and was visiting Skaguay. In June, Mattie reported to the authorities in Seattle, Washington, that she was in her room at Skaguay's Occidental Hotel the night after Ella died. In the next room, Mattie clearly heard Marshal Taylor, Smith, and two men named Tanner (sometimes spelled Tener) and Bowers talking. The men were chatting about Ella's death while divvying up thirty-eight hundred dollars among themselves. Mattie gathered the money had been taken from Ella's house after Tanner and Bowers killed her "at the instigation and with the consent of Taylor and 'Soapy Smith.'" The madam's heart surely skipped a beat as she listened to the men plan a second attack—on Mattie herself. The frightened woman had then fled Skaguay for Seattle.[16]

When Mattie's story broke in the *Seattle Times* on June 4, it was initially met with doubt and acrimony. Mattie had known Smith in Denver and was well aware of his antics there. One theory is that Smith and his cohorts coordinated the conversation for Mattie's ears only, in order to scare her out of town and keep her from telling what she knew to others.[17] Whether or not the threat was real, Soapy Smith and Marshal Taylor each filed a libel suit against the *Seattle Times*, demanding twenty-five thousand dollars. The *Times* responded in its Independence Day issue and defended Mattie (who, as an astute and prominent madam, was not likely to voluntarily tell a whopper to authorities in any town, anywhere). In teasing tones, the *Times* further commented that the article "made 'Soapy' so sad that it will take $25,000 to brighten him up again" and challenged Smith to "prove that he had a reputation that was capable of being smirched that much."[18] The article had likely not yet reached Skaguay, where Smith had now formed his own volunteer Skaguay Military Company and proudly marched in the town's Fourth of July parade, even sharing a podium with Governor John Brady.[19]

Not everybody appreciated Smith's new military company, or his feigned heroism before the people of Skaguay. Three days later, nobody was really surprised to learn that Smith's gang had relieved one John Stewart of almost three thousand dollars in gold during a crooked poker game in a back alley. Alas, the mystery of who killed Ella Wilson might have been solved but for the killing of Soapy Smith himself on July 8. Smith had been warding off threats and arguing with various "factions against him" while holding court with libations at Jeff Smith's Parlor. Just before nine p.m. he received a note telling him he was urgently needed down at the wharf, where a big meeting was taking place in a warehouse. Smith duly headed that way with a rifle, but guard Frank Reid blocked his way into the meeting. In the ensuing scuffle, both men shot each other. Soapy died immediately; Reid died two weeks later. Ironically, Soap was buried in Skaguay's Gold Rush Cemetery within "just a few dozen feet" of Ella Wilson.[20]

Skaguay went on without Soapy Smith. The town's shady ladies went on too. "Paradise Alley" near Broadway and Seventh Street now offered a bevy of soiled doves from which to choose. But changes were coming as the gold rush slowed; the post office changed the spelling of the name to Skagway, and in about 1899 the town's cribs and brothels were relocated by officials to Seventh Street. Next, in 1900, Skagway incorporated as a city with more than three thousand residents. But there were still around seventy bars and brothels in town.[21]

Two known women of the demimonde were Rose Arnold and Ruth Brown, who showed up in town shortly after the census was taken. The women, who were African American, rightfully expected to make good money in Skagway. Their focus was Company L, a regiment of Buffalo Soldiers who had been assigned to northern Lynn Canal since 1899. Certain white prostitutes of Skagway were known to turn away black customers, a boon to Rose and Ruth. The women established their own brothel at the east end of Sixth Avenue next door to Company L's barracks and enjoyed a steady flow of business for two years. When the soldiers were sent elsewhere in 1902, however, the ladies suffered a substantial loss of income. For one thing, they were now just two of hundreds of prostitutes plying their trade in Skagway. For another, their brothel was now far from Paradise Alley, their only neighbors being a group of Peniel Missionaries.[22]

The missionaries' feelings toward prostitution echoed those of the authorities, who now were arresting prostitutes in the hopes the women would leave Skagway altogether. Over the next three years, Magistrate Josiah Tanner would launch a campaign to sweep Skagway clean of its soiled doves. As a matter of course, prostitutes of Skagway were required to pay twenty-five dollars, plus court costs, each quarter. Ruth and Rose duly paid the required fees until January 25, 1905, when the women decided to try a new tactic: Both pleaded not guilty to "being an inmate of a house of ill-repute." Surprisingly, Rose was acquitted the next day as Ruth continued fighting the charge of "keeping a house of ill repute in connection with Rose Arnold." She was found guilty on January 29 and paid her twenty-five dollars to the court. Both girls, however, had had enough and left town for Juneau.[23]

Skagway was not finished with its soiled doves. Between 1908 and 1910, officials worked to refurbish the downtown area around the White Pass & Yukon Railroad line. In the way were the detested brothels, which were commanded to either move or close. Accordingly, larger places like the Red Onion Saloon and The Cottage literally moved their buildings. Other places closed their doors altogether, their proprietresses heading out for less-restrictive pastures. Next, in 1915, the Alaska Woman's Temperance Union met in Skagway and penned the "Alaska Bone Dry Act," encouraging the state to outlaw liquor. The ploy worked, and in 1918 Skagway's saloons closed up too.[24]

Around this time, businessman Martin Itjen began recognizing Skagway's colorful history as a means of attracting tourists to town. Itjen started a taxi and coal delivery business and acquired the old Jeff Smith's Parlor building to open a museum. By 1924 visitors were flocking to Skagway. Ten years later, Itjen thought to capitalize on the town's bawdy history by successfully inviting Mae West, siren of the big screen, to come for a visit.[25] Skagway's successful tourism trade continued. Today Skagway remains a premier tourist destination during the summer months, complete with a few surviving brothels serving as museums and quaint bed-and-breakfasts.

CHAPTER 20

—•◆•—

Dolly Arthur,
the "Sporting Lady" of Ketchikan

"I never could stand a whore!" exclaimed Dolly Arthur, Ketchikan's last surviving prostitute. Indeed, to Dolly, such women were "tasteless and crude." Prostitutes of her own caliber, she opined, were of a higher class. For that reason, Dolly always called herself a "sporting woman"— never a "whore." And although other women of the night worked in pairs, Dolly found working alone to be much easier, and a better way to maintain her freedom and control over her own life and affairs.[1]

Dolly was christened Thelma Dorotha Copeland when she was born on October 5, 1888, to James and Ida Copeland. Just where her birth occurred is up for speculation, but it was somewhere in the Northwest. Some historians say she was born near McCall, Idaho. More-official documentation gives her birthplace as Madison County, Montana. At different times, Dolly herself claimed to have been born both in Clear Creek, Montana, and in Idaho. All that is known for sure is that her parents married in Idaho in 1877 and were still there during the 1880 census, eight years before Dolly came along. But the family moved around so much and was in so much turmoil that perhaps even Dolly herself had no idea where she first came into this world.[2]

Dolly was only five years old when James Copeland left his family (presumably to go prospecting, since that was his later profession) and never came back. Ida Copeland would later claim that James "without cause left and deserted" her and her four children: Willie, Elizabeth, James Jr., and Thelma, who already was affectionately known as Dolly. Ida left the three older children with her mother, Mrs. L. J. Kessler, but for some reason kept Dolly with her. Mother and daughter began traveling extensively as Ida looked for gainful employment. By June 1896 they lived in Dillon, Montana, then Butte. They next moved to an unknown location in Gallatin County, where they remained until May 5, 1897. The twosome had relocated again, to Park County, when Ida finally filed for divorce from James on August 14.[3]

Ida stated that her husband had provided no support to the family. Furthermore, the woman was so poor that she could not even pay court costs for the divorce. The court sided with her and tried to summon James through the *Bozeman Chronicle*. He never answered, and Ida got her divorce. The last anyone knew of James Copeland, he was still toiling as a prospector in Washington County, Idaho, in 1900 and died in 1901. In 1900 Ida remarried, to Wellman Blanchard. Her married life may have been less than ideal; in the 1910 Montana census, Ida stated she had given birth to six children, but only three still lived.[4]

Dolly, meanwhile, apparently had had enough with her unhappy homelife. In about 1901, at the age of thirteen, she set out on her own. For the next several years she spent time in Montana and also Vancouver, British Columbia, where she worked as a waitress.[5] One day, Dolly had an epiphany. "By the time I was 18 or 19," she said, "I realized that I could make a lot more money from the attention of men than I could waiting on tables."[6] Dolly's first foray into making money "from the attention of men" was not by working as a prostitute; rather, she decided to try marriage first. On July 1, 1907, she married Josef Krausz in far-off Des Moines, Iowa. When the union fizzled, she apparently made her way back west where she married again, to John Peshak, in 1908. The couple's marriage certificate verifies they both lived in Spokane and

Dolly Arthur's bedroom in Ketchikan remains much the way it was when she still lived in her house.

Courtesy Jan MacKell Collins

were united at the M. E. Church in Davenport, Washington. The newlyweds were still together as of the 1910 census, renting an apartment in Tacoma. John worked as a plasterer. A lodger, sixty-five-year-old Albert Kendall, lived with the couple.[7] But that marriage failed too. Historians say that Dolly had an "unhappy love affair in Vancouver," which was perhaps really one or both of her marriages.[8]

Either way, Dolly took to the road once more. She is believed to have worked as a prostitute in Seattle and Spokane, Washington, during 1914 before moving to Ketchikan. The sleepy fishing village had opened its first cannery in 1886, and the post office opened in 1892. Mining endeavors during the 1890s brought more men to the blossoming town.[9] It was probably around the time that Ketchikan was incorporated, in 1900, that the city was referred to as "Uncle Sam's Wickedest City." When the red-light ladies who found a niche among the fishermen and miners became too noticeable in 1903, Ketchikan's city council voted to move them to one central area on Creek Street.[10]

Upon her arrival, Dolly observed fourteen brothels, but they were so cramped together that she decided to try Petersburg, some 150 miles north, instead. In Petersburg, Dolly secured employment with "Black Mary" Thomas, who was running a dance-hall.[11] Mary was quite a character, and a large one at that. They say that during a fire in Petersburg, the fire department feared the creek was so low that there was not enough water to pump and extinguish the flames. Mary heard about it and "shed her clothes on the spot and sat in the creek, damming it so that firefighters could extinguish the blaze."[12]

When Black Mary relocated to Ketchikan and bought the Star Dance Hall in 1917, Dolly apparently came with her. The Star was near the footbridge used to access Creek Street, while a clandestine footpath dubbed "Married Man's Trail" skirted the bushes behind the brothels. Because a state law decreed that more than two "female boarders" in a house constituted a brothel, most of Ketchikan's good time girls tended to work solo or in pairs. The Star, however, dared to defy the law, with two stories and twelve bedrooms. The place was fine enough; a five-pointed star of dark wood was inlaid on the dance floor. Outside, a star-shaped light perched on the east gable for all to see at night.[13]

Black Mary bought the Star from madam Mattie Wilkes for a whopping four thousand dollars. It was a hefty price, even for 1917, but it came with a good clientele and was the most popular brothel on Creek Street. Mary was already experienced in running a brothel. Her girls called her "Mama," and she was known for treating them well. Like most madams, Mary split the ladies' fees with them. She invested her money in real estate and was always willing to help those in need. Dolly watched and learned as she worked her way up at the Star. When the state passed the Bone Dry Law, which outlawed alcohol in 1917, Mary and others simply began bootlegging. In spite of the occasional raid, as well as "publicly embarrassing rides to the police station in the open benches" of the paddy wagon, the ladies were able to do quite well.[14]

By 1919 Dolly had saved enough money to build her own house. For reasons unknown, the house proved unsatisfactory, so Dolly purchased a different building at 24 Creek Street. The new house had formerly been owned by a schoolteacher, who had turned briefly to prostitution before going mad. Dolly was now known as Dolly Arthur. Notably, although other women paired up and shared a common brothel, Dolly always preferred to work alone. She had little trouble drawing business, as Creek Street was alive with activity every night. Customers could saunter down the boardwalk in front of the bordellos, find a drink, dance, and pick from their choice of scantily-clad women making shadows behind the silhouetted curtains of their parlors. Prostitution was wide open and legal, the only catch being that all women were required to register with the police.[15]

Dolly's little brothel also constituted her home. When author June Allen interviewed Dolly in 1972, she remembered that the first floor had "what had been the original first floor bedroom" and a simply furnished living room. The kitchen was small and quaint. A hallway revealed a "tiny" restroom, as well as a "thick, padlocked drawer in which [Dolly] kept her money." Allen guessed that when it was built, the second floor was meant to be a second, separate two-room apartment, but the dividing wall had since been torn down and the whole floor converted to Dolly's bedroom. Layers of flowered wallpaper from years gone by covered the walls, and the single small closet included a hidden cupboard for keeping illegal hooch. When Allen saw the place, Dolly's "bedroom furniture was heavy and no doubt elegant in its era—a gift from a gentlemen in Petersburg, she said."[16]

Allen's observations are likely representative of the way other brothels of Ketchikan appeared. There were no fancy parlor houses here; rather, simply furnished bordellos doubled as homes for the women.

They were quaint, cute and stylish, plainly and practically furnished for a working-class population. The men who purchased services in these places were rugged and dressed in "diesel-and-fish-scented wool gear, and were shod in boots well flecked with fish scales." The fabled millionaire miners and madams sporting expensive furs and jewelry of other places in the Pacific Northwest had no place in Ketchikan. Allen noticed the presence of linoleum floors at Dolly's, which likely covered the original hardwood boards with washable rugs, not carpet, to weather snowy winters, damp summers, and the accompanying slush and mud that surely made its way into the house.[17] Like other towns, Ketchikan's officials occasionally cracked down on and even closed their bawdy houses, and were probably more likely to do so after some crime or another had occurred. In time, the houses would reopen and continue business as usual. During 1920 there were twenty-one brothels and thirty-one women on Creek Street. Dolly was one of them.

When national prohibition began in 1920, everyone, it seemed, jumped on the bootleg bandwagon.[18] Everyone knew that illegal hooch could be found on Creek Street. Occasional busts were made; in 1923 prostitute Thelma Baker was arrested in a raid. A newspaper identified as the *Chronicle Reporter* had great fun reporting the incident on December 23. "Percolator Is Now for Sale at Cost," read the headline, with a tongue-in-cheek article: "For Sale: One percolator. As the owner is going out of business this percolator will be sacrificed at just what it has cost the owner—$257.50. Thelma Baker, she of the percolated Rhoderic Dhu [sic] and erstwhile proprietress of the Bungalow, where Deputy Marshal Handy accidentally ran across a percolator filled with whiskey and a cold bottle of beer for the morning, appeared before the U.S. Commissioner yesterday afternoon and pleaded guilty to a violation of the Alaska Bone Dry Law. She was fined $250.00. She liquidated."[19]

Unabashed, Thelma purchased Black Mary's Star Dance Hall in 1924. She was thirty-two years old, having come from Washington State, where she was born Linda Ruth McCowan in 1892. Thelma's other pseudonym was Linda Graham, and she had been working in Ketchikan for some time before she bought the Star. In time, the dance-hall became known simply as "Thelma's Place."[20] Mary, meanwhile, retired. On May 9, 1925, the *Ketchikan Chronicle* reported that Mary had died of heart failure while sitting in her chair at her home in a suburb known as Newtown. Dolly Arthur would remember the story differently, recalling that "it was a strangely pink morning" when Mary was found. She was, as the newspaper said, sitting in her chair. But Dolly said Mary was in a house on Barney Way, not in Newtown, and also revealed that the woman was counting a roll of bills in her lap when she passed. When she told the story many years later, tears came to Dolly's eyes as she remembered the woman who had given her a job and remained her friend.[21]

Thelma's Place was not the only hopping joint on Creek Street during the 1920s. By 1925 Ketchikan's red-light district was so well known that James Wickersham dubbed it "Alaska's Tenderloin" and, more important to the girls of the row, "the Barbary Coast of the North."[22] Even so, some women, like Dolly, had paramours or special friends who provided protection and company. Historians name a longshoreman identified only as "Lefty" who lived with Dolly "on and off over a period of 26 years." Lefty might have been George Christenson, a Norwegian fisherman who was identified as living at Dolly's during the 1930 census. Whoever he really was, Lefty was described as "a charming rake who flitted about town surrounded by a coterie of admiring women." Although the two had the occasional spat, Dolly gave Lefty the money to settle his debts and seemed to overlook his indiscretions. "He fooled around," she allegedly acknowledged, "but he always came back." If nothing else, Dolly "genuinely liked Lefty, and considered him a good buddy."[23]

Men like Lefty were convenient during the 1930s especially, as more and more proper folk looked down their noses at Creek Street. But the

Great Depression was on, and the girls of the row not only spent their hard-earned cash in town but also attracted hundreds of fishing fleets to town. The men might have come anyway, seeing as Ketchikan was the "Canned Salmon Capital of the World," but they also bought supplies and paid for repairs to their boats before heading to Creek Street. Unfortunately, Ketchikan was not safe from the modern world, where drugs, violence, and crime were becoming more common. These maladies eventually made their way to the city, complete with the occasional stabbing "and a body or two found floating at the mouth of the creek."[24]

Dolly was still working in 1940. The census finds her living in her Creek Street house, with no occupation listed. With her, however, was a thirty-nine-year-old truck driver named Horace Scholls, who also might have been the mysterious Lefty. Scholls, however, was a good thirteen years younger than Dolly and was possibly one of her customers. A year later, Dolly's mother, Ida Blanchard, died in Portland, Oregon. But Dolly had abandoned her new family back when she really was just a child, and it is unknown whether she attended the funeral. Also unknown is how she occupied her time during World War II, when the girls of Creek Street were officially off-limits to everyone, including soldiers who might wander into town. After the war, however, thirty-three brothels opened back up for business. During this time, the houses were numbered in a neat little row—the exception being unlucky number thirteen, which was simply known as "The End."[25]

The reopening of Creek Street might have pleased the red-light ladies and their customers, but not the respectable citizens of the town. At last, in 1953 or 1954, a federal grand jury tried and rendered a guilty verdict against the "corrupt" police department and city officials for being "tolerant" of the Creek Street brothels. The houses were closed for good, and twenty-two women found themselves unemployed. Most of the ladies of Creek Street moved on, their former bordellos rented out to respectable folks when possible. Other women, including Dolly Arthur,

Annie Watkins, and Thelma Baker, stayed put and simply stopped doing business. Annie died in January 1966. Then, on August 7, 1972, smoke was spotted on the roof of Thelma's Place. When firemen broke into the building, they discovered that Thelma had apparently tried to start a fire in her oil stove and caught herself on fire. Both Thelma and her little black dog were killed. The body was taken to Anchorage and cremated, while a memorial service was held for her in Ketchikan.[26]

That same year, June Allen had the honor of meeting and interviewing Dolly Arthur, Ketchikan's last surviving prostitute. Allen's husband, John Grainger, had been bringing Dolly her groceries, including "a continuous supply of hot chocolate mix," for some time. Still, Allen was shocked at "the deplorable condition of an elderly, ill and almost totally blind woman living alone." Dolly, she said, "had to climb up her stairs on her hands and knees" and apparently spent much of her time in her room. The former bedroom on the first floor contained Dolly's "beautiful needlework," her best dishes, and "other treasures." The living room "was furnished simply—except for one beaded lampshade—and long-unused."

Allen was especially excited to meet Dolly, whom others said had gained enough weight in her old age to be nicknamed "Big Dolly." Upon meeting her, however, Allen observed that "she did not look like a Big Dolly to me. She looked small, a white-haired woman wearing what would have been called a housedress in her day. . . . She lay, propped on her pillows, and waited for the questions to start. She looked lonely, and she was." There was a time, Allen said, that Dolly had kept a series of little dogs that she loved dearly. The animals were long gone, but "remained in a sense. The perimeter of every room in the house was thick with a wide band of doghair fluff, and the smell of their urine hung over each room." After chatting with Dolly and touring her home, Allen and Grainger said their goodbyes. Dolly, Allen said, pulled a string of keys from the neck of her dress. "If you feel like a visit," she told the couple, "just call up from down on the boardwalk and I'll throw the keys out the window down to you!"[27]

A year and a half after June Allen met Dolly, the elderly woman was taken to a nursing home. When she died in July 1975, her last words were quite prophetic. "I'm going a long trip," she said.[28] Several newspapers published her obituary, and she received a proper burial in Ketchikan's Bayview Cemetery.[29] As for her home, Dolly's House is now a premier brothel museum in Ketchikan. Other Creek Street bordellos survive, but Dolly's remains untouched in the way of her furnishings, decor, and personal belongings. It is quite a tribute to the lady who took Ketchikan by storm—and survived.

CHAPTER 21

Zula Swanson,
"Alaska's Richest Black"

T he story of Zula Swanson is unique, for many reasons. Born into blatant racism at Jackson Gap, Alabama, in 1891, Zula managed to shed the customary conditions doled out to African Americans of the turn of the last century. Relegated to labor as a plantation worker, she soon became "disgusted" with the United States' treatment of her race and decided she wanted something far better. And in a time when most blacks were hopelessly ensconced in a life with little future, Zula got it.[1]

Much of Zula's early life is relatively unknown. She identified her parents as Gilbert and Matilda Swanson, but virtually nothing is known about the couple or any other children they may have had.[2] What is known for sure is that by 1918, Zula had somehow made her way to Oregon. There she married John Lowe, a chauffeur she presumably met in her new hometown of Portland. The couple was already living together; John worked as a mechanic and Zula was a dressmaker. They married at the Lutheran church in Vancouver, Washington.

The Lowes were still in Portland as of the 1920 census, and John continued working as a chauffeur. By 1923 John was working at the Rose City Apartments. But the couple moved around a lot, and the 1924 directory does not indicate that either John or Zula was employed. The couple also parted ways sometime afterward. One source verifies that

Zula had entered the prostitution industry after her "pimp" had been sent to jail in Washington for bootlegging in about 1927. As for Zula, she had just "narrowly escaped drunk-driving charges in Washington involving the death of another woman."[3]

Zula herself later said she moved to Anchorage in 1929. She was off by a year, for the 1930 census documents her as divorced and still living in Portland, where she was employed as a housekeeper for a private family. Most historians agree that Zula was at some point involved in prostitution in Oregon and continued in the same profession when she reached Anchorage. At the time, there were only about three thousand people in Anchorage, mostly fishermen and prospectors.[4] The large male population was ripe for a brothel or two, and there was little doubt that Zula intended to make money at her profession. She did encounter at least some prejudice in Anchorage, but it didn't seem to bother her much. "There's prejudice I don't care where you go," she once said.[5]

Upon her arrival in Anchorage, or soon after, Zula managed to save two thousand dollars. She used the money to purchase a burned-out building and a piece of land "along the town's one street." She also was able to rebuild the structure into a "rooming house," a polite euphemism in this case for a brothel.[6] "Anchorage wasn't nothing then," she said. "But the land is flat and you got the Cook Inlet. I could see it was going to be something." Once her first property was up and running, Zula was able to purchase other lots for as little as seven hundred dollars.[7] One of her businesses was the Rendezvous Bar, located "in the old red-light district."[8]

Zula's financial affairs were greatly assisted by her love affair with one of the "most respected financiers" in Anchorage. She invested wisely and "soon owned more property than any other woman in town." Her relationship with the unidentified man, and her wealth, quickly made her one of the most powerful people in Anchorage.[9] By 1940 she owned her own home, and the census that year records her as sharing it with one Betty Parrish. Zula was now forty-nine years old; Betty was forty-three. The women's ages are curious, since they were pretty much too old to be working as prostitutes. But like so many things with Zula, the details of her business in the prostitution industry remain a secret, even today. Likewise, the shady ladies of Anchorage remain equally mysterious; one source only briefly mentions madam Gladys Happybottom, who ran a place called the House of Joy.[10]

By the time Zula's financial-wizard lover died in the 1950s, the woman was so wealthy and powerful that she was able to forge on without him. She was now highly respected in Anchorage, not because of her profession but rather because she was a civic-minded participant of her community. She was a card-carrying member of the Northern Lights Civic and Social Club and Daughters of the Elks. She also helped organize the Anchorage Chapter of the National Association for the Advancement of Colored People (NAACP). Her fine reputation was tarnished but one time, when she put up a twenty-thousand-dollar bond for one Edgar Lewis, who had been arrested on a narcotics charge in 1951. Lewis fled, but was arrested in Chicago in 1953 and sentenced to seventeen years in prison. In the end, however, Zula somehow got her money back.[11]

Nobody paid much attention to the Lewis case, but plenty of people were paying attention to Zula as she continued amassing a fortune. In 1953 *Color* magazine published an article about her and politely reported that Zula "operated a hotel." It was commonly known in Anchorage, however, that "a variety of services, in keeping with the Alaskan tradition, were available at the hotel."[12] Zula appears to have stopped having any direct relation to her hotel and what went on there by about 1960, when she had leased the Rendezvous Bar to a white couple and visited the place only on occasion.[13] It may have been around that time that Zula purchased "a boarding house and some property on the banks of Goose Lake," a small but scenic lake which was a favored swimming spot among locals.[14]

In about 1962 Zula sold her original rooming house, located on a prominent corner downtown, to J. C. Penney. The selling price is presumed to have been more than the 250,000 dollars she was once offered for the property.[15] She was living in her hundred-thousand-dollar home on Goose Lake in 1969 when another magazine, *Ebony*, interviewed her. The article called her "Alaska's Richest Black." It was true; Zula now owned roughly twenty properties. In spite of her wealth, it was noted that Zula lived frugally and also suffered from arthritis. Her advice to others was simply to "come up here and work hard. The money will come dribbling in and soon ya won't have to work so hard." One "white sourdough" who knew Zula commented, "She's did a lot for this country around here. She put her money back out to work to give other people jobs. Everybody just loves her here."[16]

In 1971, at the ripe age of eighty years, Zula married again. This time her chosen mate was William "Bill" Wester, a man decades younger than she.[17] Although she officially retired, Zula and Bill continued investing in Anchorage properties. Zula also remained active in organizations like the NAACP. Tarea Pittman, the organization's West Coast regional director in 1961, said in a 1972 interview that Zula was still a stockholder in the Bank of Alaska, also that she had been able to overcome prejudices that enabled her to buy "property where other black people did not." Pittman also commented that Zula's home at Goose Lake "is, of course, a very beautiful place overlooking a lake. And, you know, she has fabulous things."[18]

In January 1973 the Westers filed a million-dollar lawsuit against six people, including State Representative Tom Fink. Also named in the suit were six businesses, including a real estate agency, an insurance company, a bank, and a trust company. At issue were the Terrace Apartments, which the Westers had bought with the understanding that the property was bringing in between twelve hundred and two thousand dollars in monthly revenues. In reality, the apartments were actually losing between two thousand and thirty-five hundred dollars per month.[19] The outcome of the suit remains unknown, if only because Zula died just a few weeks later. Her obituary in the *Fairbanks Daily News-Miner* couldn't resist pointing out that "Zula Swanson Webster [sic], reputed to have been the city's leading madam during the 1930s, is dead at the age of 81." The story only merited page-two coverage, although Zula's real estate holdings alone were worth half a million dollars.[20]

Zula was buried in Angeles Memorial Park in Anchorage. Her Rendezvous Bar had been torn down long before her death.[21] Bill Wester remained at the Goose Lake house through at least 1975, when a group of tourists were treated to "a picnic at the home and grounds of Bill Wester."[22] The house eventually burned.[23] What became of Wester also remains a mystery, but Anchorage does occasionally remember Zula—a woman who defied the odds against her to reign as the queen madam of Anchorage.

NOTES

INTRODUCTION

1 Tom Nash and Twilo Scofield, *The Well-Traveled Casket: A Collection of Oregon Folklife* (Salt Lake City, UT: University of Utah Press, 1992), 59.

2 Alaska.org.

3 "Oregon" and "Washington," wikipedia.com; Pierre Berton, *The Klondike Fever: The Life and Death of the Last Great Gold Rush* (New York: Carroll & Graf Publishers, Inc., 1997), 5.

4 Walter O'Meara, *Daughters of the Country: The Women of the Fur Traders and Mountain Men* (New York: Harcourt, Brace & World, Inc., 1968), 153, 159.

5 Ibid, 153–54, 170.

6 Ibid, 150.

7 Volney Steele, MD, *Bleed, Blister and Purge: A History of Medicine on the American Frontier* (Missoula, MT: Mountain Press Publishing Company, 2005), 58.

8 O'Meara, *Daughters of the Country*, 159.

9 Steele, *Bleed, Blister and Purge*, 59–60.

10 Lambert Florin, *Oregon Ghost Towns* (Seattle, WA: Superior Publishing Company, 1970), 28.

11 *Trails End*, December–January 1998, 21.

12 Alexy Simmons, "Red Light Ladies: Settlement Patterns and Material Culture on the Mining Frontier," *Anthropology Northwest* (Corvallis, OR: Department of Anthropology, Oregon State University, Number 4, 1989), 14.

13 Lawrence Powell, "Early California Society," *Westways*, August 1965, 17.

CHAPTER 1

1 Arthur R. Kruckeberg, *The Natural History of Puget Sound Country* (Seattle, WA: University of Washington Press, 1991), 427–28; Sylvia Van Kirk, "The Role of Native Women in the Creation of Fur Trade Society in Western Canada, 1670–1830," Karen J. Blair, ed., *Women in Pacific Northwest History* (Seattle, WA: University of Washington Press, 1998).

2 O'Meara, *Daughters of the Country*, 151; Leslie Gourse, *Native American Courtship and Marriage* (Summertown, TN: Native Voices Book Publishing Company, 2005), 70; Colin G. Calloway, "Venereal Disease and the Lewis and Clark Expedition (review)," *Journal of Interdisciplinary History 38*, no. 2, 2007, 297–98, https://muse .jhu.edu, accessed November 18, 2018.

3 Van Kirk, "The Role of Native Women"; Stewart Holbrook, *Wildmen, Wobblies & Whistle Punks*: Stewart Holbrooks Lowbrow Northwest, edited by Brian Booth Corvalis, OR: Oregon State University Press, 1992, 83.

4 Holbrook, *Wildmen, Wobblies & Whistle Punks*, 83–84.

5 Gary Meier and Gloria Meier, *Those Naughty Ladies of the Old Northwest*, Bend, OR: Maverick Publications, 1990, 108.

6 Lambert Florin, *Ghost Town Trails: Third in the Western Ghost Town Series* (Seattle, WA: Superior Publishing Company, 1963), 53–54.

7 Ibid., 50–51.

8 Jeremy Agnew, *Brides of the Multitude: Prostitution in the Old West* (Lake City, CO: Western Reflections Publishing Company, 2008), 216; Donald C. Miller, *Ghost Towns of Washington and Oregon* (Boulder, CO: Pruitt Publishing, 1977), 9.

9 Florin, *Ghost Town Trails*, 59; Miller, *Ghost Towns of Washington and Oregon*, 46; Loretta Louis, "Ruby City: The Life and Death of a Mining Town," June 1963, Ghosttown USA, http://www.ghosttownsusa.com/ruby2.htm, accessed November 12, 2018; Meier and Meier, *Those Naughty Ladies of the Old Northwest*, 5–7.

10 Louis, "Ruby City: The Life and Death of a Mining Town."

11 Ibid.

12 Florin, *Ghost Town Trails*, 59; Miller, *Ghost Towns of Washington and Oregon*, 46.

13 Louis, "Ruby City: The Life and Death of a Mining Town."

14 David L. Chapman, "Everything Rolled Downhill: A Brief History of the Okanogan County Courthouse," *Columbia*, Winter 1999, 13:4, http://www.wshs.org/wshs/columbia/articles/0499-a1.htm, accessed September 26, 2006; Louis, "Ruby City: The Life and Death of a Mining Town"; Florin, *Ghost Town Trails*, 59; Miller, *Ghost Towns of Washington and Oregon*, 46.

15 Meier and Meier, *Those Naughty Ladies of the Old Northwest*, 29.

16 Charles P. LeWarne, "The Anarchist Colony at Home, Washington 1901–1902," *Journal of the Southwest*, vol. 14, Summer 1972, 155–68.

17 Holbrook, *Wildmen, Wobblies & Whistle Punks*, 99–100, 103; Lambert Florin, *Western Ghost Town Shadows, Fourth in the Western Ghost Town Series* (Seattle, WA: Superior Publishing Company, 1964), 147.

18 Ibid., 101, 103–4, 105–6.

19 Justin Wadland, *Trying Home: The Rise and Fall of an Anarchist Utopia on Puget Sound* (Corvallis, OR: Oregon State University Press, 2014), 148; Holbrook, *Wildmen, Wobblies & Whistle Punks*, 109–10; "Home, Washington," wikipedia.com.

20 Meier and Meier, *Those Naughty Ladies of the Old Northwest*, 11, 50–53.

21 *Morning Leader* (Port Townsend), March 4, 1904, 4, and August 23, 1904, 4.

22 *Morning Leader*, August 4, 1904, September 23, 1904, 4, October 8, 1904, 4, December 23, 1904, 2, and December 30, 1904, 4; *Daily Leader* (Port Townsend), April 17, 1906, 4:3.

23 Laura Bell McDaniel died in January 1918. Estate of Laura Bell McDaniel, Probate File #M311, El Paso County Courthouse, Colorado Springs, CO; Jan MacKell, *Brothels, Bordellos and Bad Girls: Prostitution in Colorado 1860–1930* (Albuquerque, NM: University of New Mexico Press, 2004), 133; "Columbia River Station," Tacoma Public Library, http://cdm17061.contentdm.oclc.org/cdm/singleitem/collection/p17061coll4/id/1541/rec/, accessed November 12, 2018.

24 Linda Carlson, *Company Towns of the Pacific Northwest* (Seattle, WA; University of Washington Press, 2003), 189.

25 Ibid., 98.

26 Ron Strickland, *"Whistlepunks & Geoducs: Oral Histories from the Pacific Northwest"* (New York: Paragon House, 1990), 29.

27 Ibid., 134–35.

28 Ibid.

29 Ibid.,136.

CHAPTER 2

1 Anne Seagraves, *Soiled Doves: Prostitution in the Early West* (Hayden, ID: Wesanne Publications, 1994), 93–94; Mary Ann Boyer, "Hochalter Family Tree," Ancestry.com; "Conklin, Mary Ann (1821–1973) aka Mother Damnable," Essay 1934, HistoryLink .org, accessed July 30, 2006.

2 "Conklin, Mary Ann (1821–1973) aka Mother Damnable."

3 Seagraves, *Soiled Doves*, 93–94.

4 "A Red Light History of Seattle," *Seattle Met*, February 2010, https://www.seattlemet .com/articles/2010/1/29/red-light-history-0210, accessed June 11, 2018; Seagraves, *Soiled Doves*, 93–94; "Conklin, Mary Ann (1821–1973) aka Mother Damnable."

5 Seagraves, *Soiled Doves*, 93–94; "Conklin, Mary Ann (1821–1973) aka Mother Damnable."

6 "Group pays homage to Seattle foremother," Associated Press, SpokesmanReview .com, accessed July 31, 2006.

7 "Conklin, Mary Ann (1821–1973) aka Mother Damnable."

8 "A Red Light History of Seattle"; Agnew, *Brides of the Multitude*, 213.

9 Ibid.; William C. Speidel, *Sons of the Profits, or, There's No Business Like Grow Business: The Seattle Story 1851–1901* (Seattle, WA: Nettle Creek Publishing Company, 1967), 113.

10 Speidel, *Sons of the Profits,* 114; Christopher T. Bayley, *Seattle Justice: The Rise and Fall of the Police Payoff System in Seattle* (Seattle, WA: Sasquatch Books, 2015), 2; Agnew, *Brides of the Multitude*, 213–14.

11 Speidel, *Sons of the Profits,* 116–23, 130.

12 Meier and Meier, *Those Naughty Ladies of the Old Northwest,* 110–11; Bayley, *Seattle Justice,* 3.

13 "The decision was repealed in 1887. Washington Secretary of State, "Voting Rights for Women, Women's Suffrage", https://www.sos.wa.gov/elections/timeline/suffrage.htm, accessed July 28, 2019.

14 Meier and Meier, *Those Naughty Ladies of the Old Northwest,* 66–67.

15 Ibid., 67; "A Red Light History of Seattle."

16 Meier and Meier, *Those Naughty Ladies of the Old Northwest,* 111–14.

17 Ibid., 17–18; Agnew, *Brides of the Multitude,* 215; Bayley, *Seattle Justice,* 5.

18 Meier and Meier, *Those Naughty Ladies of the Old Northwest,* 22–23.

19 Bayley, *Seattle Justice,* 3; Agnew, *Brides of the Multitude,* 215; Meier and Meier, *Those Naughty Ladies of the Old Northwest,* 117–18.

20 Meier and Meier, *Those Naughty Ladies of the Old Northwest,* 6, 30–31, 82–83, 116.

21 "A Red Light History of Seattle"; "Washington State carries out its first execution on May 6, 1904," Essay 5476, HistoryLink.org, http://www.historylink.org/essays/output.cfm?file_id=5476, accessed May 14, 2018.

22 Strickland, *Whistlepunks & Geoducs,* 13; Seagraves, *Soiled Doves,* 92.

23 Seagraves, *Soiled Doves,* 92; Seattle City directories for 1904, 1905, 1907, 1908, "U.S. City Directories 1822–1995," Ancestry.com; *Thirteenth Census of the United States, 1910.*

24 Meier and Meier, *Those Naughty Ladies of the Old Northwest,* 5, 33, 75–76; *Thirteenth Census of the United States, 1910* (NARA microfilm publication). T9, 1, 198

25 "A Red Light History of Seattle"; Jay Moynahan, *Forty Fallen Women: Western Doves and Madams, 1885–1920* (Spokane, WA: Chickadee Publishing, 2008), 44–46.

26 "A Red Light History of Seattle"; Meier and Meier, *Those Naughty Ladies of the Old Northwest,* 120; "Gill, Hiram C. (1866–1919)," Essay 2755, HistoryLink.org, http://www.historylink.org/essays/output.cfm?file_id=2755, accessed July 30, 2006.

27 "Gill, Hiram C. (1866–1919)"; "B-50 Bomber crashes into the Lester Apartments near Boeing Field, killing 11, on August 13, 1951," Essay 3969, HistoryLink.org, http://www.historylink.org/essays/output.cfm?file_id=3969; Meier and Meier, *Those Naughty Ladies of the Old Northwest,* 118, 120–122; Bayley, *Seattle Justice,* 7.

28 Strickland, *Whistlepunks & Geoducs,* 13; "Gill, Hiram C. (1866–1919)"; "A Red Light History of Seattle."

29 Bayley, *Seattle Justice,* 9–10.

30 "West Seattle Memories Part 7: Businesses," Essay 3499, HistoryLink.org, http://www.historylink.org/essays/output.cfm?file_i=3499, accessed July 30, 2006.

31 Bayley, *Seattle Justice,* 12–14, 31.

CHAPTER 3

1 Moynahan, *Forty Fallen Women*, 33; Dorothea Georgine Eile Ohben, "Ohben Family Tree," Ancestry.com; "A Red Light History of Seattle."

2 Meier and Meier, *Those Naughty Ladies of the Old Northwest*, 56–58.

3 Ibid., 58–59.

4 Lou Graham, "Washington, Wills and Probate Records, 1851–1970," Ancestry.com; Meier and Meier, *Those Naughty Ladies of the Old Northwest*, 60.

5 Meier and Meier, *Those Naughty Ladies of the Old Northwest*, 60.

6 *Washington Territorial Census Rolls, 1857–1892* (Olympia, WA: Washington State Archives), M1, 20 rolls; *Post-Intelligencer* (Seattle), July 21, 1889, 8:6, and August 16, 1889, 4:6.

7 *Post-Intelligencer*, January 1, 1890, 29:2; Meier and Meier, *Those Naughty Ladies of the Old Northwest*, 61, 63.

8 *Post-Intelligencer*, June 7, 1890, 8:4, November 1, 1890, 8:2, January 13, 1891, 5:2, July 21, 1891, January 14, 1892, 5:2, April 13, 1892, 8:5, December 16, 1892, 5:4, and October 6, 1890, 7:2; *Morning Call*, November 20, 1890, 3:3.

9 Meier and Meier, *Those Naughty Ladies of the Old Northwest*, 61, 79; *Post-Intelligencer*, February 15, 1891, 8:3, February 17, 1891, 7:5, and February 21, 1891, 2:6; *Morning Call*, February 21, 1891, 8:5.

10 *Post-Intelligencer*, October 30, 1892, 3:5, and February 20, 1894, 5:5.

11 Meier and Meier, *Those Naughty Ladies of the Old Northwest*, 58; *Post-Intelligencer*, September 15, 1894, 3:1.

12 *Post-Intelligencer*, January 13, 1896, 7:7, and January 31, 1896, 7:7; Seattle City Directory for 1902, "U.S. City Directories, 1822–1995," Ancestry.com; "Lou Graham," *Washington, Wills and Probate Records, 1851–1970*.

13 *Post-Intelligencer*, March 12, 1903; Moynahan, *Forty Fallen Women*, 33.

14 "Lou Graham," *Washington, Wills and Probate Records, 1851–1970*; *Seattle Star*, March 17, 1903, 1:2.

15 "Lou Graham," findagrave.com; "Lou Graham," *Washington, Wills and Probate Records*.

16 *Seattle Star*, March 17, 1903, 1:2; "Lou Graham," *Washington, Wills and Probate Records, 1851–1970*.

17 "Lou Graham," *Washington, Wills and Probate Records, 1851–1970*; *Evening Statesman* (Walla Walla), July 22, 1904, 3:4; *Seattle Republican*, August 26, 1904, 5:2.

18 Meier and Meier, *Those Naughty Ladies of the Old Northwest*, 59, 63; "Lou Graham," findagrave.com.

CHAPTER 4

1 *Evening Statesman*, April 15, 1909, 5:5; Bill Gulick, *Outlaws of the Pacific Northwest* (Caldwell, ID: Caxton Press, 2000), 55.

2 *1860 U.S. Census.*

3 Gulick, *Outlaws of the Pacific Northwest*, 56; *The Lewis and Dryden Marine History of the Pacific Northwest*, E. W. Wright, ed. (Portland, OR: Lewis & Dryden Publishing Co., 1895), 80–81.

4 Gulick, *Outlaws of the Pacific Northwest*, 57–62.

5 Mary Meeker, "History of 202–212 West Main Street, Walla Walla, WA," January 1, 2002, Walla Walla, 2020, http://ww2020.net/202-212-w-main/, accessed November 19, 2018; Gulick, *Outlaws of the Pacific Northwest*, 62, 100–101; *Evening Statesman*, April 15, 1909, 5:5.

6 Gulick, *Outlaws of the Pacific Northwest*, 62; *Evening Statesman*, April 15, 1909, 5:5; Alissa Antilla and Alex Brockman, "Walla Walla: Sin City. Looking at the Brothels of the 19th and 20th Centuries," Whitman Wire, May 4, 2017, https://whitmanwire.com/feature/2017/05/04/walla-walla-sin-city/, accessed November 15, 2018.

7 Gulick, *Outlaws of the Pacific Northwest*, 62–63.

8 *Evening Statesman*, April 15, 1909, 5:5.

9 *1870 U.S. Census,* Population Schedules (NARA microfilm publication) M593, 1,761 rolls; Meeker, "History of 202–212 West Main Street, Walla Walla, WA."

10 *Tenth Census of the United States, 1880.* (NARA microfilm publication)

11 Ibid.; Gulick, *Outlaws of the Pacific Northwest*, 64; Antilla and Brockman, "Walla Walla: Sin City"; *Puget Sound Mail*, January 29, 1881, 3:2.

12 Gulick, *Outlaws of the Pacific Northwest*, 63–64; *Territorial Census for Walla Walla, Washington, 1885 and 1887, Washington Territorial Census Rolls, 1857–1892*; Sanborn Fire Insurance Map for Walla Walla, Walla Walla County, Washington, Sanborn Map Company, March 1888, Library of Congress, www.loc.gov/item/sanborn09361_002/, accessed November 20, 2018.

13 *Twelfth Census of the United States, 1900* (Washington, DC: NAtional Archives and Records Adminsitration, 1990), T623, 1854 rolls; Walla Walla Washington City Directory for 1902, "U.S. City Directories, 1822–1995," Ancestry.com; *Evening Statesman*, April 15, 1909, 5:5.

14 "Josephine 'Dutch' Wolfe" and "Josephine Wolfe," Findagrave.com; *Evening Statesman*, April 12, 1909, 1:5, and April 15, 1909, 5:5.

15 *Evening Statesman*, April 15, 1909, 5:5, and April 17, 1909, 5:1; *Yakima Herald*, April 21, 1909, 8:6.

16 *Evening Statesman*, May 21, 1909, 5:6.

17 *Yakima Herald*, April 21, 1909, 8:6; Gulick, *Outlaws of the Pacific Northwest*, 62, 64–65.

CHAPTER 5

1 "Tacoma, Washington," wikipedia.com; Speidel, *Sons of the Profits*, 116–23.

2 "Harry Morgan's Place," Jack Cameron's Tacoma Stories, June 2, 2005, https://tacomastories.com/2005/06/02/harry-morgans-place/, accessed November 20, 2018;

Judith Kipp, "Yesteryear," *News Tribune* (Tacoma), March 21, 1986, and Randolph Radebaugh, "The Crime Wave of 1888," *News Tribune*, no. 46 in a series, accessed at https://commons.wikimedia.org/wiki/File:Morgan%27s_Theatre_Comique,_Tacoma,_January_4,_1893_(WAITE_43).jpeg, November 13, 2018.

3 *Daily Post-Intelligencer* (Seattle), January 30, 1885, 1:1; *Post-Intelligencer*, February 1, 1885, 1:4, and February 20, 2885, 1:3.

4 *1885 Washington Territorial Census*, "Washington State and Territorial Censuses, 1857–1892," Ancestry.com; "Harry Morgan's Place."

5 *Post-Intelligencer*, September 20, 1885, 3:4, October 23, 1885, 4:5, March 3, 1887, 3:4, and May 5, 1887, 3:3; "Harry Morgan's Place."

6 "Morgan's Theatre Comique, January 4, 1893," notes, University of Washington Libraries Digital Collections, http://content.lib.washington.edu, accessed July 30, 2006; "Harry Morgan's Place"; Meier and Meier, *Those Naughty Ladies of the Old Northwest*, 77.

7 Kipp, "Yesteryear," and Radebaugh, "The Crime Wave of 1888"; *Post-Intelligencer*, June 29, 1887, 2:3.

8 Ibid.; "Morgan's Theatre Comique, January 4, 1893"; *Olympia Standard*, April 18, 1889, 3:3.

9 Kipp, "Yesteryear," and Radebaugh, "The Crime Wave of 1888"; *Post-Intelligencer*, June 22, 1888, 8:1, and October 26, 1888, 4:1.

10 "Harry Morgan's Place"; *Post-Intelligencer*, October 26, 1888, 4:1.

11 *Post-Intelligencer*, November 16, 1888, 4:1, and January 6, 1889, 8:1.

12 *Post-Intelligencer*, January 20, 1889, 8:1, January 23, 1889, 8:1, January 25, 1889, 8:1, and February 2, 1889, 8:1; Lewis O, Saum, "William Lightfoot Visscher and the 'Eden of the West,' Part One," *Pacific Northwest Quarterly*, January 1980, http://www.skagitriverjournal.com/wa/library/newspaper/visscher/visscher4-saum1.html, accessed November 10, 2018.

13 "Figaro—1889," https://archive.org/stream/figaro188900unse/figaro188900unse_djvu.txt, accessed November 12, 2018; *Post-Intelligencer*, October 11, 1892, 2:1; Sherry Monahan, *The Wicked West: Boozers, Cruisers, Gamblers and More* (Tucson, AZ: Rio Nuevo Publishers, 2005), 107; Meier and Meier, *Those Naughty Ladies of the Old Northwest*, 77.

14 Harry Morgan, "Washington, Death Records, 1883–1960," Ancestry.com; *Yakima Herald*, May 1, 1890, 2:3; Kipp, "Yesteryear," and Radebaugh, "The Crime Wave of 1888."

15 *Post-Intelligencer*, April 29, 1890, 2:1.

CHAPTER 6

1 Laura Arksey, "Spokane Falls (later renamed Spokane) is incorporated as a first-class city on November 29, 1881," Essay 9176, October 3, 2009, HistoricLink.org, http://www.historylink.org/File/9176, accessed November 12, 2018; Paul Burgarino,

"Spokane's hidden history lies right under your nose," *Gonzaga Bulletin*, March 30, 2005, https://www.gonzagabulletin.com/spokane-s-hidden-history-lies-right-under-your-nose/article_8e519457-d1e4-5688-b018-a31b104c2a68.html, accessed November 10, 2018; Meier and Meier, *Those Naughty Ladies of the Old Northwest*, 4.

2 Meier and Meier, *Those Naughty Ladies of the Old Northwest*, 34–36; "Tenderloin, Manhattan," wikipedia.com; Edward Winslow Martin, *The Secrets of the Great City* (Philadelphia: National Publishing Company, 1868), 293–94.

3 "The 1880s: Early Settlement & Pioneer Life," Spokane City Council Historic Preservation Office, http://www.historicspokane.org/riverfront-park-history-1880, accessed November 10, 2018; Arksey, "Spokane Falls."

4 Burgarino, "Spokane's hidden history lies right under your nose."

5 Meier and Meier, *Those Naughty Ladies of the Old Northwest*, 47–48.

6 Ibid., 48.

7 "The Great Spokane Fire—1889," Spokane History Timeline, https://discoveryrobots.org/spokanehistory/greatfire.html, accessed November 16, 2018; Anna Harbine, "The Great Fire of 1889," SpokaneHistorica.org, lhttps://www.spokanehistorical.org/items/show/356, accessed November 16, 2018; Caitlin M. Shain, "The Death of Irish Kate," SpokaneHistorical.org, https://spokanehistorical.org/items/show/456, accessed November 16, 2018.

8 Meier and Meier, *Those Naughty Ladies of the Old Northwest*, 89.

9 In Cripple Creek, Colorado, dance-hall girl Jennie LaRue set a fire when she and her man tangled and a gas heater was overturned. MacKell, *Brothels, Bordellos & Bad Girls*, 162.

10 Spokane City Directory, 1892, "Spokane, Washington Directories, 1889–93," Ancestry.com; *Post-Intelligencer*, May 28, 1892, 4:5; Shain, "The Death of Irish Kate"; "Kate Barrett," findagrave.com.

11 Annika Herbes, "Rescuing the Destitute: The Salvation in Spokane, 1891–1920," *Columbia*, Fall 2004, 18:3, http://www.wshs.org/wshs/columbia/articles/0304-a2.htm, accessed September 26, 2006; Meier and Meier, *Those Naughty Ladies of the Old Northwest*, 40.

12 Burgarino, "Spokane's hidden history lies right under your nose"; letters written by Abbie Widner, North West Museum of Arts and Culture, from Keith Shelton, "Prostitution in Early Spokane," SpokaneHistorical.org, https://www.spokanehistorical.org/items/show/204, accessed November 12, 2018.

13 Letters written by Abbie Widner.

14 "Prostitution in Early Spokane."

15 Herbes, "Rescuing the Destitute: The Salvation in Spokane, 1891–1920."

16 Burgarino, "Spokane's hidden history lies right under your nose."

NOTES

CHAPTER 7

1 "U.S., Social Security Death Index, 1935–2014," Ancestry.com; *Sixteenth Census of the United States, 1940* (Washington DC: National Archives and Records Administraion, 1940), T627, 4, 643: Sandra Wagner Wright, "Naughty Nellie—'A Madam of Legendary Proportion,'" Sandrawagnerwright.com, May 11, 2015, http://www.sandrawagnerwright.com/naughty-nellie-a-madam-of-legendary-proportion/, accessed November 20, 2018.

2 Seattle City Directories for 1932–1940, "U.S. City Directories, 1822–1995," Ancestry.com; Wright, "Naughty Nellie"; United States Department of the Interior, National Park Service, National Register of Historic Places Registration, "Pike Place," Seattle, Washington, https://www.seattle.gov/Documents/Departments/Neighborhoods/HistoricPreservation/HistoricDistricts/PikePlaceMarket/PikePlace-National-Register-Nomination.pdf, accessed November 21, 2018.

3 *Sixteenth Census of the United States, 1940.*

4 National Register of Historic Places, "Pike Place"; Wright, "Naughty Nellie."

5 National Register of Historic Places, "Pike Place"; *George S. Ikeda et al., Respondents and Cross-appellants, v. Nellie Curtis, Appellant*, no. 32436, Supreme Court of Washington, Department Two, October 6, 1953, Justia Law, https://law.justia.com/cases/washington/supreme-court/1953/32436-1.html, accessed November 19, 2018; Wright, "Naughty Nellie."

6 Wright, "Naughty Nellie," also "Naughty Nellie and The Honest Cop," Sandrawagnerwright.com, May 18, 2015, http://www.sandrawagnerwright.com/naughty-nellie-and-the-honest-cop/, accessed November 20, 2018.

7 *George S. Ikeda v. Nellie Curtis.*

8 Wright, "Naughty Nellie."

9 *George S. Ikeda v. Nellie Curtis.*

10 Ibid.

11 "History of Washington," wikipedia, accessed July 30, 2006; John C. Hughes and Ryan Teague Beckwith, *On the Harbor: From Black Friday to Nirvana* (Las Vegas, NV: Stephens Press, LLC, 2005), 128.

12 Robert A. Weinstein, *Grays Harbor, 1885–1913* (New York: Penguin Books, 1978), 25.

13 Agnew, *Brides of the Multitude*, 216.

14 Wright, "Naughty Nellie and The Honest Cop."

15 *Spokane Press*, October 16, 1903, 1:1; Hughes and Beckwith, *On the Harbor*, 128; Pamela Dean Aho, "Billy Was the Ghoul of Grays Harbor," *Daily World* (Aberdeen), July 29, 1989; Murray Morgan, *The Last Wilderness* (Seattle, WA, and London: University of Washington Press, 1955), 124.

16 Aho, "Billy Was the Ghoul of Grays Harbor"; "Grays Harbor County Auditor, Marriage Records, 1871-2013-William Gohl-Bessie Hager," Washington State Archives-Digital Archives, www.digitalarchives.wa.gov/Record/View/37DA3E4C9FC

7C2284A24B3A89EBB9E15?Print=true, accessed November 14, 2018; Hughes and Beckwith, *On the Harbor*, 20.

17 *Thirteenth Census of the United States, 1910*; "Gohl Taken to Walla Walla," *Grays Harbor Post*, June 18, 1910.

18 "State News," *Tacoma Times*, February 19, 1912; "Washington, Death Records, 1883–1960," Ancestry.com.

19 Wright, "Naughty Nellie" and "Naughty Nellie and the Honest Cop."

20 Ibid.; "U.S., Social Security Death Index, 1935–2014," Ancestry.com.

CHAPTER 8

1 Meier and Meier, *Those Naughty Ladies of the Old Northwest*, 64.

2 Ibid., 124–27; "Jane Barnes Robson," *The Oregon Encyclopedia*, https://oregonencyclopedia.org/articles/barnes_robson_jane_c_1790_/#.W8ept2hKjIU, accessed October 5, 2018.

3 Meier and Meier, *Those Naughty Ladies of the Old Northwest*, 124–27; "Jane Barnes Robson"; Kenneth W. Porter, "Jane Barnes, First White Woman in Oregon," *Oregon Historical Quarterly Review*, vol. 31, no. 2, June, 1930, 125–35.

4 Porter, "Jane Barnes, First White Woman in Oregon," 125–35.

5 Ibid.

6 "Jane Barnes Robson."

7 Porter, "Jane Barnes, First White Woman in Oregon," 125–35.

8 Meier and Meier, *Those Naughty Ladies of the Old Northwest*, 124–27; Porter, "Jane Barnes, First White Woman in Oregon," 125–35.

9 Ibid.

10 Ibid.

11 Porter, "Jane Barnes, First White Woman in Oregon," 125–35.

12 Meier and Meier, *Those Naughty Ladies of the Old Northwest*, 124–27.

13 Porter, "Jane Barnes, First White Woman in Oregon," 125–35.

14 Ibid.

15 Ibid; "Jane Barnes Robson."

CHAPTER 9

1 "Astoria, Oregon," wikipedia.com; Chelsea Gorrow, "Astoria Embraces Chinese Legacy," *Daily Astorian*, April 16, 2012, https://www.opb.org/news/article/astoria_embraces_chinese_legacy/, accessed March 1, 2018.

2 Matt Winters, "Is it time to pull the oldest profession out into the sunshine?" *Chinook Observer*, May 29, 2014, http://www.chinookobserver.com/article/20140529/ARTICLE/140529999/1925, accessed March 15, 2018.

3 Elleda Wilson, "In One Ear: Swilltown, 1893 Astoria Fire Anniversary," *Daily Astorian*, July 3, 2015, http://www.dailyastorian.com/ear/20150703/in-one-ear-swilltown, accessed March 16, 2018.

4 "Social and Economic History of Astoria," https://archive.org/stream/jstor-20609567/20609567_djvu.txt, accessed March 16, 2018.

5 Wilson, "In One Ear: Swilltown, 1893 Astoria Fire Anniversary."

6 "Social and Economic History of Astoria."

7 *Daily Morning Astorian*, May 15, 1885, 3:2, June 4, 1887, 3:1, and June 30, 1888, 3:1.

8 "The Most Wicked Place on Earth," Astoria/Warrenton, Oregon, https://www.travelastoria.com/trip-ideas/the-most-wicked-place-on-earth.html, accessed March 12, 2018; "Social and Economic History of Astoria," accessed March 18, 2018; Meier and Meier, *Those Naughty Ladies of the Old Northwest*, 48.

9 *Dalles Daily Chronicle*, October 8, 1891, 2:2.

10 *Daily Astorian*, May 9, 1895, n.p.

11 Newspaper index files, Astoria Public Library, Astoria, Oregon.

12 *Morning Astorian*, December 18, 1904, 5:3.

13 *Sunday Oregonian* (Portland, OR), December 18, 1904.

14 *La Grande Evening Star*, December 13, 1906, 1:1; *Morning Astorian*, December 14, 1906, 8:1.

15 *Morning Astorian*, June 23, 1903, 3:4, and July 26, 1904, 8:4; Spokane City Directory, 1902, "U.S. City Directories, 1882–1995," Ancestry.com.

16 *Morning Oregonian* (Portland) July 27, 1904, 4:3.

17 *Morning Astorian*, July 26, 1904, 8:4.

18 Ibid; *Morning Oregonian*, July 27, 1904, 4:3.

19 *Morning Oregonian*, July 27, 1904, 4:3.

20 *Morning Astorian*, July 26, 1904, 8:4, and July 27, 1904, 5:3.

21 *Morning Oregonian*, July 27, 1904, 4:3; *Morning Astorian*, July 27, 1904, 5:3.

22 "Oregon, Wills and Probate Records, 1849–1963," and Astoria City Directory for 1904, "U.S. City Directories, 1882–1995," Ancestry.com; *Twelfth Census of the United States, 1900*.

23 "Oregon, Wills and Probate Records, 1849–1963"; *Morning Oregonian*, August 1, 1904, 4:2; "Hope Clayton" and "Shirley Rowe," findagrave.com.

24 *Morning Astorian*, February 25, 1908, 5:3, February 26, 1908, 5:1, and March 15, 1908, 4:1.

25 *Morning Oregonian*, October 9, 1911, 1:2; *Daily Eastern Oregon*, October 11, 1911, 6:4; *Daily Capital Journal* (Salem), May 2, 1912, 4:2.

26 Edwin D. Culp, *Yesterday in Oregon: A Pictorial Scrapbook* (Caxton, ID: The Caxton Printers, Ltd., 1990), 20; "John Jacob Astor Hotel," wikipedia.org; "The Most Wicked Place on Earth."

NOTES

CHAPTER 10

1 "North Bend, Oregon" and "Coos Bay, Oregon," wikipedia.org; Andie E. Jensen, *Law on the Bay: Marshfield, Oregon 1874–1944* (Coos Bay, OR: Lawman Publishing, 2010), 1–2, 4.

2 Jensen, *Law on the Bay: Marshfield, Oregon 1874–1944,* 3, 5, 18–19.

3 Meier and Meier, *Those Naughty Ladies of the Old Northwest,* 54.

4 Jensen, *Law on the Bay: Marshfield, Oregon 1874–1944,* 20.

5 Ibid., 19–20.

6 Ibid., 22.

7 *Coast Mail* (Marshfield), January 3, 1879, 2:1; *Tenth Census of the United States, 1880* (NARA microfilm publication), T9, 1,454 rolls.

8 Meier and Meier, *Those Naughty Ladies of the Old Northwest,* 53–54.

9 Jensen, *Law on the Bay: Marshfield, Oregon 1874–1944,* 6, 32, 35.

10 *Coquille City Herald,* November 16, 1897, 2:3.

11 Dick Wagner, *Louie Simpson's North Bend* (North Bend-on-Coos Bay, OR: *North Bend News,* 1986), 22–23.

12 Wagner, *Louie Simpson's North Bend,* 23; *Coos Bay Times,* March 30, 1911, 4:1.

13 Ibid., 19.

14 *Coos Bay Times,* March 8, 1911, 1:3, and April 6, 1911, 1:1.

15 Ibid., August 5, 1911, 1:2; Jensen, *Law on the Bay: Marshfield, Oregon 1874–1944,* 53–54.

16 Jensen, *Law on the Bay: Marshfield, Oregon 1874–1944,* 54.

17 *Coos Bay Times,* September 7, 1911, 2:2.

18 *Morning Oregonian,* December 23, 1911, 3:3; *Coos Bay Times,* December 21, 1911, 1:3.

19 *Sunday Oregonian,* December 24, 1911, 11:6.

20 Jensen, *Law on the Bay: Marshfield, Oregon 1874–1944,* 151–54.

21 *Morning Oregonian,* December 27, 1911, 6:5, and December 30, 1911, 5:4; *Coos Bay Times,* December 29, 1911, 1:2, and December 30, 1:5.

22 *Daily Capital Journal,* April 19, 1912, 5:2.

23 Jensen, *Law on the Bay: Marshfield, Oregon 1874–1944,* 151–54.

24 *Coos Bay Times,* May 4, 1912, 5:3, and June 18 1912, 5:4.

25 Wagner, *Louie Simpson's North Bend,* 45.

26 Nathan Douthit, *The Coos Bay Region 1890–1944: Life on a Coastal Frontier* (Coos Bay, OR: River West Books, printed for the Bandon Historical Society Press, 1981), 65.

27 Wagner, *Louie Simpson's North Bend,* 15.

28 Jensen, *Law on the Bay: Marshfield, Oregon 1874–1944,* 8.

29 Boyd Stone, *You Are the Stars: History of the Coquille Area* (Myrtle Point, OR: Myrtle Point Printing, 1995), 51.

30 Wagner, *Louie Simpson's North Bend,* 21.

31 Douthit, *The Coos Bay Region 1890–1944*, 65; *Coos Bay Times*, December 31, 1915, 1:1.

32 Jensen, *Law on the Bay: Marshfield, Oregon 1874–1944*, 68–69.

33 Wagner, *Louie Simpson's North Bend*, 15, 23; *Coos Bay Times*, January 12, 1916, 3:3, and January 21, 1916, 6:4.

34 Historical Notes, "More on the fires that burned Barbette," OSHU Historical Collections and Archives, http://ohsu-hca.blogspot.com/2010/01/more-on-fires-that-burned-barbette.html, accessed April 3, 2018; Jensen, *Law on the Bay: Marshfield, Oregon 1874–1944*, 8–9, 77.

35 Al Sandine, *Plundertown USA: Coos Bay Enters the Global Economy* (Blaine, WA: Hancock House Publishers, 2003), 99; Jensen, *Law on the Bay: Marshfield, Oregon 1874–1944*, 11.

36 Boyd Stone, *My Valley: History of the Coquille River Valley, Outlying Areas and More* (Myrtle Point, OR: Myrtle Point Printing, 2008), 106.

CHAPTER 11

1 Holbrook, *Wildmen, Wobblies & Whistle Punks*, 61.

2 Brad Lockwood, "Bend's Brothels: The Sin-Dustry That Built Our City," *Source Weekly*, July 21, 2010, http://www.bendsource.com/bend/bendandaposs-brothels-the-sin-dustry-that-built-our-city/Content?oid=2135926, accessed September 2, 2018.

3 "Baker County: Oregon's Gold Country," *1859 Oregon Magazine*, November 1, 2012, https://1859oregonmagazine.com/explore-oregon/travel/2012-november-december-1859-oregon-from-where-i-stand-baker-county/, accessed April 12, 2018; Meier and Meier, *Those Naughty Ladies of the Old Northwest*, 72–73.

4 Meier and Meier, *Those Naughty Ladies of the Old Northwest*, 28.

5 Ibid., 79.

6 Florin, *Oregon Ghost Towns*, 41.

7 *Twelfth Census of the United States, 1900*.

8 *State Rights Democrat* (Albany), October 8, 1886, 3:4; "Human Skulls, Freak Calves—Grant County Historical Museum," Roadside America, https://www.roadside-america.com/story/11017, accessed January 3, 2018.

9 *Grant County News*, November 1, 1888, 3:4, May 16, 1889, 3:4, and September 12, 1889, 3:4.

10 *Grant County News*, December 23, 1891, 2:2; *Twelfth Census of the United States, 1900*; "Human Skulls, Freak Calves—Grant County Historical Museum."

11 *Plaindealer* (Roseburg), March 10, 1904, 2:1. The *babi humayun* is the name of the imperial gate of Topkapi Palace in Istanbul, constructed in 1459 for use by the Ottoman sultans of the Ottoman Empire. "Topkapi Palace," wikipedia.org.

12 Meier and Meier, *Those Naughty Ladies of the Old Northwest*, 55–56.

13 *Thirteenth Census of the United States, 1910*

14 J. D. John Finn, "Midnight Murder of a Logger," http://mckenzieriverreflection-snewspaper.com/News/midnight-murder-logger, accessed September 7, 2018.

15 Ibid; *Evening Herald* (Klamath Falls), December 4, 1911, 1:6, and January 9, 1912, 1:1.

16 *Evening Herald*, January 9, 1912, 1:1.

17 Finn, "Midnight Murder of a Logger."

18 Ibid.; *Evening Herald*, February 5, 1912, 1:6.

19 "Sally Stanford," wikipedia.com; Sally Stanford, *The Lady of the House: California's Most Notorious Madam* (New York: Ballantine Books, 1972), 5–7.

20 Ibid.

21 "Pendleton, Oregon: Statue of Beloved Brothel Madam," Roadside America, https://www.roadsideamerica.com/tip/44804, accessed July 15, 2015; Jade McDowell, "History in Action: The Pendleton Underground comes to life with the help of actors," *East Oregonian* (Salem), May 27–28, 2017, 21; "Cozy Rooms," Mark & Teri's Travels, August 19, 2017, http://markteri.blogspot.com/2017/08/cozy-rooms.html, accessed October 23, 2018.

22 Pendleton Underground Tours, http://www.pendletonundergroundtours.org/main/, accessed July 7, 2018.

23 Nash and Scofield, *The Well-Traveled Casket*, 162.

24 Mark Monmonier, "From Squaw Tit to Whorehouse Meadow: How Maps Name, Claim and Inflame" (excerpt), University of Chicago Press, https://www.press.uchicago.edu/Misc/Chicago/534650.html, accessed February 3, 2018.

25 "Whorehouse Meadow," wikipedia.org.

CHAPTER 12

1 Holbrook, *Wildmen, Wobblies & Whistle Punks*, 73–74; *Oregon Daily Journal* (Portland), April 6, 1907, 8:7.

2 Gary Deilman, "Copperfield," Oregon Encyclopedia, https://oregonencyclopedia.org/articles/copperfield/#.Wkcg4t-nFpk, accessed June 11, 2018; *Morning Oregonian*, March 11, 1907, 12:4, and June 28, 1909, 15:1.

3 Deilman, "Copperfield"; Lewis L. McArthur, *Oregon Geographic Names*, 7th ed. (Portland, OR: Oregon Historical Society Press, 2003), 230; *Oregon Daily Journal*, April 6, 1907, 8:7.

4 Nash and Scofield, *The Well-Traveled Casket*, 129–30.

5 Holbrook, *Wildmen, Wobblies & Whistle Punks*, 73; *La Grande Evening Observer*, January 7, 1909, 7:4.

6 *Morning Oregonian*, June 28, 1909, 15:1.

7 Nash and Scofield, *The Well-Traveled Casket*, 130.

8 Holbrook, *Wildmen, Wobblies & Whistle Punks*, 74.

9 Nash and Scofield, *The Well-Traveled Casket*, 130.

10 *Morning Oregonian*, July 27, 1909, 1:2; *Sunday Oregonian*, December 19, 1909, 6:2.

11 Holbrook, *Wildmen, Wobblies & Whistle Punks*, 74; *Morning Oregonian*, December 22, 1913, 1:5.

12 Holbrook, *Wildmen, Wobblies & Whistle Punks*, 75.

13 Ibid.; *Morning Oregonian*, December 22, 1913, 1:5.

14 Holbrook, *Wildmen, Wobblies & Whistle Punks* 75; *Morning Oregonian*, December 22, 1913, 1:5; *East Oregonian*, December 29, 1913, 1:7.

15 Holbrook, *Wildmen, Wobblies & Whistle Punks*, 75–76; *Morning Oregonian*, December 31, 1913, 5:1.

16 Holbrook, *Wildmen, Wobblies & Whistle Punks*, 76.

17 Ibid., 77.

18 Ibid., 78; *Morning Oregonian*, January 3, 1914, 1:1.

19 Holbrook, *Wildmen, Wobblies & Whistle Punks*, 79; *Morning Oregonian*, January 3, 1914, 10:3.

20 *Eastern Oregonian*, January 3, 1914, 1:7; *Morning Oregonian*, January 5, 1914, 11:1; "Livermore Family Tree," Ancestry.com; "Fern Hobbs," findagrave.com.

CHAPTER 13

1 "City of Coquille," Living Places, http://www.livingplaces.com/OR/Coos_County/Coquille_City.html, accessed October 5, 2018; City of Coquille, Facebook.com, https://www.facebook.com/pg/CityOfCoquille/about/?ref=page_internal, accessed June 5, 2018; *Coquille City Herald*, September 11, 1883, 2:1 and 2:5.

2 Boyd Stone, *My Valley*, 200, and *Living in the Past Lane* (Myrtle Point, OR: Coquille Valley Sentinel), 45; Patti and Hal Strain, eds., *The Coquille Valley: Memories—Moccasins to the Moon, Volume One* (Myrtle Point, OR: Myrtle Point Printing, 2007), 408–09.

3 Strain and Strain, *The Coquille Valley, Memories*, 422; Marilee Miller, "When 'Entertainments' Were in Vogue," *History of the Local Area, Book 4*, assignments written by the classes of Gertrude A. Currier, 1979, 1980, 1984 (Coos Bay, OR: Southwestern Oregon Community College, 1984.).

4 *Coquille City Herald*, March 12, 1901, 1:4.

5 Stone, *My Valley*, 108, and *Living in the Past Lane*, 45; *Coquille City Herald*, May 12, 1903, 3:6.

6 *Coquille City Herald*, February 23, 1904, 1:3; *Coquille Herald*, September 12, 1912, 3:4.

7 Stone, *My Valley*, 108.

8 Ibid., 36–37.

9 Stone, *You Are the Stars*, 47, 49.

10 *Fifteenth Census of the United States, 1930* (Washington, DC: National Archives and Records Administration, 1930), T626, 2,667 rolls; 1938 Marshfield City

Directory, Coquille section, "U.S. City Directories, 1822–1995," Ancestry.com; Stone, *You Are the Stars*, 47, 50–51.

11 Stone, *You Are the Stars*, 49.

12 Ibid., 50.

13 Strain and Strain, *The Coquille Valley, Memories*, 445; Stone, *You Are the Stars*, 50–51.

14 Patti and Hal Strain, eds., *The Coquille Valley: Ancestor Review, Wagon Wheels to Wireless* (Myrtle Point, OR: Myrtle Printing, May 2009), 741.

15 Stone, *You Are the Stars*, 50–51; interview with Joanie Bedwell, Hazel M. Lewis Library, Powers, OR, September 2017.

16 Dorothy Taylor, "Did You Know This," *Coquille Valley Sentinel*, February 25, 2009, 2:1.

17 Stone, *You Are the Stars*, 51; correspondence with Bert Dunn, Coos County, OR, November 2018; *Sixteenth Census of the United States, 1940*

18 Correspondence with Bert Dunn, July 15, 2019.

19 Ibid.

20 "Alleged Houses of Prostitution in Cities in Oregon, from information gathered during 1941," January 7, 1942, https://sos.oregon.gov/archives/exhibits/ww2/Documents/life-vice3.pdf, accessed October 2, 2018; Strain and Strain, *The Coquille Valley, Memories*, 766; Stone, *You Are the Stars*, 51, and *My Valley*, 106.

21 *Sixteenth Census of the United States, 1940*; Stone, *My Valley*, 106; correspondence with Deb Woosley, Powers, OR, July 2018; correspondence with Bert Dunn, Coos County, OR, June 11, 2019; Stone, *My Valley*, 106.

22 Stone, *You Are the Stars*, 51, 106.

23 Strain and Strain, *The Coquille Valley, Memories*, 290–91.

24 Victor H. Stevens, *Powers, Oregon* (Myrtle Point, OR: Vic Stevens, printed by Wegford Publications, North Bend, OR, n.d.), 31.

25 Curt Beckham, "The Myrtle Point Herald's Kurt's Korners," supplement to the *Myrtle Point Herald*, May, 1980, large print edition, 11.

26 Ibid.

27 Stone, *You Are the Stars*, 51, and *My Valley*, 106; interviews with Joanie Bedwell, Jill Moore, Tish Moore, Lacey Pearce, and Phyllis Pearce, Powers, OR, summer 2018.

CHAPTER 14

1 Holbrook, *Wildmen, Wobblies & Whistle Punks*, 63.

2 "Portland, Oregon," wikipedia.com; Nash and Scofield, *The Well-Traveled Casket*, 58; Jan MacKell, *Red Light Women of the Rocky Mountains* (Albuquerque, NM: University of New Mexico Press, 2009), 194.

3 *1860 U.S. Census*, Population Schedule (NARA microfilm publication), M653, 1,438 rolls; 1865 and 1868 Portland City Directories, "U.S. City Directories, 1822–1995," Ancestry.com; Meier and Meier, *Those Naughty Ladies of the Old Northwest*,

90–92; Finn J. D. John, "The original floating bordello of 1880s Portland," July 25, 2010, http://www.offbeatoregon.com/H1007d_floating-bordello-in-portland.html, accessed April 30, 2018.

4 John, "The original floating bordello of 1880s Portland."

5 Ibid.; Meier and Meier, *Those Naughty Ladies of the Old Northwest*, 90–92.

6 Meier and Meier, *Those Naughty Ladies of the Old Northwest*, 92; *Portland, New Northwest*, November 8, 1872, 2:2, March 17, 1876, 3:1, and December 6, 1880, 5:5; *Tenth Census of the United States, 1880.*

7 "Fire Area, Portland, 1873," Oregon History Project, https://oregonhistoryproject .org/articles/historical-records/fire-area-portland-1873/#.W9uCbZNKjIU, accessed October 12, 2018; *Portland Oregonian*, December 15, 1915; "The Guide," Café Unknown, March 23, 2011, http://unknown59.rssing.com/browser.php?indx=83490 63&last=1&item=7, accessed September 12, 2018; Meier and Meier, *Those Naughty Ladies of the Old Northwest*, 3, 100.

8 Meier and Meier, *Those Naughty Ladies of the Old Northwest*, 11, 77, 92–95.

9 Ibid., 79.

10 "The Guide."

11 Ibid.; *Twelfth Census of the United States, 1900*; Portland City Directories 1885–1909, "U.S. City Directories, 1822–1995," Ancestry.com; *Oregon Daily Journal*, July 23, 1904, 5:3.

12 "The Guide"; Meier and Meier, *Those Naughty Ladies of the Old Northwest*, 79; *Twelfth Census of the United States, 1900*; Portland City Directory for 1891, "U.S. City Directories, 1822–1995," Ancestry.com; City of Portland, Bureau of Planning, "Midtown Blocks Historic Assessment," September 2004, 165, 169, https://www.portland-oregon.gov/bps/article/137474, accessed October 31, 2018.

13 Meier and Meier, *Those Naughty Ladies of the Old Northwest*, 79, 95; *Twelfth Census of the United States, 1900.*

14 "The Guide"; Portland City Directories, 1893–1895, "U.S. City Directories, 1822–1995," Ancestry.com; *Morning Oregonian*, August 18, 1909, 9:1; *Thirteenth Census of the United States, 1910.*

15 "The Guide"; J. D. John Finn, "Early anti-prostitution crusade was an embarrassing fizzle," Offbeat Oregon, March 3, 2013, http://www.offbeatoregon.com/1303a-open-door-for-wayward-girls-and-fallen-women.html, accessed October 5, 2018.

16 Meier and Meier, *Those Naughty Ladies of the Old Northwest*, 92–93.

17 Finn, "Early anti-prostitution crusade was an embarrassing fizzle"; Portland City Directory for 1896, "U.S. City Directories, 1822–1995," Ancestry.com.

18 "The Guide"; Meier and Meier, *Those Naughty Ladies of the Old Northwest*, 85.

19 "The Guide"; Portland City Directories for 1894 and 1895, "U.S. City Directories, 1822–1995," Ancestry.com; *Daily Journal* (Salem), September 28.1899, 4:5; *Morning Oregonian*, April 3, 1900, 4:2; *Twelfth Census of the United States, 1900.*

20 "The Guide."

21 Ibid.; Meier and Meier, *Those Naughty Ladies of the Old Northwest*, 95.

22 Meier and Meier, *Those Naughty Ladies of the Old Northwest*, 43, 45.

23 Ibid., 97, 99; Agnew, 214; *Sunday Oregonian*, August 30, 1903, 10:1.

24 Agnew, *Brides of the Multitude*, 214; Nash and Scofield, *The Well-Traveled Casket*, 58–59; Meier and Meier, *Those Naughty Ladies of the Old Northwest*, 104.

25 Meier and Meier, *Those Naughty Ladies of the Old Northwest*, 100; *Morning Oregonian*, February 11, 1903, 14:1.

26 *Morning Oregonian*, February 11, 1903, 14:1, April 16, 1903, 8:4, and April 26, 1903, 9:3.

27 Meier and Meier, *Those Naughty Ladies of the Old Northwest*, 100; *Morning Oregonian*, June 3, 1903, 14:3, July 8, 1903, 14:2, September 9, 1903, 14:3, September 16, 1903, 10:4, December 17, 1903, 10:4, and February 2, 1904, 10:5; *Sunday Oregonian*, August 30, 1903, 10:1.

28 *Morning Oregonian*, October 17, 1904, 7:5, and January 14, 1905, 7:1; *Oregon Daily Journal*, November 30, 1904, 3:2, February 7, 1905, 1:2, February 10, 1905, 16:3, and February 18, 1905, 10:4; Meier and Meier, *Those Naughty Ladies of the Old Northwest*, 100; "Lewis and Clark Centennial Exposition," wikipedia.com.

29 Meier and Meier, *Those Naughty Ladies of the Old Northwest*, 100; "The Guide"; *Morning Oregonian*, January 14, 1906, 8:4, and November 15, 1906, 14:1.

30 Portland City Directories, 1912–1918, "U.S. City Directories, 1822–1995," Ancestry.com; *Thirteenth Census of the United States, 1910*; Meier and Meier, *Those Naughty Ladies of the Old Northwest*, 100.

31 *Morning Oregonian*, December 31, 1909, 9:1, and August 3, 1911, 11:5; *Thirteenth Census of the United States, 1910*.

32 *Morning Oregonian*, September 15, 1911, 14:5, August 12, 1912, 16:4, and December 6, 1917, 14:1; *Sunday Oregonian*, June 23, 1912, 9:5; Portland City Directory for 1918, "U.S. City Directories, 1822–1995," Ancestry.com.

33 Meier and Meier, *Those Naughty Ladies of the Old Northwest*, 99; *Morning Oregonian*, August 27, 1912, 4:4, and August 28, 1912, 6:5.

34 Meier and Meier, *Those Naughty Ladies of the Old Northwest*, 100–105; *Morning Oregonian*, November 29, 1912, 13:2.

35 "Early 1900s Republicans Suspected of Colluding with Bawds," Capital Taps: Fine Beer in Salem, Oregon, June 28, 2010, http://capitaltaps.blogspot.com/2010/06/early-1900s-republicans-suspected-of.html, accessed October 4, 2018; Meier and Meier, *Those Naughty Ladies of the Old Northwest*, 49–50.

36 "The Guide."

CHAPTER 15

1 "Salem, Oregon," wikipedia.org; Meier and Meier, *Those Naughty Ladies of the Old Northwest*, 76.

2 *Daily Capital Journal*, September 8, 1914, 1:4; Lewis E. Judson, *Reflections on the Jason Lee Mission and the Opening of Civilization in the Oregon Country* (Salem, OR: Wynkoop-Blair Printing Service, 1971), n.p.

3 *Evening Capital Journal* (Salem), November 1, 1892, 3:2, and November 2, 1892, 3:4.

4 *Evening Capital Journal*, November 16, 1892, 3:1.

5 *Evening Capital Journal*, December 10, 1892, 3:5.

6 *Capital Journal* (Salem), November 12, 1894, 4:5.

7 Capital Taps: Fine Beer in Salem, Oregon, "Not in my Neighborhood: Downtown Tries to Fend off 'Ill Fame' and 'Moral Defamation,' 1893," http://capitaltaps.blogspot .com/2010/01/not-in-my-neighborhood-downtown-tries.html, accessed October 5, 2018.

8 *Capital Journal*, July 15, 1893, 4:3.

9 *Capital Journal*, September 2, 1893, 4:3.

10 Capital Taps: Fine Beer in Salem, Oregon, "Chinatown's 'Bell Tower'—Brothel or Just False Alarm?" January 20, 2010, http://capitaltaps.blogspot.com/2010/01/ chinatowns-bell-tower-brothel-or-just.html, accessed October 5, 2018.

11 *Statesman Journal* (Salem), October 5, 1895; *Capital Journal*, October 25, 1895, 4:4.

12 *Capital Journal*, November 16, 1895, 6:4.

13 Capital Taps, "Chinatown's 'Bell Tower'—Brothel or Just False Alarm?"; Ben Maxwell, "The Chinese in Salem," *Historic Marion County*, vol. 7 (1961), 9–15.

14 Daniel J. Fry Jr., "The Saga of Daniel J. Fry, Part 3 . . . My Youth on Gaiety Hill," *Historic Marion County*, Winter 1998, 12.

15 *Statesman Journal*, July 20, 1900, 4:3; *Daily Capital Journal*, August 26, 1898, 2:3, and September 13, 1898, 1:8.

16 *Capital Journal*, June 12, 1900, 4:2.

17 *Morning Oregonian*, June 13, 1900, 4:2.

18 Ibid., July 6, 1900, 10:4.

19 *Daily Journal*, July 21, 1900, 2:4.

20 "Early 1900s Republicans Suspected of Colluding with Bawds."

21 Ibid.

22 *Daily Capital Journal*, March 2, 1905, 5:2.

23 *Twelfth Census of the United States, 1900*; Capital Taps: Fine Beer in Salem, Oregon, "Peppermint Flat & Potiphar's Wife: Madam Hattie McGinnis in 1909," November 2, 2009, http://capitaltaps.blogspot.com/2009/11/peppermint-flat-poti- phars-wife-madam.html, accessed October 8, 2018.

24 *Capital Journal*, October 6, 1909, 7:4, and October 16, 1909, 7:4.

25 Capital Taps, "Peppermint Flat & Potiphar's Wife: Madam Hattie McGinnis in 1909"; *State v. McGinnis*, taken from "John S. Foote, Mary Elledge, and Deborah Mapes-Stice v. State of Oregon," Appellate Court Records, https://web.courts.oregon

.gov/records/sccalendar.nsf/b29dd44d01dffea088256c91005b3a5b/d3b3f278fbedb
95588258274007fca82/$FILE/SC065883BRACaclu.pdf, accessed October 7, 2018;
Capital Taps: Fine Beer in Salem, Oregon, "Madam McGinnis Goes to the Oregon
Supreme Court," November 6, 2009, http://capitaltaps.blogspot.com/2009/11/
madam-mcginnis-goes-to-oregon-supresme.html, accessed October 7, 2018.

26 Salem City and Marion County, Oregon, Directory, 1911, "*U.S. City Directories,
1822–1995*," and Hattie McGinnis and James McGinnis, "California, Death Index,
1905–1939," Ancestry.com; *Twelfth Census of the United States, 1900; Thirteenth
Census of the United States, 1910; Fourteenth Census of the United States, 1920* (Washington, DC: National Archives and Records Administration, 1920), T630, 1,712
rolls; Martha (Pearce) Martin, "Edgemoore, the Not so Poor, Farm," Save Our Heritage Organization, http://www.sohosandiego.org/reflections/2009-1/edgemoor.htm,
accessed October 9, 2018.

27 "Early 1900s Republicans Suspected of Colluding with Bawds"; "Madam McGinnis Goes to the Oregon Supreme Court"; Meier and Meier, *Those Naughty Ladies of
the Old Northwest*, 78; *Daily Capital Journal*, April 23, 1919, 6:3.

CHAPTER 16

1 Robert Swanson, "The Ballad of the Soiled Snowflake," *Bunkhouse Ballads, Book 3*
(Toronto: Thomas Allen, Limited, 1945), 11.

2 Berton, *The Klondike Fever*, 6–9.

3 "Chilkoot Pass," wikipedia.org, accessed October 1, 2018; Berton, *The Klondike
Fever*, 15–16.

4 Berton, *The Klondike Fever*, 21–22.

5 Lael Morgan, *Good Time Girls of the Alaska-Yukon Gold Rush* (Fairbanks, AK, Epicenter Press, 1998), 22, 26–27.

6 Berton, *The Klondike Fever*, 28, 32–33; Agnew, *Brides of the Multitude*, 217–81.

7 Agnew, *Brides of the Multitude*, 217–81.

8 "Prostitution, 'Advertising,'" Box 48A ff 2, Mazzulla Collection, Amon Carter
Museum, Fort Worth, Texas, accessed 1992; Berton, *The Klondike Fever*, 160–61.

9 Jay Moynahan, *The Good Time Girls' Guide to Gold Rush Cuisine* (Spokane, WA:
Chickadee Publishing, 2006), 71; Correspondence with Jay Moynahan, Spokane, WA,
December 2007.

10 Kay Reynolds Blair, *Ladies of the Lamplight* (Ouray, CO: Western Reflections Publishing Company, 2000), 37.

11 Ronald Dean Miller, *Shady Ladies of the West* (Los Angeles: Westernlore Press,
1964), 96; Hadley Meares, "Baldwin's Belvedere: The Queen Anne Cottage at the
L.A. Arboretum," History & Society, KCET, August 31, 2015, https://www.kcet.org/
history-society/baldwins-Belvedereee-the-queen-anne-cottage-at-the-la-arboretum,
accessed October 1, 2018.

12 Blair, *Ladies of the Lamplight*, 37–38.

13 Ibid., 38; Meares, "Baldwin's Belvedere"; MacKell, *Brothels, Bordellos and Bad Girls*, 67–68.

14 Meares, "Baldwin's Belvedere"; Edgar F. Losee, "Elias Jackson 'Lucky' Baldwin," The Fornightly Club, Meeting no. 1734, October 19, 2006, http://www.redlandsfortnightly.org/papers/losee06.htm, accessed October 1, 2018.

15 Berton, *The Klondike Fever*, 111; Blair, *Ladies of the Lamplight*, 39.

16 Losee, "Elias Jackson 'Lucky' Baldwin."

17 Glenn G. Boyer, ed., *I Married Wyatt Earp: The Recollections of Josephine Sarah Marcus Earp* (Tucson, AZ: University of Arizona Press, second printing, 1979), 148 n.8, 149 n.10; Ann Kirschner, "Wyatt Earp's Alaskan Adventure," *True West*, March 28, 2014, https://truewestmagazine.com/wyatt-earps-alaskan-adventure/, accessed June 30, 2014.

18 Losee, "Elias Jackson 'Lucky' Baldwin."

19 Ibid.

20 Olive Barber, *Meet Me in Juneau* (Portland, OR: Binfords & Mort, Publishers, 1960), 13–14.

CHAPTER 17

1 "Dawson City," Alaska.org, http://www.alaska.org/detail/dawson-city, accessed September 29, 2018.

2 Agnew, *Brides of the Multitude*, 217–18; Berton, *The Klondike Fever*, 385.

3 Sara Bornstein, "Women of the 1898 Alaska-Klondike Gold Rush," Senior History Thesis, 2009, 28, https://scholarship.tricolib.brynmawr.edu/bitstream/handle/10066/3588/2009BornsteinS.pdf?sequence=2, accessed October 2, 2018.

4 Berton, *The Klondike Fever*, 385.

5 Alfred Brooks, *Blazing Alaska's Trails* (Fairbanks, AK: University of Alaska Press, 1953), 363.

6 Chad Evans, *Frontier Theater* (Victoria, BC: Sono Nis Press, 1983), 236; Agnew, *Brides of the Multitude*, 220; Berton, *The Klondike Fever*, 186; Bornstein, "Women of the 1898 Alaska-Klondike Gold Rush."

7 Berton, *The Klondike Fever*, 88–89, 314; Marriage of Emile C. Leglise and A. F. Busch, August 13, 1894, "California, Marriage Records from Select Counties, 1850–1941," Ancestry.com.

8 Berton, *The Klondike Fever*, 313–15, 374–75.

9 Ibid., 314; Agnew, *Brides of the Multitude*, 219–20.

10 Berton, *The Klondike Fever*, 186–87, 382.

11 Ibid., 325–26, 382–83, 405.

12 Agnew, *Brides of the Multitude*, 218; Berton, *The Klondike Fever*, 301–2; *Anaconda Standard* (Montana), September 4, 1895, 1:2.

13 Berton, *The Klondike Fever*, 375, 383–84.

14 Ibid., 384–85.

NOTES

15 Bornstein, "Women of the 1898 Alaska-Klondike Gold Rush"; Berton, *The Klondike Fever*, 384–85.

16 Forbes Parkhill, "The Scarlet Lady: Mattie Silks made over a half million dollars from the world's oldest profession, but a good-for-nothing broke her heart," *Denver Post, Empire Magazine*, June 10, 1951, http://blogs.denverpost.com/library/files/2012/11/MattieSilks.pdf, accessed October 1, 2018; Agnew, *Brides of the Multitude*, 220.

17 "Turner McWilliams 3.4 Family Tree," Ancestry.com; "Eliza Jane Duckett Monroe" and "Sarah A. 'Sadie' Oatley," findagrave.com.

18 MacKell, *Brothels, Bordellos & Bad Girls*, 180.

19 Berton, *The Klondike Fever*, 303.

20 Ibid., 395–96, 418; "California, Federal Naturalization Records, 1843–1999," Ancestry.com.

21 "Mary Jane 'Pollie' Oatley" and "Lottie Oatley Casley," findagrave.com; "California, Federal Naturalization Records, 1843–1999."

22 Jan MacKell Collins, *Lost Ghost Towns of Teller County* (Charleston, SC: The History Press, 2016), 112–13; Jan MacKell, *Cripple Creek District: Last of Colorado's Gold Booms* (Charleston, SC: Arcadia Publishing 2003), 51.

23 Berton, *The Klondike Fever*, 372, 378.

24 Ibid., 322, 385; Agnew, *Brides of the Multitude*, 217–18.

25 Berton, *The Klondike Fever*, 385–86.

26 *San Francisco Call*, November 15, 1898, 1:1.

27 Berton, *The Klondike Fever*, 395, 406–7, 412; Agnew, *Brides of the Multitude*, 218.

28 Agnew, *Brides of the Multitude*, 218; Berton, *The Klondike Fever*, 385.

29 Ken Spotswood, "The History of Dawson City, Yukon Territory," Explore North, http://explorenorth.com/yukon/dawson-history.html, accessed September 30, 2018; Berton, *The Klondike Fever*, 368.

CHAPTER 18

1 Morgan, *Good Time Girls of the Alaska-Yukon Gold Rush*, 139.

2 *Tenth Census of the United States, 1880*; Morgan, *Good Time Girls of the Alaska-Yukon Gold Rush*, 140; Frank A. Bettis, "1890 Veterans Schedule," and 1890 Spokane City Directory, "U.S. City Directories, 1822–1995," Ancestry.com; "Martha Alice Murphy Bettis," findagrave.com.

3 Meier and Meier, *Those Naughty Ladies of the Old Northwest*, 18–22; Morgan, *Good Time Girls of the Alaska-Yukon Gold Rush*, 140.

4 Morgan, *Good Time Girls of the Alaska-Yukon Gold Rush*, 140.

5 Rolv Schillios, "Dance Hall Girl," *Alaska*, March 1956, 9.

6 Meier and Meier, *Those Naughty Ladies of the Old Northwest*, 18–22.

7 Schillios, "Dance Hall Girl," 9.

8 Morgan, *Good Time Girls of the Alaska-Yukon Gold Rush*, 145–46.

9 Meier and Meier, *Those Naughty Ladies of the Old Northwest*, 18–22; Morgan, *Good Time Girls of the Alaska-Yukon Gold Rush*, 139.

10 Kate Rockwell Matson, "I Was Queen of the Klondike," as told to Mary Mann, *Alaska Sportsman* magazine, August, 1944, 10; Morgan, *Good Time Girls of the Alaska-Yukon Gold Rush*, 141–42; Schillios, "Dance Hall Girl," 11.

11 Jean Beach King, *Arizona Charlie: A Legendary Cowboy, Klondike Stampeder and Wild West Showman* (Phoenix, AZ: A Heritage Publishers Book, 1989), 219–20.

12 Morgan, *Good Time Girls of the Alaska-Yukon Gold Rush*, 145–46.

13 Meier and Meier, *Those Naughty Ladies of the Old Northwest*, 18–22.

14 Morgan, *Good Time Girls of the Alaska-Yukon Gold Rush*, 148–49.

15 Matson, "I Was Queen of the Klondike," 10.

16 Morgan, *Good Time Girls of the Alaska-Yukon Gold Rush*, 150; Kathleen "Klondike Kate" Eloise Rockwell, "Davidson Consadine Family Tree," Ancestry.com.

17 Morgan, *Good Time Girls of the Alaska-Yukon Gold Rush*, 149.

18 Matson, "I Was Queen of the Klondike," 30.

19 Morgan, *Good Time Girls of the Alaska-Yukon Gold Rush*, 151–53; Pericles Alexander Pantages, "David Consadine Best Family Tree" and Seattle, Washington City Directory for 1905, "U.S. City Directories, 1822–1995," Ancestry.com; Daniel Statt, "Pantages, Alexander (1876–1936)," Essay 2999, Historylink.org, March 5, 2001, http://www.historylink.org/File/2999, accessed October 4, 2018.

20 Morgan, *Good Time Girls of the Alaska-Yukon Gold Rush*, 153–54.

21 Ellis Lucia, "Klondike Kate in Central Oregon," Geoff Hill, ed., *Little Known Tales from Oregon History* vol. 1, reprinted from *Cascades East* magazine (Bend, OR: Sun Publishing, 1988), 72.

22 Ibid., 73.

23 Kate E. Rockwell, "Oregon Marriage Indexes, 1906–2009," and Floyd J. Warner, Deschutes County, Oregon, "U.S., World War I Draft Registration Cards," Ancestry.com; Bureau of Land Management Document #012391 for Kate Warner, formerly Kate Rockwell, glorecords.blm.gov; Lucia, "Klondike Kate in Central Oregon," 73.

24 *Fourteenth Census of the United States, 1920*; Lucia, "Klondike Kate in Central Oregon," 74.

25 Lucia, "Klondike Kate in Central Oregon," 74; Morgan, *Good Time Girls of the Alaska-Yukon Gold Rush*, 155; "Alexander Pantages," findagrave.com.

26 Meier and Meier, *Those Naughty Ladies of the Old Northwest*, 18–22.

27 Lucia, "Klondike Kate in Central Oregon," 75.

28 *Fifteenth Census of the United States, 1930*.

29 Lucia, "Klondike Kate in Central Oregon," 75.

30 Ibid., 75–76; Meier and Meier, *Those Naughty Ladies of the Old Northwest*, 18–22; *Sixteenth Census of the United States, 1940*; Johnny "Jack" Matson (1864–1946), from Kathleen "Klondike Kate" Eloise Rockwell, "Deschutes County Pioneers Family Tree," Ancestry.com.

31 Lucia, "Klondike Kate in Central Oregon," 75–76.

32 Ibid., 75; Standard Certificate of Death for Klondike Kate Van Duren, "Kathleen Eloise 'Klondike Kate' Rockwell," findagrave.com.

CHAPTER 19

1 "Skagway, Alaska," wikipedia.org.

2 Florin, *Western Ghost Town Shadows, Fourth in the Western Ghost Town Series*, 105–6.

3 Tobey Schmidt, "Women of Skagway," *Skaguay Alaskan*, August 12, 2017, https:// skagwaynews.com/2017/08/12/women-of-skagway/, accessed October 5, 2018.

4 Morgan, *Good Time Girls of the Alaska-Yukon Gold Rush*, 41.

5 Menu from the Red Onion Saloon, Skagway, Alaska, 2002, www.redonion1898. com; correspondence with Sara Waisanen, aka "Madam Honee DoMee," Red Onion Saloon, March 9, 2006; "Alaska: Gold Rush Train Ride Ends with Lesson in Prostitution," *Wake and Wander* (blog), https://wakeandwander.com/travel/united-states/ alaska/alaska-gold-rush-train-ride-ends-with-lesson-in-prostitution/, accessed October 2, 2018.

6 "Red Light District," Alaska.org, http://www.alaska.org/detail/red-light-district, accessed October 6, 2018; menu from the Red Onion Saloon; Correspondence with Sara Waisanen; Jeff Brady, ed., "Skagway History," originally published in *Skagway News*, New Year's edition, January 2000 (updated); "Skagway: Gateway to the Klondike," http://skagway.com/history-complete/, accessed October 2, 2018.

7 Morgan, *Good Time Girls of the Alaska-Yukon Gold Rush*, 41.

8 Ibid., 48.

9 "New Criminal Code adds laws against 'procuring,'" Docplayer.net, 15, docplayer .net/54194061-Canada-s-anti-prostitution-laws.html, accessed October 9, 2018.

10 Collins, *Lost Ghost Towns of Teller County*, 113.

11 Florin, *Western Ghost Town Shadows,* 107.

12 "Soapy's Saloons," *Alias Soapy Smith*, http://www.soapysmith.net/id21.html, accessed October 9, 2018.

13 "Soapy Smith History Part 3," *Alias Soapy Smith*, http://www.soapysmith.net/ id15.html, accessed October 9, 2018.

14 *Morning Oregonian*, June 4, 1898, 2:1.

15 Jeff Smith, *Alias Soapy Smith* (Juneau, AK: Klondike Research, 2009), 506, 508.

16 *Seattle Times*, June 4, 1898, 2:1.

17 Smith, *Alias Soapy Smith*, 509–10.

18 *Seattle Times*, July 4, 1898, 2:1.

19 "Soapy Smith History Part 4," *Alias Soapy Smith*, http://www.soapysmith.net/ id18.html, accessed October 10, 2018; "Skagway History."

20 "Soapy Smith History Part 4"; "Ella Wilson," Klondike Gold Rush National Historical Park, National Park Service, https://www.nps.gov/people/ella-wilson.htm, accessed October 7, 2018.

21 "Skagway History"; "Red Light District"; "Alaska: Gold Rush Train Ride Ends with Lesson in Prostitution."

22 "Company L 24th Infantry in Skagway," National Park Service, https://www.nps .gov/klgo/learn/historyculture/company-l.htm, accessed October 11, 2018; "Ruth Brown and Rose Arnold," Klondike Gold Rush, National Park Service, April 17, 2018, https://www.nps.gov/klgo/learn/historyculture/ruth-brown-rose-arnold.htm, accessed October 6, 2018.

23 "Ruth Brown and Rose Arnold"; *Twelfth Census of the United States, 1900.*

24 "Skagway History"; "Red Light District."

25 "Skagway History."

CHAPTER 20

1 June Allen, "Dolly Arthur: now Ketchikan's poster girl," *Sitnews*, May 7, 2002, http://www.sitnews.org/JuneAllen/050702_dolly_arthur.html, accessed October 2, 2018.

2 "Thelma Dorotha 'Dollie' Copeland," findagrave.com; "U.S., Social Security Death Index, 1935–2014," Garbe Family Tree, "Iowa, Select Marriages Index, 1758–1996," and "Washington, Marriage Records, 1854–2013," Ancestry.com; "'Cat' houses & Sporting Women," interpretive sign at Dolly's House Museum, Ketchikan, AK; *Thirteenth Census of the United States, 1910.*

3 "Montana, County Divorce Records, 1865–1950," Ancestry.com.

4 Ibid.; *Twelfth Census of the United States, 1900*; Garbe Family Tree; *Thirteenth Census of the United States, 1910.*

5 "Alaska's Villains, Vamps and Vagabonds, Part II, Dolly Arthur," http://www.margaretdeefholts.com/dollyarthur.html, accessed October 1, 2018; Morgan, *Good Time Girls of the Alaska-Yukon Gold Rush*, 277.

6 "Alaska's Villains, Vamps and Vagabonds, Part II, Dolly Arthur."

7 "Iowa, Select Marriages Index, 1758–1996"; "Washington, Marriage Records, 1854–2013"; *Thirteenth Census of the United States, 1910.*

8 "Alaska's Villains, Vamps and Vagabonds, Part II, Dolly Arthur."

9 "'Cat' houses & Sporting Women"; "The History of Ketchikan, Alaska," Explore North, http://www.explorenorth.com/alaska/history/ketchikan-history.html, accessed October 1, 2018.

10 "Ketchikan, Alaska," wikipedia.org; "'Cat' houses & Sporting Women."

11 "'Cat' houses & Sporting Women"; Morgan, *Good Time Girls of the Alaska-Yukon Gold Rush*, 279; June Allen, "Ketchikan's Creek Street Dance Hall echoes of music from the past," *SitNews*, February 21, 2004, http://www.sitnews.net/JuneAllen/Star/022104_star.html, accessed October 2, 2018.

12 Morgan, *Good Time Girls of the Alaska-Yukon Gold Rush*, 279.

13 "'Cat' houses & Sporting Women"; Allen, "Ketchikan's Creek Street Dance Hall echoes of music from the past."

14 Allen, "Ketchikan's Creek Street Dance Hall echoes of music from the past."

15 Morgan, *Good Time Girls of the Alaska-Yukon Gold Rush*, 279; "'Cat' houses & Sporting Women"; June Allen, *Dolly's House* (Ketchikan, AK: Tongass Publishing Co., 1976), 11–14, and "Dolly Arthur: now Ketchikan's poster girl"; "Alaska's Villains, Vamps and Vagabonds, Part II, Dolly Arthur."

16 Allen, "Dolly Arthur: now Ketchikan's poster girl."

17 Ibid.

18 "'Cat' houses & Sporting Women."

19 Allen, "Ketchikan's Creek Street Dance Hall echoes of music from the past."

20 "'Cat' houses & Sporting Women"; Allen, "Ketchikan's Creek Street Dance Hall echoes of music from the past."

21 Allen, "Ketchikan's Creek Street Dance Hall echoes of music from the past."

22 Morgan, *Good Time Girls of the Alaska-Yukon Gold Rush*, 276.

23 *Fifteenth Census of the United States, 1930*; "Alaska's Villains, Vamps and Vagabonds, Part II, Dolly Arthur"; Allen, "Dolly Arthur: now Ketchikan's poster girl."

24 Allen, "Ketchikan's Creek Street Dance Hall echoes of music from the past."

25 *Sixteenth Census of the United States*; "Oregon, Death Index, 1898–2008," Ancestry.com; Allen, "Ketchikan's Creek Street Dance Hall echoes of music from the past"; "'Cat' houses & Sporting Women."

26 Allen, "Ketchikan's Creek Street Dance Hall echoes of music from the past"; "'Cat' houses & Sporting Women."

27 Allen, "Dolly Arthur: now Ketchikan's poster girl."

28 "'Cat' houses & Sporting Women."

29 "Alaska's Villains, Vamps and Vagabonds, Part II, Dolly Arthur"; findagrave.com.

CHAPTER 21

1 Morgan, *Good Time Girls of the Alaska-Yukon Gold Rush*, 292–93; "Zula Swanson," *Ebony* magazine (Johnson Publishing Company), 25:1, November 1969, 126.

2 Alabama marriage records document Gilbert Swanson marrying Tilda Wester at Chambers, Alabama, in 1867. Ironically, Wester was the last name of Zula's last husband, William "Bill" Wester. But the connection, if there is any, is unknown. "Alabama Marriages, 1816–1957," Ancestry.com.

3 *Fourteenth Census of the United States, 1920*; Portland City Directory for 1923, "U.S. City Directories, 1822–1995," Ancestry.com; Morgan, *Good Time Girls of the Alaska-Yukon Gold Rush*, 292–93.

4 "Zula Swanson," *Ebony* magazine; *Fifteenth Census of the United States, 1930*.

5 "Zula Swanson," *Ebony* magazine.

6 Randall Kenan, *Walking on Water: Black American Lives at the Turn of the Twenty-first Century* (New York: Random House, 1999), 280–81.

7 "Zula Swanson," *Ebony* magazine.

8 *Fairbanks Daily News-Miner*, January 15, 1973, 2:6.

9 Morgan, *Good Time Girls of the Alaska-Yukon Gold Rush*, 292–93.

10 *Sixteenth Census of the United States*; Sarana Schell, "Anchorage is celebrating its 100th birthday with theater," *Senior Voice*, July 1, 2015, https://www.seniorvoicealaska.com/story/2015/07/01/people-and-places/anchorage-is-celebrating-its-100th-birth-day-with-theater/793.html, accessed October 3, 2018.

11 Morgan, *Good Time Girls of the Alaska-Yukon Gold Rush*, 292–93; *Fairbanks Daily News-Miner*, June 28, 1955, 6:6.

12 Kenan, *Walking on Water: Black American Lives at the Turn of the Twenty-first Century*, 280–81.

13 "Zula Swanson," *Ebony* magazine.

14 "Goose Lake (Anchorage)," wikipedia.com.

15 "Zula Swanson," *Ebony* magazine; "J.C. Penney (Anchorage, Alaska)," wikipedia.com.

16 "Zula Swanson," *Ebony* magazine.

17 Morgan, *Good Time Girls of the Alaska-Yukon Gold Rush*, 292–93.

18 Interview with Tarea Pittman, NAACP West Coast regional director in 1961, December 2, 1972, http://content.cdlib.org/view?docId=kt4h4nb06r&doc.view=frames&chunk.id=d0e2938&toc.depth=1&toc.id=d0e2938&brand=calisphere, accessed October 4, 2018.

19 *Fairbanks Daily News-Miner*, January 4, 1973, 2:7.

20 Ibid., January 15, 1973, 2:6.

21 "Zula Swanson Wester," findagrave.com; *Fairbanks Daily News-Miner*, January 15, 1973, 2:6.

22 *Kalendar* magazine, vol. 4, no. L17, September 5, 1975.

23 Kenan, *Walking on Water: Black American Lives at the Turn of the Twenty-first Century*, 280–81.

SELECTED BIBLIOGRAPHY

———————•●•———————

BOOKS

Agnew, Jeremy. *Brides of the Multitude: Prostitution in the Old West.* Lake City, CO: Western Reflections Publishing Company, 2008.

Allen, June. *Dolly's House.* Ketchikan, AK: Tongass Publishing Co., 1976.

Barber, Olive. *Meet Me in Juneau.* Portland, OR: Binfords & Mort, Publishers, 1960.

Bayley, Christopher T. *Seattle Justice: The Rise and Fall of the Police Payoff System in Seattle.* Seattle, WA: Sasquatch Books, 2015.

Berton, Pierre. *The Klondike Fever: The Life and Death of the Last Great Gold Rush.* New York: Carroll & Graf Publishers, Inc., 1997.

Blair, Karen J., editor. *Women in Pacific Northwest History.* Seattle, WA: University of Washington Press, 1998.

Blair, Kay Reynolds. *Ladies of the Lamplight.* Ouray, CO: Western Reflections Publishing Company, 2000.

Boyer, Glenn G., editor. *I Married Wyatt Earp: The Recollections of Josephine Sarah Marcus Earp.* Tucson, AZ: University of Arizona Press, second printing, 1979.

Brooks, Alfred. *Blazing Alaska's Trails.* Fairbanks, AK: University of Alaska Press, 1953.

Carlson, Linda. *Company Towns of the Pacific Northwest.* Seattle, WA; University of Washington Press, 2003.

Collins, Jan MacKell. *Lost Ghost Towns of Teller County.* Charleston, SC: The History Press, 2016.

Culp, Edwin D. *Yesterday in Oregon: A Pictorial Scrapbook.* Caxton, ID: The Caxton Printers, Ltd., 1990.

Douthit, Nathan. *The Coos Bay Region 1890–1944: Life on a Coastal Frontier.* Coos Bay, OR: River West Books, printed for the Bandon Historical Society Press, 1981.

Evans, Chad. *Frontier Theater.* Victoria, BC: Sono Nis Press, 1983.

Florin, Lambert. *Ghost Town Trails: Third in the Western Ghost Town Series.* Seattle, WA: Superior Publishing Company, 1963.

———. *Oregon Ghost Towns.* Seattle, WA: Superior Publishing Company, 1970.

———. *Western Ghost Town Shadows, Fourth in the Western Ghost Town Series.* Seattle, WA: Superior Publishing Company, 1964.

Gourse, Leslie. *Native American Courtship and Marriage.* Summertown, TN: Native Voices Book Publishing Company, 2005.

Gulick, Bill. *Outlaws of the Pacific Northwest.* Caldwell, ID: Caxton Press, 2000.

Holbrook, Stewart. *Wildmen, Wobblies & Whistle Punks: Stewart Holbrook's Lowbrow Northwest.* Edited and introduced by Brian Booth. Corvallis, OR: Oregon State University Press, 1992.

Hughes, John C., and Ryan Teague Beckwith. *On the Harbor: From Black Friday to Nirvana.* Las Vegas, NV: Stephens Press, LLC, 2005.

Jensen, Andie E. *Law on the Bay: Marshfield, Oregon 1874–1944.* Coos Bay, OR: Lawman Publishing, 2010.

Judson, Lewis E. *Reflections on the Jason Lee Mission and the Opening of Civilization in the Oregon Country.* Salem, OR: Wynkoop-Blair Printing Service, 1971.

Kenan, Randall. *Walking on Water: Black American Lives at the Turn of the Twenty-first Century.* New York: Random House, 1999.

King, Jean Beach. *Arizona Charlie: A Legendary Cowboy, Klondike Stampeder and Wild West Showman.* Phoenix, AZ: A Heritage Publishers Book, 1989.

Kruckeberg, Arthur R. *The Natural History of Puget Sound Country.* Seattle, WA: University of Washington Press, 1991.

MacKell, Jan. *Brothels, Bordellos and Bad Girls: Prostitution in Colorado 1860–1930.* Albuquerque, NM: University of New Mexico Press, 2004.

———. *Cripple Creek District: Last of Colorado's Gold Booms.* Charleston, SC: Arcadia Publishing 2003.

———. *Red Light Women of the Rocky Mountains.* Albuquerque, NM: University of New Mexico Press, 2009.

Martin, Edward Winslow. *The Secrets of the Great City.* Philadelphia, PA: National Publishing Company, 1868.

McArthur, Lewis L. *Oregon Geographic Names,* seventh edition. Portland, OR: Oregon Historical Society Press, 2003.

Meier, Gary and Gloria. *Those Naughty Ladies of the Old Northwest.* Bend, OR: Maverick Publications, 1990.

Miller, Donald C. *Ghost Towns of Washington and Oregon.* Boulder, CO: Pruitt Publishing, 1977.

Miller, Ronald Dean. *Shady Ladies of the West.* Los Angeles: Westernlore Press, 1964.

Monahan, Sherry. *The Wicked West: Boozers, Cruisers, Gamblers and More.* Tucson, AZ: Rio Nuevo Publishers, 2005.

Monmonier, Mark. *From Squaw Tit to Whorehouse Meadow: How Maps Name, Claim and Inflame.* Chicago: University of Chicago Press, Second Printing, 2007.

Morgan, Lael. *Good Time Girls of the Alaska-Yukon Gold Rush.* Fairbanks, AK: Epicenter Press, 1998.

Morgan, Murray. *The Last Wilderness.* Seattle, WA, and London: University of Washington Press, 1955.

Moynahan, Jay. *Forty Fallen Women: Western Doves and Madams, 1885–1920.* Spokane, WA: Chickadee Publishing, 2008.

———. *The Good Time Girls' Guide to Gold Rush Cuisine.* Spokane, WA: Chickadee Publishing, 2006.

Nash, Tom, and Twilo Scofield. *The Well-Traveled Casket: A Collection of Oregon Folklife*. Salt Lake City, UT: University of Utah Press, 1992.

O'Meara, Walter. *Daughters of the Country: The Women of the Fur Traders and Mountain Men*. New York: Harcourt, Brace & World, Inc., 1968.

Sandine, Al. *Plundertown, USA: Coos Bay Enters the Global Economy*. Blaine, WA: Hancock House Publishers, 2003.

Seagraves, Anne. *Soiled Doves: Prostitution in the Early West*. Hayden, ID: Wesanne Publications, 1994.

Smith, Jeff. *Alias Soapy Smith*. Juneau, AK: Klondike Research, 2009.

Speidel, William C. *Sons of the Profits, or, There's No Business Like Grow Business: The Seattle Story 1851–1901*. Seattle, WA: Nettle Creek Publishing Company, 1967.

Stanford, Sally. *The Lady of the House: California's Most Notorious Madam*. New York: Ballantine Books, 1972.

Steele, Volney, MD. *Bleed, Blister and Purge: A History of Medicine on the American Frontier*. Missoula, MT: Mountain Press Publishing Company, 2005.

Stevens, Victor H. *Powers, Oregon*. Myrtle Point, OR: Vic Stevens, printed by Wegford Publications, North Bend, OR, n.d.

Stone, Boyd. *Living in the Past Lane*. Myrtle Point, OR: The Coquille Valley Sentinel, n.d.

———. *My Valley: History of the Coquille River Valley, Outlying Areas and More*. Myrtle Point, OR: Myrtle Point Printing, 2008.

———. *You Are the Stars: History of the Coquille Area*. Myrtle Point, OR: Myrtle Point Printing, 1995.

Strain, Patti and Hal, editors. *The Coquille Valley: Ancestor Review, Wagon Wheels to Wireless*. Myrtle Point, OR: Myrtle Printing, 2009.

———. *The Coquille Valley: Memories—Moccasins to the Moon, Volume One*. Myrtle Point, OR: Myrtle Point Printing, 2007.

Strickland, Ron. *Whistlepunks & Geoducs: Oral Histories from the Pacific Northwest*. New York: Paragon House, 1990.

Swanson, Robert. *Bunkhouse Ballads, Book 3.* Toronto: Thomas Allen, Limited, 1945.

Wadland, Justin. *Trying Home: The Rise and Fall of an Anarchist Utopia on Puget Sound.* Corvallis, OR: Oregon State University Press, 2014.

Wagner, Dick. *Louie Simpson's North Bend.* North Bend-on-Coos Bay, OR: The North Bend News, 1986.

Weinstein, Robert A. *Grays Harbor, 1885–1913.* New York: Penguin Books, 1978.

Wright, E. W., editor. *The Lewis and Dryden Marine History of the Pacific Northwest.* Portland, OR: Lewis & Dryden Publishing Co., 1895.

CORRESPONDENCE AND INTERVIEWS BY THE AUTHOR

Joanie Bedwell, Hazel M. Lewis Library, Powers, Oregon, September 2017.

Bert Dunn, Coos County, Oregon, November 2018–June 2019.

Jill Moore, Powers, Oregon, summer 2018.

Tish Moore, Powers, Oregon, summer 2018.

Jay Moynahan, Spokane, Washington, December 2007, November 2018.

Lacey Pearce, Powers, Oregon, summer 2018.

Phyllis Pearce, Powers, Oregon, summer 2018.

Sara Waisanen, aka "Madam Honee DoMee," Red Onion Saloon, March 9, 2006.

Debra Woosley, Powers, Oregon, July 2018.

INTERNET

Ancestry.com

"1890 Veterans Schedule"

"Alabama Marriages, 1816–1957"

"California, Death Index, 1905–1939"

"California, Federal Naturalization Records, 1843–1999"
"California, Marriage Records from Select Counties, 1850–1941"
"Iowa, Select Marriages Index, 1758–1996"
"Montana, County Divorce Records, 1865–1950"
"Oregon, Death Index, 1898–2008"
"Oregon Marriage Indexes, 1906–2009"
"Oregon, Wills and Probate Records, 1849–1963"
"Spokane, Washington Directories, 1889–93"
"U.S. City Directories, 1822–1995"
"U.S., Social Security Death Index, 1935–2014"
"Washington, Marriage Records, 1854–2013"
"Washington State and Territorial Censuses, 1857–1892"
"Washington Territorial Census Rolls, 1857–1892"
"Washington, Wills and Probate Records, 1851–1970"
"World War I Draft Registration Cards"

Other Sites

Alaska.org.
Alias Soapy Smith, soapysmith.net.
Bureau of Land Management, glorecords.blm.gov.
Capital Taps, capitaltaps.blogspot.com.
Dawsoncityalaska.org.
Findagrave.com.
Ghosttownsusa.com.
HistoryLink.org.
National Park Service, nps.gov.
Offbeatoregon.com.
The Oregon Encyclopedia, oregonencyclopedia.org.
Oregon History Project, oregonhistoryproject.org.
Pendleton Underground Tours, pendletonundergroundtours.org.
Roadside America, roadsideamerica.com.
Skagway: Gateway to the Klondike, skagway.com/history-complete.
Spokane Historical, spokanehistorical.org.

University of Washington Libraries Digital Collections, content.lib
.washington.edu.
Wikipedia.org.

NEWSPAPERS

Alaska
Fairbanks Daily News-Miner
Senior Voice
Sitnews
Skagway News

California
Morning Call
San Francisco Call

Colorado
Denver Post

Montana
Anaconda Standard

Oregon
Capital Journal
Coast Mail
Coos Bay Times
Coquille City Herald
Coquille Valley Sentinel
Daily Astorian
Daily Capital Journal
Daily Morning Astorian
Dalles Daily Chronicle

East Oregonian
Evening Capital Journal
Evening Herald (Klamath Falls)
Grant County News
La Grande Evening Observer
La Grande Evening Star
Morning Astorian
Morning Oregonian
Myrtle Point Herald
Oregon Daily Journal
Oregonian
Portland New Northwest
Roseburg Plaindealer
Salem Daily Journal
State Rights Democrat
Statesman Journal
Sunday Oregonian

Washington
Chinook Observer
The Daily World (Aberdeen)
Grays Harbor Post
Olympia Standard
Port Townsend Daily Leader
Port Townsend Morning Leader
Puget Sound Mail
Seattle Daily Post-Intelligencer

Seattle Met

Seattle Post-Intelligencer

Seattle Republican

Seattle Star

Seattle Times

Spokane Press

Spokesman Review

Tacoma News Tribune

Walla Walla Evening Statesman

Yakima Herald

PERIODICALS

Alaska

Alaska Sportsman

Anthropology Northwest

Cascades East

Columbia

Ebony

1859 Oregon Magazine

The Gonzaga Bulletin

Historic Marion County

Journal of Interdisciplinary History

Journal of the Southwest

Kalendar

Oregon Historical Quarterly Review

Pacific Northwest Quarterly

Trails End

True West

Westways

INDEX

Bonniefield, Sam, 167

bootlegging, 55, 190, 192, 198

Bowers, 183–84

bowling alleys, 113, 114

Box Car Annie's, 116

Boyer, Mary Ann, 15–17

Brace, Ella, 22

Brace, Lottie, 22

Brady, John, 184

Brewen, Anna, 36

Bridge, Oregon, 117

Bright, Jennie, 6–7

Briscoe, Myrtle, 166–67

British North American Trading and Exploration Company, 160

Brookings, Oregon, 116

Brooks, Albert, 158

Brooks, Lottie, 122

brothels and bordellos. *See also* parlor houses

  advertising for, 12, 30, 53, 57, 123–24, 141, 157

  African-American, 185–86

  air-conditioning systems for, 13

  Alaska definition of, 190

  in beer parlors, 13

  business license requirements, 39

  children living in, 39

  closure of, 118

  descriptions, 50, 133, *189,* 191–92

  discretion and privacy, 16–17, 39, 92–93

  doll systems for prostitute selection, 180–81

  employee management, 97

  employee turnover, 57–58

  fires in, 51–52, 70–71, 71, 124

  floating, 78–79, 120–21, 122, 181

  in grocery stores, 84

  holiday popularity of, 78

  horse riding into, 5

  in hotels, 19, 25, 53, 56–60, 64, 75, 80–81, 85, 118, 122, 140–41

  laws and ordinances on, 6, 110, 122, 125, 128–29, 146–47

  in meadows, 98–99

  as modern tourist hotels, 97

  monthly raids of, 11–12

  municipal funding by, 13, 18, 28

  as museums, 196

  name display requirements, 136

  in newspaper office buildings, 12

  ownership by prominent citizens, 24, 133, 136

  payment systems, 180–81

  police protection payments, 26, 40, 133–34

  property sales and prices of, 190, 200

  robberies of, 74–75

  in saloons, 84, 132

  saloons as, 80, 84, 125, 132, 180–81

  security features, 17, 97, 132

  success, keys to, 35

  in tents, 89, 166

  theft and robberies at, 31, 40, 74–75, 78, 133, 135, 140

Brown, Ruth, 185–86

Brown, Sallie, 132

Bruno, Pete, 135
Bryant, Vlasta, 116
Bucket of Blood, The, 113
Buffalo Soldiers, 185
Bulldog Annie, 71
burlesque shows, 110, *111*
Burnell, Ida, 146
Burnett, Washington, 6
Burns, J. J., 103
Burns, Jim, 31
Burris, Della, 127–29, *128*
Busby, Mable Janice, 96–97
Bush, Ann, 14
business licenses, 18, 39, 120
Butler, William, 115
buzzer systems, 132

Cady, Pat, 11
Cahill, Madge "Big Maddy," 136
Cameron, Hazel, 82
Camille (play), 165
Campbell, Frankie, 126
camp followers, 88–89
Camp Hotel, 25, 56–57
Canada, 6, 13–14, 153, 157–68, 171–73, 182
Cantwell, Frank, 48
Canyon City, Oregon, 90–93
carbolic acid, 52–53, 144
Cardwell, Fannie, 78–79
Carmack, George Washington, 153
carriages, 30, 53, 126, 131
Carter, Jack, 112
Cartwright, Annie, 39
Cartwright, Willie, 39

Casley, Vernon, 165
Cassakes, 68
Cass Hotel, 63
cats, 90, 137
censorship, 9–10
Chambers, Mary, 19–20
Champoux, Zenon "James," 22
Chandler Hotel, 81
charitable acts, 30, 42, 89, 177
Chenago, 117
Chicken House, The, 118
chickens, 11
children
  adopted, 33
  alcohol sales to, 80
  of celebrity performers, 173–74
  delivery boys and initialed gold pieces, 38–39
  living in brothels, 39, 124–25
  newspaper sales, 22–23, 26
  as prostitutes, xiii, 38, 81–82
  red-light district perceptions, 142–43
Chilkoot Pass, Alaska, 150, 171
Chinese immigrants, xii–xiii, 45, 51, 151, 154
Christenson, George, 193
Circle City, Alaska, 152–53, 165
circuit riders, 88–89
circuit towns, 89–97, 117
City Brewery, 109
Clancy's Place, 182
Clapp, Benjamin, 67
Clark, Dora, 130
Clark, Mary, 132

NAACP (National Association for the Advancement of Colored People), 199, 200

Native Americans
Alaskan entertainment and dances with, 150, 152
alcohol sales to, 4
curfews for, 19
fear of, 16
interracial marriages, xii, 2
mythological figures of Alaskan, 179
as prostitutes, 17, 66, 67
sex trade perceptions, x–xii, 1–2
venereal diseases among, xi, 2, 66
white prostitutes' treatment by, 68, 152
women's status, 1
New Era (newspaper), 9
newspapers, 9–10, 12, 22–23
New York City, 50
Nichols, Elsworth E., 145–46
Niegmann, Henry, 30
Nightingale, Zella (Nellie Curtis), 56–64
Noble, William Henry, 77, 78
Nome, Alaska, 155–56, 168, 173
Norman, James A., 87, 118
North Bend, Oregon, 76, 80–81, 84–85, 86, 87
North End, 122–23, 136
Northern Pacific Railroad, 18, 43
North West Fur Company, 65, 68
nudity, 10, 113–14, 123

Oatley Sisters, 164–65

occupation aliases, 20, 23, 36, 41, 78, 135
O'Conners, Freda, 24
O'Day, Billy, 45
O'Donnell, Fannie, 84
Ohben, Dorothea Georgine Emile (Lou Graham), 20, 27–34 , *29*
Ohben, Johann, 34
Ohben Eberhardt, Pauline, 34
Ohben-Klaus, Joanna Henrietta Bertha, 34
OK Barbershop, 113
Ole Scott, 12
Open Door, 127, 129
Oregon. *See also* Portland, Oregon; *specific towns of Oregon*
alcohol prohibition, 85
celebrity performers living in, 174–75, 176–78
circuit riders, 88
circuit towns of, 89–97, 100–108, 117, 118
first Anglo woman in, 65–68
insane asylums of, 130–31, 140, 144
meadows as workplace locations, 98–99
money storage services, 89
prostitution prohibitions, 118
residential challenges, x
state history, x, 69
Oregon Folklore Studies, 137
Oregon Hotel, 85
Oregon Mare, 162
Oregon State Insane Asylum, 130, 140, 144

Walker, Samuel, 94–95
Walla Walla, Washington, 35–42
Wantawabe, 141–42
Wappenstein, Charles W., 24
Ward, Oren, 175
Waring, Guy, 6, 7
Warner, Floyd, 175
Warner, Tony, 103, 108
Warrenton, Oregon, 71
Washburn, Gardner and Annie, 39
Washington, 1–14, 19, 25, 55, 62–64.
    See also Seattle, Washington;
    specific towns of Washington
Washington Hotel, 19
Washington Theater, 53
Watkins, Annie, 195
Webster, Blanche (Sugar), *114,*
    114–16
Webster, Howard, 116
Weisbach, J. Robert, 43–44, 45
Welcome Saloon, 136
Wells, Minnie, 39
Wenrich, Albert, 72
West, Mae, 186
West, Oswald, 75, 104–5, 147–48
Westbrooke, Gladys, 58–59
Wester, William, 200–201
West Hill Rooms (Coquille), *114,*
    114–16, 117
West Hill Rooms (Portland), 116
White, Libby, 166
White Chapel District (Dawson), 168
Whitechapel District (Seattle), 18
Whitechapel District/North End
    (Portland), 122–23, 136

White Pass & Yukon Route Railroad,
    181, 186
Whorehouse Meadow, 98–99
Wickersham, James, 193
Widner, Abbie, 53–54
Wiegand, William, 103, 108
Wilcox, Jay, 80, 86
Wilkes, Mattie, 190
Williams, Frankie, 24
Williams, N. S., 139–40
Williams, S. P., 32
Williams, Thornton, 91
wills and estates, 33–34, 41–42, 48,
    73–74, 137, 142
Wilson, Cad, 162–63
Wilson, "Dutch Kate," 152
Wilson, Ella D., 183–84, 185
Wilson, Mary, 127
Wilson, Polly, 90–91
window breaking, 143–44
window dressings, 141, 157
Wing, Tommy, 113, 114
Wingard, Emma, 125
Wittico-Weeon, x
wives, auctions for, 158
Wolf, Dr., 160
Wolfe, Joe, 182
Wolfe, Josephine (*aka* Dutch Joe),
    35–42
Wolfe, Sam, 52
women, scarcity of white, 2–3, 150
Women's Christian Temperance
    Union (WCTU), 46–47,
    144–45, 186
Wood, Laura, 10

ABOUT THE AUTHOR

Jan MacKell Collins has been a published author, speaker, and presenter since 2003. Her focus has always been on Western history, with an emphasis on historical prostitution. Collins has published numerous articles on her subjects in such magazines as *True West*, *Montana Magazine*, *All About History*, and numerous regional periodicals. In 2016, she appeared on *Adam Ruins Everything* as an "expert" in prostitution history. Collins currently resides in Oregon, where she continues researching the history of prostitution.